Ancient Cahokia and the Mississippians

The ancient capital of Cahokia and a series of lesser population centers developed in the Mississippi valley in North America between the eighth and fifteenth centuries AD, leaving behind an extraordinarily rich archaeological record. Cahokia's gigantic pyramids, finely crafted artifacts, and dense population mark it as the founding city of the Mississippian civilization, formerly known as the 'mound builders'. As Cahokian ideas and objects were widely sought, a cultural and religious ripple effect spread across the mid-continent and into the South. In its wake, population migrations and social upheavals transformed social life along the ancient Mississippi River. In this important new survey, Timothy Pauketat outlines the development of Mississippian civilization, presenting a wealth of archaeological evidence and advancing our understanding of the American Indians whose influence extended into the founding moments of the United States and lives on today.

TIMOTHY R. PAUKETAT is Associate Professor of Anthropology at the University of Illinois at Urbana-Champaign. His publications include *The Archaeology of Traditions* (2001), *Cahokia: Domination and Ideology in the Mississippian World* (with T. Emerson, 1997), and *The Ascent of Chiefs* (1994).

Case Studies in Early Societies

Series Editor
Rita P. Wright, New York University

This series aims to introduce students to early societies that have been the subject of sustained archaeological research. Each study is also designed to demonstrate a contemporary method of archaeological analysis in action, and the authors are all specialists currently engaged in field research. The books have been planned to cover many of the same fundamental issues. Tracing long-term developments, and describing and analyzing a discrete segment in the prehistory or history of a region, they represent an invaluable tool for comparative analysis. Clear, well organized, authoritative and succinct, the case studies are an important resource for students, and for scholars in related fields, such as anthropology, ethnohistory, history and political science. They also offer the general reader accessible introductions to important archaeological sites.

Other titles in the series include:

1. *Ancient Mesopotamia*
   Susan Pollock

2. *Ancient Oaxaca*
   Richard E. Blanton, Gary M. Feinman, Stephen A. Kowalewski, Linda M. Nicholas

3. *Ancient Maya*
   Arthur Demarest

4. *Ancient Jomon of Japan*
   Junko Habu

5. *Ancient Puebloan Southwest*
   John Kantner

Ancient Cahokia and the Mississippians

Timothy R. Pauketat

University of Illinois

CAMBRIDGE
UNIVERSITY PRESS

CAMBRIDGE UNIVERSITY PRESS
Cambridge, New York, Melbourne, Madrid, Cape Town, Singapore,
São Paulo, Delhi, Dubai, Tokyo

Cambridge University Press
32 Avenue of the Americas, New York, NY 10013-2473, USA

www.cambridge.org
Information on this title: www.cambridge.org/9780521520669

First published 2004
Third printing 2007

A catalog record for this publication is available from the British Library

ISBN 978-0-521-81740-0 Hardback
ISBN 978-0-521-52066-9 Paperback

Transferred to digital printing 2010

For Susan

Contents

Figures

Boxes

Acknowledgements

Portions of my research reviewed in this book have been funded by the National Science Foundation (BNS-9305404, SBR 99-96169), National Geographic Society, Wenner-Gren Foundation for Anthropological Research, Cahokia Mounds Museum Society, Illinois Transportation Archaeological Research Program, Illinois Department of Transportation, Illinois State Museum, St. Louis District Corps of Engineers, Illinois Division of Natural Resources, University of Illinois, SUNY-Buffalo, and University of Oklahoma. I am most grateful to Tom Emerson, Mark Esarey, Hal Hassan, William Iseminger, Terry Martin, Terry Norris, Joseph Phillippe, John Walthall, Michael Wiant, and John Yellen. I also thank a host of landowners, tenant farmers, and realtors who allowed crews of students to dig on their land: Dan Davis, Terry Johnson, Don Lienesch, Ron Christ, Vernon Kombrink, Ron Stein, Connie Stohlman, and the late Hal Smith.

Since 1999, Susan Alt has directed excavations of the Richland Archaeological Project, and I am most indebted to her. We shared the distress of negotiating access to sites about to be destroyed. In this and other endeavors we were joined by Jeff Kruchten, who supervised various crews over the years. A number of other supervisors and field crew members also worked on and stressed out over these and the other digs of the Early Cahokia, Cahokia-Waterline, and Richland Archaeological Projects: Tamira Brennan, Don Dycus, Ian Fricker, Stephanie Glienke, Jenny Howe, Mike Litchford, Sherry McAlister, Phil Millhouse, Mark Rees, Katherine Roberts, Tracy Steffgen, Amber Vanderwarker, Jill Wesselmann, and Greg Wilson. Their efforts, friendship, and generosity are much appreciated. The same goes for Jeff Christ, the world's best archaeological heavy equipment operator. Students were invariably impressed when Christ's backhoe or trackhoe showed up on site (they were even more impressed by his inevitable second coming).

Others deserve credit for their help in various ways during one or more field seasons: Tom Emerson, Eve Hargrave, Mike Hargrave, William Iseminger, John Kelly, Larry Kinsella, Brad Koldehoff, Terry Norris, Lee and Lila Vick, John Walthall, and Ken Williams. That is Lee and Lila at Halliday in Fig. 1.5. Also serving as scales are Preston Miracle at Toltec (Fig. 3.2), Andy Bryan and Sarah Anderson at Grossmann (Fig. 4.8), and Susan Alt at Fatherland (Fig. 7.6). While no photo of Mike Litchford appears in the book, his house reconstruction does (Fig. 4.8, bottom), built with the help of an undergraduate university class after he, Susan, Jeff, and Tamira dug the original at the Pfeffer site in 2000. The undergraduates in the class included Ian Fricker, Stephanie Glienke, Maria Roditis, Tracy Steffgen, and Nick Wisseman, among those participants in what would become the *crème de la crème* of field schools: the 2001 season – also known as "the year of the mother" – at Grossmann.

I am most grateful to Rita Wright for making this book part of the series, and to Simon Whitmore for guiding me through to the final product. Susan Alt, David Anderson, Tom Emerson, Melvin Fowler, William Iseminger, Mike Lewis, and Robert Hall provided additional assistance with images, drawings, and other information in this book. Jack Scott's superb artwork appears in Figs. 3.1, 4.14, 6.8, 7.1, and 7.3. Anonymous readers of the book draft provided helpful commentary, as did my friends David Anderson and Tom Emerson. Of course, all omissions and errors of fact are mine alone.

Finally, allow me to note my appreciation of old friends and relatives. Brad Koldehoff and Terry Norris have provided much-needed friendly advice and feedback. Likewise, my sisters Elaine Gregson, Janice Rudert, and Cindy Walker, my mother Janet Pauketat, my daughters Regena N. Pauketat and Janet V. T. Pauketat, and my wife Susan Alt have supported me through thick and thin. I am as always most grateful.

1 Civilization in North America

This wasn't a chiefdom; it was a kingdom!

Robert Carneiro[1]

"Civilization" is not a word typically associated with ancient North America. The cities, stone pyramids, and writing systems of the Old World, Mexico, or Peru are not generally thought to have existed in the pre-Columbian Mississippi valley. However, if we define a civilization as a kind of political culture or as a great tradition associated with populated administrative centers and spread across some portion of a continent, then it is clear that there was a pre-Columbian civilization in the Mississippi valley, or at least the early stages of one. Archaeologists often call it "Mississippian culture" and refer to the many peoples of the time simply as "Mississippians."

There were political and religious centers associated with the Mississippian civilization, the largest of which was Cahokia, along the middle portion of the Mississippi (Fig. 1.1).[2] And there were historical effects emanating from each Mississippian center. Cahokia's historical effects were great. If there were founding events that kicked off Mississippian history, they happened at Cahokia. In this way, Cahokians created early Mississippian culture and they laid the groundwork for things to come, including the so-called "Southern Cult." Their descendants greeted Hernando de Soto in the twilight years of the Mississippian world, and proved worthy opponents to the westward expansion of the young United States.

The original Mississippians built huge monuments of earth, wood, and thatch. Their political capitals were home to many hundreds to thousands of people. The ideas behind their monuments, symbols, and capital towns were founded on the traditions of centuries past, but the fact of their founding forever altered the futures of many people throughout the mid-continent, the Great Plains, and the Gulf Coastal Plain over a period of several centuries, from the eleventh to well into the sixteenth and seventeenth centuries AD. In fact, the timing of the invasion of North America by Europeans in the sixteenth century meant that many of the people met

1

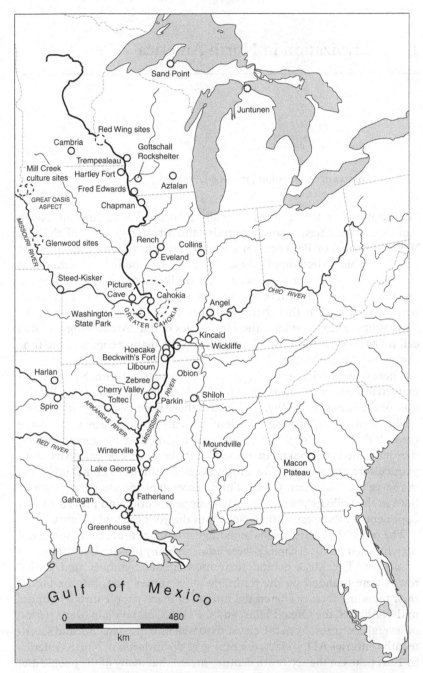

1.1 The Mississippi River valley, showing select Pre-Columbian sites

by the Old World intruders were Mississippians. The circumstances of that meeting, in one way or another, shaped the contours of the colonial experience that led up to the founding of the United States in 1776.

It also gave shape to the science of archaeology. Thomas Jefferson's well-known excavations of a Virginia burial mound and his recognition of America's Indian heritage mark the beginning of scientific archaeology, but a less enlightened view soon supplanted the Jeffersonian vision (Wallace 1999). By the end of the eighteenth century, many Indian peoples had forgotten the mound-building traditions, and westward-looking Anglo-Americans were all too eager to dispossess Indians of their lands. By the time Andrew Jackson became president, in 1829, the idea that Indians could have built the mounds was concluded to be absurd. Mythical peoples from the Old World were imagined to have built them. Indians were thought incapable of the coordinated labor necessary for construction projects.

Unfortunately, the legacy of this nineteenth-century "Moundbuilder Myth" still lurks in the dark corners of archaeology, shrouded in some of the well-meaning interpretive schemes used by archaeologists and laypersons alike (see Kehoe 1998; Patterson 1995). In plain words, that legacy is racist. But it lives wherever archaeologists understate the cultural achievements or de-emphasize the historical importance of First Nations peoples. It is hidden in words. For instance, Cahokia has been called a "mound center," a "town-and-mound" complex, or the "ceremonial center" of a "chiefdom." Few North American archaeologists call it a city. Fewer still would think it was the center of a kingdom or a state. Even the term "pyramid" is thought too immodest by many eastern North American archaeologists. They prefer to call these four-sided and flat-topped equivalents of stone pyramids in Mexico or adobe *huacas* in Peru, simply, mounds.

However, if Cahokia, Cahokians, and Cahokia's mounds had been in ancient Mesopotamia, China, or Africa, archaeologists might not hesitate to identify pyramids in a city at the center of an early state. Certainly, as the Near Eastern archaeologist Norman Yoffee has succinctly put it, when it comes to thinking about the big picture, many North American archaeologists are "downsizers" (Yoffee *et al.* 1999:267). We have inherited the conservative and subtly racist terminology of the nineteenth century (Kehoe 1998). So perhaps it is justifiable if a little cynical to wonder if Cahokia might be more easily conceptualized as a city if only Cahokians had built with stone instead of earth and wood, or if Cahokia had been in Asia or the Near East, instead of North America. If so, then cultural biases have crept into our interpretations of New World people, and the Moundbuilder Myth lives.

Goal of the book

If the first challenge of North American archaeology is to avoid the biases of the shared heritage of Indian removal and cultural disenfranchisement, the second challenge is to figure out what places such as Cahokia were all about. To that end, we have to admit that no two archaeologists in any part of the world completely agree on how to identify a city, a chiefdom, or an early state. Was early Monte Albán a chiefly capital, a city-state, or an early imperial capital? What about Eridu, Great Zimbabwe, or Chavín de Huantar? Was the Predynastic Egyptian "Scorpion King" actually just a chief?

Chiefdoms, city-states, and kingdoms come in various shapes and sizes. Those in China may have been quite unlike those in Mesopotamia, Peru, or Ghana. To get around this obvious problem, archaeologists tend to assume that while the shapes and sizes of their territories may vary, the governing bodies at the heart of any polity were similar and thus so were their developmental histories. Unfortunately, this is seldom actually proven (see chapter 8). For this reason, if no other, Cahokia and the Mississippian peoples of North America can provide much-needed perspective from which to view other civilizations. How did Mississippian North Americans govern themselves? How did diverse Mississippi valley peoples become *a people*, living under the moral authority of Mississippian rules or rulers? To what degree did government suppress or celebrate community, or vice versa? Did group identities and ethnicities develop hand-in-hand with a division of labor, warfare, social stratification, or economic centralization? Did Mississippian civilization emerge as part of a struggle among politically motivated people with divergent interests *or* was it an outcome of forces beyond anyone's control? The answers to these questions are the answers to civilization itself. Archaeologists hotly debate them.

The debates between archaeologists, especially as they involve the Mississippians, often boil down to differences of opinion about the importance of people, material culture, places, and historical events in shaping the North American experience. Fortunately, the opinions of archaeologists are only as good as the archaeological data that we have on hand. New finds and excavations keep changing our minds about what happened in the past. Thus, I am confident that present-day disagreements will be laid to rest with more of the kinds of archaeological data summarized in this book. But whatever the final answers to the questions posed, most can agree that the processes of civilization were under way in the Mississippi valley.

The goal of this book is to allow the reader to weigh the evidence for how and why ancient Cahokia and the Mississippians developed over a six-century span. This is the story of the early Mississippian peoples. I begin with an overview of the cultural chronology of the Mississippi valley and then turn to the archaeologists, their discoveries, and their projects. The chapter ends with some notes on the theoretical framework of this book. The rest of the book examines the economic, social, religious, and political underpinnings of the Mississippian world.

Time and place

At AD 900, a diverse array of peoples lived along the Mississippi River and its tributaries large and small. Most were living what archaeologists generally refer to as "Woodland" cultural traditions. The people lived these traditions to the extent that they actively incorporated remembrances of their forebears into their own cultural creations and daily practices. But change was also a part of these lived traditions. In the centuries leading up to the day that Hernando de Soto's army crossed the cypress-lined Mississippi in 1541, populations had segmented, recombined, and migrated into or out of regions where native governments had arisen or fallen.

Mississippi valley archaeologists track their movements and the passage of time using pottery styles, absolute dates, horizon markers, and cypress tree-rings. In regions yet to see significant archaeological excavations, the chronologies remain coarse-grained and reliant on very general pottery stylistic changes and a few radiocarbon, archaeomagnetic, or thermoluminscence dates. The chronologies of these regions consist of a series of one or two century-long phases, too lengthy to permit observations of anything but the most general economic or cultural change. However, in the greater Cahokia region, archaeologists use the temporally sensitive pottery attributes of stratified or superimposed deposits of garbage to create micro-chronologies for specific places, obtaining suites of radiocarbon dates to frame the time-series at sites like Cahokia. Here, extensive excavations allow archaeologists to measure change between decades and, sometimes, years or even seasons. Indeed, there is a series of historical events or moments that can be isolated owing to their appearance in multiple media at multiple places. In this way, archaeologists begin to approach the historical event as a real unit of observation (e.g., Pauketat *et al.* 2002).

Such time-series data can be compared across and between regions if anchored by absolute dates or *horizon markers*. Radiocarbon assays are most widely used to tie cultural sequences to real time. However, even the best dates have one-sigma error values of plus-or-minus sixty years. Dendrochronology offers another way to anchor portions of the later Mississippian period, although coverage is spotty at best. There are a few

UPPER MIDWEST	GREATER CAHOKIA	OHIO-MISSISSIPPI	LOWER MISSISSIPPI	AD
	VACANT QUARTER		Parkin	1400
			Nodena	1350
ONEOTA	SAND PRAIRIE	POWERS		1300
			Winterville	
	MOOREHEAD	TINSLEY HILL CAIRO LOWLANDS	Lake George	1250
pan-regional horizon				1200
	LATE STIRLING	CHERRY VALLEY		1150
Aztalan Chapman	EARLY STIRLING	KINCAID I–II	Lake Providence	
Trempealeau	LOHMANN	Obion	Greenhouse	1100
pan-regional horizon				1050
		Zebree Hoecake		
TERMINAL LATE WOODLAND EFFIGY MOUND CULTURE	TERMINAL LATE WOODLAND	Toltec PLUM BAYOU	COLES CREEK	1000
				950
				800

1.2 Chronology chart

floating tree-ring sequences showing possible correlations between major events and climatic fluctuations (see Lopinot 1994; Ollendorf 1993).

Thus, horizon markers are highly useful in tying the Mississippian regions together. Such temporal anchors in the Mississippi valley include specific craft objects or decorative motifs associated with particular sites, schools of artisans, or centrally sponsored distribution events. Because of their wide distribution, Cahokia's horizon markers serve to calibrate other less secure Mississippian chronologies up and down the Mississippi, and give us a sense of the importance of the place in Mississippian cultural histories (Fig. 1.2). For instance, Thomas Emerson and colleagues (2003) have discovered that some famous carved-stone figurines were not made over a long timespan in the various places where they were discovered, but were made at Cahokia in the early 1100s and later carried to distant places. Similarly, James Stoltman (2000) has used petrographic techniques to identify Cahokian pots and thereby link a series of sites to twelfth-century Cahokia. Likewise, Phillip Phillips and James Brown (1978) isolated a "Braden" style that they associated with Cahokia (see also Brown and Kelly 2000).

Archaic and Woodland periods

Six millennia after the first known human "Paleo-Indian" inhabitants arrived in the Mississippi valley, Archaic period peoples in present-day

Louisiana built some of the first public monuments in the New World. These were the mounds at the Watson Brake site, raised around an oval plaza, indicating some kind of social complexity already at about 3400 BC (Saunders *et al.* 1997; Sassaman and Hackenberger 2001). There were other such sites over the subsequent centuries, including the well-known Poverty Point site at about 1600 BC. Besides mounds, the Late Archaic Poverty Point culture in Louisiana is defined by a suite of ritual or craft objects and practices that seem to have diffused well up the Mississippi River by 800 BC or so. By this time, the beginning of the Early Woodland period, pottery had been adopted across much of the Southeast and interior Midwest (Sassaman 1995).

The subsequent Woodland period can be demarcated by the intensification of horticulture and the use of pottery by families to cook the seeds of native grasses. On the heels of the Late Archaic, semi-sedentary "base camps" seem to have disappeared across much of the Midwest, even as the people of distinctive corporate groups engaged in elaborate mortuary rituals and, in the Ohio valley, built impressive "Adena" burial mounds. In the lower Mississippi valley, mound construction on the scale of Poverty Point had ceased. But mortuary rites became complicated central affairs there and elsewhere during the Middle Woodland period (200 BC–AD 400).

The Mesoamerican cultigen, maize, made its first appearance in eastern North America during the Middle Woodland period, although its adoption was tentative and discontinuous across the east (Fritz 1990; Hart 1999; Riley *et al.* 1990). By this time, the well-known Hopewell culture(s) had coalesced along the Ohio River. The lesser-known Marksville and Havana cultures, among others, were the Hopewellian counterparts along the Mississippi River, stretching from Louisiana to Wisconsin. Tomb burials and village sites dating to this well-known period are frequently associated with specific horizon markers of the period: obsidian knives, hammered copper axes and ornaments, carved-stone smoking pipes, antler headdresses, and "Hopewell" pots boldly incised with abstract eyes, long-necked birds, and perhaps bodily representations (e.g., Benn and Green 2000:467).

Late Woodland period (AD 400–900)

Hopewellian-style artifact types and mortuary rituals disappeared by or were heavily remodeled during Late Woodland times (AD 400–900). The peoples of these "good gray cultures" could be said to have experienced a cultural "collapse" or a sweeping transformation of "technologies, ideologies, and organization[s]" (Benn and Green 2000:479; McElrath *et al.* 2000:15; Williams 1963). The period is marked by population expansion, possible migrations, localized isolationism, the introduction of the bow and arrow, food production intensification and, to the south, mound-and-plaza constructions (Anderson and Mainfort 2001; McElrath *et al.* 2000). Rock cairns and possibly defensive "hill forts" are found through the interior hills of Missouri, southern Illinois, and Kentucky. Effigy mounds of birds, bears, water spirits, and such are found in special places from Iowa to Ohio, but no mounds were built in the region soon to see the rise of Cahokia. Settlement locations and sizes shift in different ways, by locality, perhaps related to social and defense exigencies associated with the widespread adoption of the bow and arrow around AD 600. Sites decreased in size in some parts of the central Mississippi valley, nucleated in others, and became major "ceremonial centers" in the central Arkansas and lower Mississippi river valleys. Much pottery from the midcontinent was cordmarked or cord-impressed and minimally decorated, while southern ceramic traditions appear to continue in intricate Gulf Coast modes.

Along the middle stretch of the Mississippi, pottery seems to have changed little for centuries, meaning that archaeologists there necessarily rely on absolute dating techniques to track change. Carefully calibrated radiocarbon assays, taking the fluctuations in atmospheric carbon isotopes into account, show that the Late Woodland period lasted up to AD 1050 in southwestern Illinois. In other Midwestern and Midsouthern locations, there were Late Woodland people at least up to AD 1200, while in far-off Great Lakes, Great Plains, or northeastern areas the period lasted until European contact.

Crushed mussel shell temper in pots, a major "Mississippian" hallmark, appears to have been an innovation of southeast Missouri potters in the eighth century AD, based on a suite of thermoluminescence dates (Lynott 1987). However, this technological novelty may not have been as readily "selected" by people up and down the Mississippi as occasionally asserted (O'Brien *et al.* 1994). Shell-tempered pots make up only a fraction of ceramic refuse both of northern "Mississippianized" and of southern "Coles Creek" and "Baytown" peoples even at AD 1100. Michael Nassaney (1991) years ago recognized the persistence of various Late Woodland attributes to comprise a kind of cultural resistance to Mississippian changes. It seems they were selecting *against* the ideas, meanings, or practices embodied by this so-called innovation.

Likewise, the adoption of maize has been used as a hallmark of the Mississippian period, and yet it was differentially adopted before, during, and after the Mississippian period in eastern North America. The growing of maize, or the decision not to grow maize, may have been quite intentional. Maize intensification lagged especially in the more "insular" Coles Creek region of the lower Mississippi valley (see Kidder 1992, 2002; Kidder and Fritz 1993; Lynott *et al.* 1986). There, people built elaborate flat-topped pyramids around rectangular plazas long before adding corn to their diets. In fact, the intensified production of maize appears to have co-occurred with the introduction of shell-tempered pottery only in a restricted zone of southeast Missouri and northeast Arkansas (e.g., Morse and Morse 1983). So, was there really a gradual emergence of Mississippian ways of life? Perhaps not. However, it is likely that new cultural boundaries if not distinct cultural identities were under construction during the "terminal Late Woodland" period, as indicated by the adoption of or resistance to agricultural intensification, technologies, settlement forms, and material-cultural forms after AD 900 (Fortier and McElrath 2002).

The terminal Late Woodland Red-Filmed Horizon (AD 900–1050)

From the central alluvial valley northward, the terminal Late Woodland period is a time of notable changes in settlement form and location. Certain villages grew larger as populations gravitated toward the agricultural resources of rich floodplain localities. At this time, Cahokia was one of several villages in a 120 km stretch of floodplain or "bottom" called, in colonial times, the "American Bottom." A similar minimally centralized settlement pattern characterizes a series of floodplain localities or variously named "bottoms" during the tenth century north of Thebes Gap south to Memphis (Kreisa 1987; Lafferty and Price 1996; Mainfort 1996).

Here, the people also intensified maize production after AD 800 (Kelly 1990a; Mainfort 1996; D. Morse and P. Morse 1990a), leading some to call these the "Emergent Mississippian" people (but see Fortier and McElrath 2002; Muller 1997:118). This maize intensification did not continue south of the Toltec site, where there was only a "slight use of maize" (Rolingson 1998:132, 2002:55; Schambach 2002:103–8). From the American Bottom south to Reelfoot Lake, Tennessee, the fact of food-production intensification was accompanied by the use of pottery coated with red films, particularly in the area around the confluence of the Ohio and Mississippi rivers. Red films or "slips" involve the application of a thin coat of liquefied clay premixed with pulverized hematite for color (see Rice 1987). This phenomenon was in no way uniformly adopted across the Midsouth, but seems nonetheless to represent both a temporal horizon and a series of interacting peoples, at least some of whom may have relocated from one part of the middle Mississippi area to another.

This "Red-Filmed Horizon" also witnessed the introduction of a new chipped-stone hoe blade type. These were large and durable versions of older and more modest Woodland digging tools, now made from "Mill Creek" chert in Union County, Illinois (Cobb 2000). In years to come, many Cahokian and Midsouthern farmers would use these widely traded Mill Creek hoe blades.

Newly calibrated radiocarbon assays suggest that the terminal Late Woodland period or the Red-Filmed Horizon did not end until the eleventh century AD in the American Bottom. In other parts of the Mississippi valley, the terminal Late Woodland period ended abruptly when Cahokians or their representatives contacted local people. Even in the American Bottom itself, Cahokia's abrupt appearance represents a historical disjuncture. Increased exchange or culture contact, particularly between people living in the lower Mississippi valley and those occupying the growing village of Cahokia, also characterizes the terminal Late Woodland period (Kelly 1991). Cahokian novelties were overlaid on the local material-cultural repertoires of mid-continental Late Woodland peoples. Some populations may have been displaced as a direct or indirect result of terminal Late Woodland and early Mississippian changes emanating from the American Bottom. In any case, the abrupt historical character of this contact ensures archaeological difficulties when attempting to use conventional radiometric techniques to pinpoint it in time. Complicating the matter further are the blips in the radiocarbon curve between AD 1000 and 1200 (Stuiver and Pearson 1986). There are several possible calendar dates for any one individual radiocarbon assay during this time, owing to erratic fluctuations in the amount of atmospheric radiocarbon.

The Early Mississippian period (AD 1050–1200)

The formation of Cahokia is synonymous with the beginning of the early Mississippian period (Pauketat 1994). A suite of horizon markers denote this rapid development: triangular Cahokia-type arrowheads, Cahokia-style "chunkey" stones, the predominance of shell-tempered pottery, a novel wall trench architectural style, pyramidal mound construction, and a suite of icons depicting supernatural themes. The appearance of these attributes is not uniform outside of Cahokia itself, although a distinctive set of early Mississippian pottery attributes (incurved-rim jars, bi-knobbed loop handles, blank-faced hooded bottles, etc.) has been used to delineate an early Mississippian horizon stretching from eastern Oklahoma to western Tennessee, and down into the oddly out-of-place Ocmulgee region of central Georgia (Griffin 1952, 1967). Given the pan-Mississippi valley appearance of a distinctive type of decorative earpiece, the early portion of the Mississippian period has also been termed the "Long-Nosed God Horizon" (Williams and Goggin 1956).

The Mill Creek hoe blade industry in southern Illinois and its counterpart chert quarry and lithic workshop complexes in the Ozarks (near Cahokia) and in Tennessee are salient features of the early Mississippian landscape. Cahokians and others at lesser regional centers may have attempted directly to monitor production of the hoe blades, chipped-stone knives, scepters, and axe heads (also known as "celts"). Equally clear, however, is the fact that the chipped-stone artisans and their local communities had considerable day-to-day autonomy (Cobb 2000). Then again, the levels of lithic tool production were doubtless a function of an emerging network linking Cahokia and other large Mississippian polities at places such as Kincaid and Angel in the lower Ohio valley, Obion in northwestern Tennessee, and Shiloh in southwestern Tennessee (Koldehoff and Carr 2001). Smaller mounds centers punctuate the major floodplains (or bottoms) between these sites and Cahokia.

Elsewhere in portions of the Midsouth, the early Mississippian period is marked by apparent regional abandonments, or "vacancies" (House 1996; Nassaney 2001). At the same time, in northwestern Illinois, southwestern Wisconsin, and eastern Iowa, the early Mississippian period is actually a continuation of the Late Woodland occupations, albeit with the complicating factors of population displacement and "Mississippianization" (Emerson 1991; Pauketat and Emerson 1997; Stoltman 1991). Cahokian pots or copies complement local cord-impressed pottery forms. Arrowheads, beads, and stone axe heads probably originating at Cahokia are among the artifacts found in these northern places. A Cahokian microlithic tool technology and Cahokia area raw materials also seem to have been transferred to some Midsouthern peoples. Cahokian pottery types, some of which were probably fine-wares made exclusively by a few potters for specific purposes, are readily identifiable from Lake Superior to Louisiana (see summaries by Hall 1991; Pauketat 1998b). Carved red-stone statuettes or figurines made at or near Cahokia ended up in Alabama, Arkansas, Louisiana, Missouri, Oklahoma, and Wisconsin (Emerson and Hughes 2000; Emerson et al. 2002, 2003).

Given the far-flung Cahokian objects, archaeologists in other parts of the Mississippi valley use Cahokian dates and Cahokian phase names to synchronize regional chronologies. Cahokia's "Lohmann" phase is currently dated to AD 1050–1100, bracketing the dramatic events of Cahokia's political consolidation and the first Mississippian outposts or clear contacts between Cahokians and northerners. The "early Stirling" phase encapsulates the next half-century climax of Cahokian influence

(AD 1100–1150), easily identifiable owing to the Cahokian red-stone figurines and to the unique and widely distributed and emulated "Ramey
Incised" pots (Emerson 1997a, 1997c; Emerson and Hughes 2000;
Pauketat and Emerson 1991). The "late Stirling" phase (AD 1150–1200)
sees the initial waning of Cahokia's regional dominance and interregional
prominence that culminates in a reorganized and reduced "Moorehead"
phase polity (AD 1200–1275).[3]

The Late Mississippian period (AD 1200–c. 1600)

Cahokia's Moorehead phase is of less importance for synchronizing regional chronologies since Cahokian influence had faded considerably.[4]
Radiocarbon dates for this period are supplemented by a cypress and
cedar wood dendrochronology for certain localities. First introduced at
the Kincaid site, the potential of dendrochronology still exceeds the realized benefits (Stahle and Wolfman 1985). However, the beginnings of
a pan-regional Mississippian dendrochronology exist that will ultimately
synchronize chronologies according to real calendar years.

Fortunately, archaeologists working on sites up and down the Mississippi River have found that AD 1200 begins a phase of notable change
across the mid-continent and the Coastal Plain. This fact may be the most
telling acknowledgement of the former importance of Cahokia as an interregional cultural force. To the south, the beginning of the thirteenth
century saw new or expanded Mississippian polities and political capitals,
as peoples appear to have undergone their own political consolidations at
about this time. This includes the large and spacious Moundville site in
Alabama. The regional consolidation there occurred at or shortly before
AD 1200, with effects that included a political and economic shadow
several thousand km^2 (or greater) in extent, similar to early Cahokia's
even longer shadow, within which no major centers existed (see Knight
and Steponaitis 1998; Steponaitis 1991:226). In southeast Missouri and
southern Illinois, the new central sites of modest polities were compact,
with steep earthen pyramids surrounded by wooden palisades and moats.
Many of these smaller Mississippian capitals appear more like the guarded
compounds of a few high-ranking families than the spacious ceremonial
grounds of their early Mississippian forebears. This seems true also of
larger sites in the Yazoo Basin of southwestern Mississippi, Winterville
and Lake George, where twenty-three and twenty-five (or more) pyramids were crowded into site areas of 20 and 22 ha respectively (Brain
1989; Williams and Brain 1983). To the north of Cahokia, palisaded villages were built, and frequently incinerated in conflagrations, beginning
at AD 1200 (see Conrad 1991).

1.3 Select Southeastern Ceremonial Complex motifs

This general Mississippian expansion produced a distinctive Mississippian iconography termed the "Southeastern Ceremonial Complex" (also known as the Southern Cult). This complex is often correlated with temple rites, earth-fertility symbolism, ancestor worship, and a falcon-warrior ideology. Suites of icons, motifs, and decorative elements have been recognized across the Mississippian world, albeit in distinctive local variants (Fig. 1.3). Some think Cahokia is the original inspiration behind the southeastern iconography (e.g., Emerson *et al.* 2003). Certainly, each Mississippian polity served as a filter through which cultural meanings and icons took on new meanings or new forms such that, in a sense, there was a series of Southeastern Ceremonial Complexes (Knight *et al.* 2001; Muller 1989:26).

Thus Mississippian artisans and politicians altered the media and meanings of Southern Cult symbols, and thus archaeologists use the forms and associations of the symbols to date rock art, monument construction, and site occupation history (e.g., Diaz-Granados *et al.* 2001; Muller 1989). The dénouement of this cultural history might be said to have occurred at the famous Spiro site, in eastern Oklahoma. There, the Southeastern Ceremonial objects and icons from generations past and from far-flung sites were hoarded, revalued, and ultimately interred in an extravagant mortuary complex at about AD 1400. The fifteenth and sixteenth centuries would not see anything comparable, and Southern Cult symbolism seems to have lost its currency. Indeed, the "communalization" of formerly exclusive imagery became commonplace after AD 1200, epitomized by the placing of falcon and earth-monster icons and "Ramey" iconography on the everyday cooking pots of people in the south and the north (Knight 1997).

Contact period Mississippian (AD 1600 ± 100)

Archaeologists use stylistic elements of material culture to link textual accounts of historic groups with presumed pre-Columbian traditions, but not without uncertainty and some controversy (e.g., Hoffman 1990; Schambach 2002). The problems associated with the process include the fact that traditions are contingent on the social memories of people, and things remembered in such group contexts are always subject to politics (Pauketat and Alt 2003). Tribal identities as we know them are products of history, and are not necessarily pre-Columbian realities. Given the changes and chaos of the times, the most difficult period to track chronologically may be the contact period. Unmistakable signs of Hernando de Soto's army in the Midsouth between AD 1541 and 1543 take the form of a miscellany of trade items and cast-offs (notably a particular kind of metal bell) – never mind the clear signs of depopulation, violence, and migration (Ramenofsky 1987; Young and Hoffman 1993).

Of course, migrations had been a feature of social life at least since the terminal Late Woodland period. Likewise, an increase in endemic violence – even what we could call a village-level form of ethnic cleansing – accompanied the formation of ethnicities in portions of the eastern Plains and central Mississippi valley since at least AD 1400 (see Santure et al. 1990; Willey and Emerson 1993). So the migrations and intergroup violence of the European contact era, linked with coastal slave trading and apparent attempts to bolster locally flagging populations, exacerbated a pre-contact pattern. The severity of depopulation and migration complicates archaeological attempts to track change through time.

Archaeologists, explorers, and historians

European explorers witnessed the culmination of Mississippian history, as written in accounts of their expeditions. There were also other French, Spanish, English, and Anglo-American missionaries, traders, artists, and military officers who made written accounts of the final days of Mississippian governments and the profound changes of the post-contact period. French colonial surveyors made the first maps of "anciens tombe aux des sauvages" or mounds near St. Louis (Finiels 1989; Marshall 1992). Later, men with a heightened concern for natural history followed the French: James Adair, William Bartram, George Rogers Clark, and others (James 1928; Schoolcraft 1860; Williams 1930). Clark's Virginia neighbor, Thomas Jefferson, consulted these explorers and doubtless learned of the mounds and plazas of southeastern towns (Waskelkov and Braund 1995). As president, Jefferson began inviting Indian leaders and representatives to Washington DC. He monitored explorers', naturalists', and Indian agents' accounts of western peoples. He requested or oversaw the expeditions of William Dunbar, Thomas Freeman, Zebulon Pike, and Meriwether Lewis and William Clark (the brother of George Rogers

1.4 St. Louis and the Big Mound in 1840 (lithograph by John Casper Wild, Missouri Historical Society, St. Louis)

Clark), advising them always to describe the Indian cultures and archaeological remains that they encountered. He doubtless read William Clark's notes of an Indian "fortress" of nine mounds "forming a Circle" made in January 1804 before the Corps of Discovery left the American Bottom; Clark may have been describing a Cahokian outlier – the Mitchell site (Moulton 1986:153–4). And Jefferson read Henry Marie Brackenridge's description of the arrangements of earthen pyramids today called the St. Louis, East St. Louis, and Cahokia sites, published in an 1811 newspaper account and sent in an 1813 letter to then ex-president Thomas Jefferson (Brackenridge 1818).

In 1819, the same year that naturalist Thomas Nutall discovered the eighteen pyramids of the Toltec site in central Arkansas, Major Stephen Long headed an expedition west to the Rockies. Delayed in St. Louis, expedition members mapped the twenty-six mounds of the St. Louis group, as had Brackenridge before them (Peale 1862).[5] Continuing west, Long and his men encountered many Indian tribes, the first of which were those whom Thomas Jefferson in 1804 described as "the great nation South of the Missouri" – the Osage (Rollings 1992:215). In subsequent years, artists, wayfarers, and engineers from Karl Bodmer and John Casper Wild to Lieutenant Robert E. Lee sketched, painted, and mapped the mounds of St. Louis, Cahokia, or East St. Louis (Fig. 1.4). Perhaps a few wondered what Indian nations had built these mounds.

However, a few short years later, the identities of American Indians if not their impressive mounds were irrelevancies in the Anglo-American vision of Manifest Destiny. Instead, the dominant "theory" was that American Indians were not the builders of the mounds. A race of Moundbuilders was thought to have been responsible, dreamily believed to have originated in ancient Israel, India, Wales, or even Atlantis. One version had the ancestors of the Aztecs as the Moundbuilders, driven out by later savage races of Indians; the Aztalan site in Wisconsin was thus named in 1837 for the mythical Aztec homeland.

The Moundbuilder Myth, although pre-dating the founding of the United States, increasingly became the common sense of the new republic. The myth undergirded much nineteenth-century thought, including early well-known surveys of mounds in the Ohio and Mississippi valleys (DeHaas 1869; McAdams 1887; Schoolcraft 1860; Squier and Davis 1848). This common sense was doubtless helped along by the Anglo-American battles with American Indians: campaigns against the native people of the old Northwest during the War of 1812, Andrew Jackson's 1813–14 campaign against the Creek, and the suppression of uprisings in Florida and elsewhere. President Andrew Jackson saw to the defeat of Blackhawk in 1832, and to the removal of northwestern and southeastern Indians to Oklahoma territory with the Congressional Removal Act of 1830 (Boewe 2000).

Mississippian descendants actively resisted the cultural dispossession embodied in the Moundbuilder Myth, perhaps most notably by fighting as soldiers from Oklahoma territory for the Confederacy (e.g., Moulton 1985). And, while the Union emerged victorious, the 1861–65 War between the States nevertheless hastened the end of the Moundbuilder Myth (Williams 1991:61). Civil War soldiers marched by, floated past, camped on, and fought over Indian grounds, most famously at Shiloh, Tennessee, where the Union casualties included one Major John Wesley Powell. After the war, the one-armed Powell, now director of the Smithsonian's Bureau of American Ethnology, commissioned a fellow Illinoisian, Cyrus Thomas, to muster sufficient data to prove that American Indians themselves were the Moundbuilders. During the 1880s, Cyrus Thomas did just that, laying the Moundbuilder Myth to rest, at least officially (Thomas 1985).

Civil War veterans conducted additional systematic surveys and studies of key Mississippi valley sites and artifacts (e.g., C. Jones 1999; J. Jones 1876; Putnam 1878; Thruston 1897). These surveys included the mapping of the St. Louis, East St. Louis, and Cahokia sites by Dr. John J. R. Patrick, a dentist who had returned from the war to practice in the town of Belleville, Illinois a few kilometers southeast of the Cahokia site (J. Kelly 2000:9). Patrick witnessed the expansion of the railroads west and accelerated commercial and industrial development that accompanied the end of the war. The former frontier town and then gateway city of St. Louis was perhaps the most thoroughly transformed at this time. The last of the twenty-six Indian pyramids in St. Louis, up to then colloquially called "Mound City," was a large *ridge-top* mound – locally called the "Big Mound" or "Le Grange de Terre" (the earthen barn) – flattened by 1869. The expansion and grading of the floodplain city of East St. Louis resulted in the removal of the many pyramids that Brackenridge had seen there, including in 1870 the 12m high "Cemetery Mound," another of the unique ridge-top tumuli. Shortly thereafter, men building a new railroad grade in 1876 destroyed a probable ridge-top mound containing presumed elite tombs at the Mitchell site (Howland 1877). Sadly, an even larger ridge-top mound, the second largest of the Cahokia group, was destroyed as late as 1930.

In 1899, the Shiloh National Military Park Commission funded excavations into a small mound at Shiloh, Tennessee, reminiscent of the greater Cahokian ridge-top tombs (Welch 2001). The excavators found a carved-stone smoking pipe in a log-lined tomb that has proven a key piece of Mississippian history (see chapter 6). This discovery was followed in the early 1900s by many more made by men such as Clarence B. Moore, who excavated into the earthen pyramids of Mississippian sites from Florida to Arkansas (e.g., Moore 1998). Scientific excavations also were funded by the Peabody Museum at Obion in 1911 and 1912. These were followed by the large-scale digs by men such as Samuel Barrett at Aztalan and Warren King Moorehead at Cahokia in the early 1920s (see Kehoe 1997; J. Kelly 2000). Moorehead's techniques were questionable even for their day, but his lobbying efforts to save the site as a state park were successful. At the time, professional geologists did not believe that the great earthen pyramids – so obviously human constructions to Brackenridge – were anything but natural hillocks left behind by the Ice Age and the meandering Mississippi River.

In northwestern Illinois up to Minnesota, William Nickerson had been conducting controlled stratigraphic excavations at Cahokia era settlements, perfecting the "Peabody Museum Method" advocated by Frederic Ward Putnam in his correspondence with Nickerson (Bennett 1942; Browman 2002; Johnson 1991).[6] However, Nickerson's techniques and concerns surpassed those of Putnam, and were prescient for twenty-first-century archaeology. In a manuscript submitted to the Peabody Museum in 1913, he states that a region

to be properly studied should be looked at not only from the standpoint of the archaeologist but also with the eye of the topographist and geologist, and never losing sight of the light which contemporary ethnographical research in America has thrown upon all archaeological research... the aim is to demonstrate how some vexing problems can be solved if we have reports of intensive work in detail as systematic as this from every locality where such material exists, and to leave the facts I have gathered in a shape where they may be available to any student following me desiring to take up the work where I have left it. (Nickerson 1913:1–2)

Borrowing some of Nickerson's techniques, an early center of archaeological science emerged at the University of Chicago with Fay Cooper Cole's archaeological survey in 1926. The Chicago field school, first in northwestern Illinois and later at the Kincaid site in southern Illinois, trained a generation of field workers in the latest scientific techniques (Cole and Deuel 1937; Cole *et al.* 1951). Many of these men, and a few women, were hired by the federal government to participate in the great excavations of the so-called "New Deal" archaeology during the Great Depression of the 1930s, generating the first programmatic research in the Mississippi valley and beyond. Robert McCormick Adams and Winslow Walker dug Missouri and Louisiana sites, Jesse Wrench and Carl Chapman surveyed portions of Missouri, Madeline Kneberg operated the Works Progress Administration lab, James B. Griffin analyzed much of the pottery in Ann Arbor, Arthur Kelly and Charles Fairbanks took on the odd Mississippian site of Ocmulgee in Georgia, John Bennett worked in the Upper Mississippian area, and Robert Bell excavated Oklahoma Mississippian sites. Of the non-Chicago archaeologists, Glenn Black dug the Angel site, Frank Roberts worked at Shiloh, James Ford, George Quimby, Gordon Willey, and Preston Holder dug in the Deep South, and Harriet Smith worked at Cahokia (about the northernmost site to see New Deal funding, given the inability to keep work crews busy through the cold winters). Finally, Kenneth Orr salvaged what remained of the elaborate mortuary tombs of Spiro, Oklahoma, after locals used dynamite to blast to the center of the Brown and Craig mounds in 1933–35. Calling themselves the "Pocola Mining Company," these looters happened upon what was dubbed by the *Kansas City Star* newspaper "A 'King Tut' Tomb in the Arkansas Valley" and "the greatest puzzle of this continent" (Brown 1996:43, 45).

To all intents and purposes, this period of the Chicago-method and public-funded archaeology ended when the Empire of Japan bombed Pearl Harbor in 1941. Following the war, the New Deal archaeology bore significant synthetic fruit based in the wealth of comparative data generated. For instance, Antonio Waring and Preston Holder came up with the idea of the Southeastern Ceremonial Complex in 1938 (published in 1945). Even more importantly, Philip Phillips, James Ford, and James B. Griffin produced the landmark survey of the lower Mississippi valley, defining for generations to come the sites and artifacts of an area that some considered the Mississippian heartland (Phillips 1970; Phillips *et al.* 1951). In 1940–41, these men attempted to locate the major pre-Columbian sites between Memphis and New Orleans and in so doing laid the foundations for future studies of settlement patterns and cultural regions.

Their work, and the excavations of the New Deal archaeologists, served as the model for later work in the eastern Plains "River Basin Surveys," in other midwestern reservoir excavations, and in the interstate highway archaeology that began in the 1960s. Preston Holder landed a teaching job in St. Louis and, owing to the ongoing urban expansion in that area, conducted emergency digs in his spare time on the weekends with little or no funding. He would salvage what he could prior to destruction by earthmoving equipment and subsequent development. In fact, he was the first to use heavy equipment in the service of salvage archaeology in the greater Cahokia region. He asked a tractor operator who was pulling an earthmoving "belly scraper" to take a few passes over what he suspected were the remains of a Mississippian house near St. Louis in 1953. He continued to dig as he had in the New Deal days, by opening up large horizontal areas, including the buried floors of a Cahokia pyramid in 1955 and 1956 (Pauketat 1993b).

In 1960 and 1961, Warren Wittry stripped bare large portions of two neighborhoods at Cahokia (Pauketat 1998a; Young and Fowler 2000). At this time, several interstate highways were to intersect one another in the American Bottom, slicing through villages and cemeteries and cutting across the large sites of Cahokia, Mitchell, East St. Louis, and St. Louis. Much of the archaeology of this area had to be salvaged by a new breed of tireless archaeologists cutting their teeth on the complexities of American Bottom archaeology. Charles Bareis, James Porter, Warren Wittry, and others used heavy machinery to strip open large excavation blocks, beginning a new phase of site data accumulation. With their work, a new ethic of salvage archaeology emerged that blended scientific desperation with a belief in massive data recovery projects (Fig. 1.5).

Alongside the ongoing salvage operations began the first major National Science Foundation projects in the Mississippi valley. One was James B. Griffin and James Price's "Powers Phase" project in southeast Missouri, where an entire settlement pattern was defined and entire Mississippian settlements were laid open and nearly all the houses excavated (Price and Griffin 1979). Another was Melvin Fowler's Cahokia Mapping Project (Fowler 1997). A former surveying engineer, Fowler used crews to map the Cahokia site, locate and excavate portions of Cahokia's palisade wall, excavate into the largest pyramid at the site, and

1.5 Salvage archaeology at the Halliday site, St. Clair County, Illinois

open the spectacular tombs of Mound 72, in retrospect the single most significant find at the site. Entire theories and philosophical positions hinge on the interpretation of the dead buried there.

There was one extraordinary volunteer dig at this time. By 1974, Lawrence Conrad and Thomas Emerson had salvaged 200 Mississippian houses and 1300 pit features at the successively burned and rebuilt village of Orendorf in the central Illinois River valley. A coal mining company had bought the land to shovel away the earth to extract the buried coal. While Orendorf was left unprotected from such mining by the public laws of the day, historic preservation legislation was passed in the United States in the 1960s and 1970s that protected many other sites and permitted a second wave of public archaeology. The results of this legislation would far surpass those of New Deal archaeology.

In the American Bottom, former salvage archaeologists Charles Bareis and James Porter directed what would become the model of interstate highway archaeology. This was the so-called "Federal Alignment Interstate (FAI) 270" project that bisected the American Bottom. Although skirting the central Cahokia site itself, the excavations along this interstate corridor altered views of Mississippian history almost as radically as Mound 72. Because of their salvage hardened ethic, the project directors and site supervisors – Thomas Emerson, Andrew Fortier, John Kelly, Dale McElrath, George Milner, and others – exposed whole villages and farmsteads of the Cahokian era, discovering, for the first time, details of settlement and everyday life to measure the causes and effects of Mississippian civil society. The well-planned and then published archaeological excavations of the FAI-270 project produced an unbroken history of occupation from the Archaic through post-contact periods, redefining the regional chronology and laying the groundwork for a new understanding of the Mississippi valley (Bareis and Porter 1984).

The programmatic federally funded archaeology of the American Bottom continues today, a tribute to the earlier settlement archaeologists of the lower Mississippi valley survey, especially James B. Griffin (Walthall *et al.* 1997). A consultant on the FAI-270 project, Griffin was the "great synthesizer" of eastern North American archaeology. Griffin witnessed the sweep of twentieth-century archaeology and was known for his photographic memory, biting wit, and intellectual sarcasm (displayed at professional conferences to the consternation of those on the receiving end). He linked archaeological cultures with American Indian peoples from the beginning, and sought knowledge for its own sake (Griffin 1936, 1960). He was a walking archaeological encyclopedia who promoted archaeology and assisted young archaeologists, making him the undisputed champion of twentieth-century Midwestern and Southeastern archaeology. He reflected on the FAI-270 project:

The most stimulating excavation program in my recent experience has been, and still is, that of the Federal Highway I-270 project along the east side of the Mississippi flood plain opposite St. Louis...In 1977 the University of Illinois at Urbana-Champaign signed an agreement as prime contractor, with Charles J. Bareis as the general director, and I use the adjective "general" advisedly...It is certainly the most extensive continuing program in a concentrated area in eastern archaeology and has produced the most important results in regard to society adaptation and structure...I am most grateful in my retired, but not retiring, years to have contributed in a small way to the major results it has produced. (Griffin 1985:16–17)

Recent trends in Mississippian archaeology

Recent theoretical developments in archaeology are reevaluating the cultural-historical data that so concerned Griffin and that have been generated by the large federally funded archaeological programs. These theoretical changes have at least two primary sources: (1) the rise of a historical archaeology that concerns itself with cultural contacts, cultural diversity, and unique historical change, and (2) the acceptance of alternative, more humanistic (or "post-processual") theories to explain human history. The latter have benefited from points of view one might call feminist, cognitive, phenomenological, Marxist, or symbolic, but most importantly these viewpoints pick up where Griffin and others left off. In today's archaeology, horizon markers, settlement histories, pottery styles, and iconographies of the Mississippians have greater explanatory potential than even Griffin realized.

Today, Mississippian images and icons are being seen as more than benign representations of beliefs or myths. Chipped-stone tools, weapons, and cooking utensils are much more than utilitarian technologies. And places, architecture, and monuments are more than the mere sites of human activities. The material, spatial, corporeal, and temporal dimensions of the activities, practices, and experiences of American Indians are increasingly recognized to be the processes through which both culture and history were made (see Pauketat 2001b). Artifacts, representations, and constructions are themselves the creative media through which American Indians gave meaning to their worlds. Spaces are the contexts wherein peoples came together and constructed places of cultural significance. Archaeological sites are also, literally, the sites of cultural production (see Box 1).

Box 1. History, ethnographic analogies, and the myth of the unchanging Indian. How useful are the written accounts, legends, and oral histories of the descendants of Mississippians for understanding the cosmologies, organizations, symbolic meanings, ceremonies, legends, and games of their forbears? Archaeologists have struggled with the conundrum of ethnographic analogy (interpreting one group with reference to another) and with the limitations of the direct-historical approach (using descendants to interpret a parent population). Along with the Moundbuilder Myth, archaeologists have had to contend with the related myth of the unchanging Indian. In theories created in part by twentieth-century anthropology, American Indians have been said to be a ritual people, a conservation-minded people, and a traditional people. Such sayings unfortunately imply that all Indians were alike (and these underlie the "rituality" and "adaptationist" explanations reviewed later in the book).

However, my position is that cultures, meanings, and "traditional" practices are themselves the media of change. They are not static. So, how can we interpret the past using the present? How can we know, for instance, that a round smooth stone was a chunkey stone or that a special building was a religious temple? The answer is that the cultures, meanings, and traditions of later people certainly were contingent on or memorialized those of their forbears, so that we can analyze the historical trajectories (genealogies, biographies, etc.) of cultures, meanings, and traditional practices. We must avoid using analogies to fill in gaps in our knowledge, but we can expect to find the antecedents of later practices in earlier time periods. Certain analogies (including those in the following chapters) are very general, and thus are appropriate first steps in a historical analysis. If we begin by assuming, for instance, that round discoidal stones in the seventh through eighteenth centuries all may have been "chunkey" gaming stones, detailed study should reveal to us how the meanings and rules of the game(s) – if not the very idea of what constituted "gaming" – changed through time. Likewise, forked eye motifs from the twelfth century versus similar icons from the sixteenth century probably referenced a supernatural bird of some sort, even though the contexts in which such motifs created meaning, never mind the meanings themselves, doubtless were very different. The initial analogy allows us to begin to examine the forked eye motif through time. But to avoid the pitfalls of ethnographic analogy, we must go beyond the analogy to attempt to comprehend cultural history.

Some places were at the center of cultural regions. These regions were defined by the experiences of people rather than predetermined by nature. Understanding them means obtaining better controls over the production and distribution of material culture and the "spatiality" of experience that embodies the ideas, cultural values, memories, and traditions of people (Soja 1989). This means that archaeologists require well-founded multiple lines of evidence from many contexts and at multiple scales of analysis in order to answer the large questions of civilization. Mississippian archaeologists, particularly Cahokia archaeologists with their hefty datasets, may be uniquely situated to answer these questions.

In American anthropology today, such ideas would be arrayed under the banners of theories of practice, human agency, corporeality, landscape, and "historical-processualism" (Pauketat 2001b, 2003b). Archaeologists advocating these theories study the material, spatial, and temporal dimensions of how people make history via their own bodies, artifact biographies, *chaînes opératoires*, architectural genealogies, and the constructions of monuments and landscapes. They seek to understand culture contact, population displacement, creolization, and ethnogenesis as forms of the process of cultural construction. Pluralism, migration, and diaspora have emerged as foci in the study of the tensions within and inequalities between social groups. Therein lie the mechanisms whereby reciprocity and communities became tribute and hierarchies.

Such perspectives provide potent modes of interpreting the past when used in conjunction with more traditional studies of settlement, subsistence, production, and exchange. They enable us to understand that American Indians were diverse people all of whom did not act or think alike. Today, there is a greater appreciation of the importance of how multiple perspectives and diverse people shaped the past and, not incidentally, shape the present (see Watkins 2000). This is not to say that the past is unknowable or that archaeological findings are always open to multiple interpretations. Clearly, many interpretations are not supported by archaeological data and need not be seriously considered (Brumfiel 1996; Trigger 1991).

Equally clear is that archaeologists *have* answered certain questions. Did American Indians build the mounds? Yes. Were Archaic Indians the simple forerunners of later complex peoples? No. Did North Americans independently invent agriculture? Yes! These formerly controversial issues are now closed. But in closing them, we have moved further along to ask other questions that, in turn, are more or less controversial at the present time. Did Mississippians adopt directly or indirectly ideas from Mesoamerica? Was Cahokia a founding city and did Cahokians spread their Mississippian ideas across the Mississippi valley?[7] Were pyramids statements of elite authority or constructions of resistant communities?

I remain optimistic that present-day disagreements will be laid to rest with more of the kinds of archaeological data reviewed in this book. In the meantime, the debates surrounding the questions are themselves valuable, as they force archaeologists to rethink carefully even their nearest and dearest assumptions. To begin to rethink these assumptions, we turn first to the environment.

2   Geography, resources, and the Mississippian ethnoscape

The Mississippi River has been likened to the Nile of North America. It is the principal physiographic feature of the American mid-continent, and it gave shape to landforms and peoples alike. It was a major transportation corridor, a political boundary, a rich resource zone, and a living symbol of the Mississippian cosmos. Like the people along its banks, it was dynamic. In 1796, it was described as follows:

This great, this magnificent Mississippi...is a very bad neighbor. Strong in a body of yellowish muddy water, two or three thousand yards in breadth, which it annually rolls over its banks to a height of five to twenty feet, it urges this mass over a loose earth of sand and clay; forms islands and destroys them; floats along trees, which it afterwards overturns; varies its course through the obstructions it creates for itself; and at length reaches you at distances, where you would have supposed yourself perfectly secure. (Alvord 1965:5)

The Mississippi's dynamism owes itself to the river's size. The river is 3744 km long and drains 3.2 million km². It is joined by the 4000 km Missouri River near St. Louis, and the combined Missouri-Mississippi system is the third longest river in the world, draining 40 percent of North America's landmass. By the time it reaches the Gulf of Mexico, the volume of water moving through the river is about 18,000 m³ per second. The Mississippi River at flood stage carries considerably more water than this, forcing the channel to breach natural levees, scour new channels, and back up abandoned oxbow channels, backwater marshes, and slow-moving yazoo tributaries (Fig. 2.1). Sedentary life on the banks of the river would always have been precarious because of the river's dynamism.

However, behind the natural levees and along the old oxbow lakes of the floodplain, a more resource-rich life could not be imagined. Floods seldom threatened human inhabitants; a parochial assumption that people built mounds to escape the Mississippi's floodwaters is absolutely false! In fact, only a few floods in historic times covered the entire floodplain of the wide American Bottom near St. Louis and the most recent of these did so

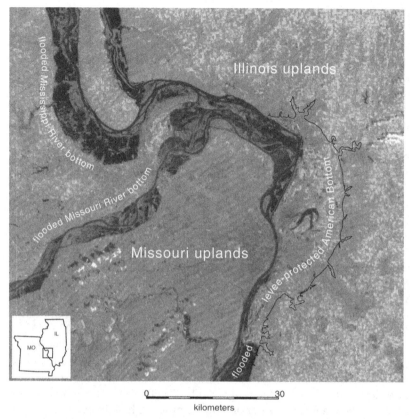

2.1 Aerial view of the Mississippi River at flood stage, 1993 (source: NASA/Goddard Space Flight Center Scientific Visualization Studio)

owing to twentieth-century alterations to drainage ways. Otherwise, the lakes, marshes, swales, and tributary streams of the floodplain regularly absorbed the floodwaters. Because of such a renewal process, in fact, the floodplain's watery places teemed with aquatic, terrestrial, and avian life. The alternating ridges and swales of well-drained flood-deposited sands and organically rich backwater silts and clays were in some ways ideal for hoe agriculturalists, who survived by spreading the risks of crop failure across the full range of tillable bottomland soils.

In fact, the entirety of the middle stretch of the Mississippi is marked by its resource availability, productivity, and diversity. Within the 35–44 degrees North latitude and 87–90 degrees West longitude, annual average temperatures range from winter lows of 15 to 30 degrees Fahrenheit to summer highs of 67 to 85 degrees Fahrenheit. For most of this area, the four seasons are well delineated, particularly in the north. Average precipitation ranges from just over 30 inches in the north to over 50 inches in the south, obviating the need for pre-Columbian irrigation. Snowfall makes up some of the precipitation in the north, but little to none in the warmer south. Excessive summer humidity levels and extreme temperatures in excess of 100 degrees Fahrenheit characterize the entire middle-river area.

The warmer greenhouse climate of today is probably comparable to that of the "Medieval Warm Period" of AD 800 to 1300, sometimes called the "Neo-Atlantic episode" (Anderson 2001; Bryson *et al.* 1970). However, the winter season inhibited the growth of crops, even into the southern latitude range. The mean number of frost-free days is less than 200 in the north and up to 300 in the south, so that the growing season everywhere extends from no earlier than late March to no later than mid-November. Farmers in the past were limited to one major crop per year. This growing season may have been shortened considerably with the beginning of the chilly climatic regime of the "Little Ice Age" after AD 1300 (Anderson 2001; Griffin 1961). A hundred years earlier, crop production may also have been curtailed by two twenty-five-year droughts (Ollendorf 1993:175).

Ordinarily, there is plenty of summertime moisture. Particularly violent in the south are the mid-latitude summer cyclones, spiraling weather cells produced when the warm and moist Gulf of Mexico air mass slams into the colder and dryer continental air. These cells spin off tornadoes and produce heavy downpours of rain and pummeling hail that generate flash floods. Corn crops can be flattened by winds, shredded by localized hail events, and washed out by rushing run-off. Engelke (1983:58) recounts one storm system that spawned a monster tornado in 1805:

At first there was complete darkness, which was followed by a terrific roaring wind which carried limbs and branches of trees through the air. This storm destroyed everything in the area, about three-fourths of a mile wide. The great force of the wind swept the water out of the Mississippi River. Fish were found around the lakes after the storm.

Physical geography and earth-shaking events

Over millions of years, weather events wore away the central geological feature of the middle-river area, the Ozark anticline, exposing basement granite magmas and ancient lava flows of Precambrian volcanoes 1.3 billion years old, known as the St. François Mountains (Fig. 2.2). Around this ancient core, the Ozark dome consists of the weathered

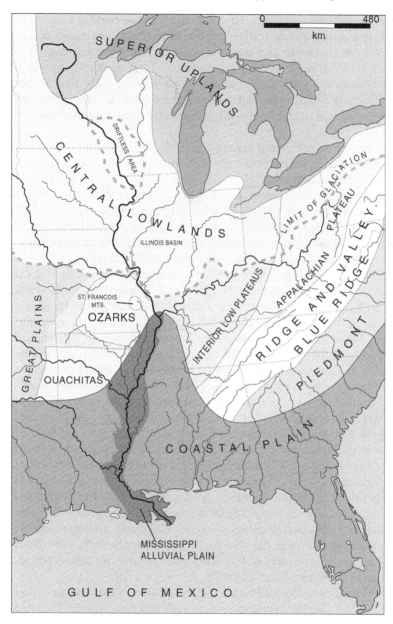

2.2 Physiographic provinces of the American mid-continent

exposures of folded and fractured sedimentary rocks, ranging from high-quality quartz sandstones to chert-bearing limestones, sometimes coated with iron ore (hematite and limonite) that had been carried deep into the rock by downward-moving groundwater. In at least one restricted location, lead ore or galena crystallized in the eroding rock. The surface run-off incised deep stream valleys down through these strata, draining east and southeast into the Mississippi River and north into the Missouri River.

Hardwood forests covered the entirety of the Ozark uplift and met the Great Plains in Oklahoma north through Missouri. An isolated stand of southern pines grew amongst these hardwoods in the rugged St. François Mountains, the northernmost stand of pine south of Wisconsin. Game was abundant, the area serving as a hunting territory for many groups during historic times. However, soils were thin in the unglaciated and steep terrain of the Ozarks, save in the narrow floodplains of major rivers such as the St. François, the Meramec, and the Big Rivers.

Soils thickened considerably to the north and east of this geological anticline. Above the 37 degrees North line of latitude and north of the Missouri River, soil thickness owed a debt to the huge glacial ice sheets that covered these "Central Lowlands" during the Pleistocene epoch, or Ice Age. These broad and relatively flat lowlands were both a geological feature and a result of the ice masses that pushed southward from Canada. The same ancient geological event that buckled and uplifted the Ozarks had bowed downward the sedimentary bedrock of the so-called "Illinois Basin" immediately to the northeast. Subsequently, the upper Midwest gave little resistance to the southward push of three sequential ice sheets during the Pleistocene. The glacial advance was halted, however, both by the warmer weather and by the formidable hills of the Missouri Ozarks and the heavily dissected "Interior Low Plateau" to the south (Fenneman 1914; Thornbury 1965). The Interior Low Plateau, called the "Shawnee Hills" in southern Illinois, extends into western Kentucky and Tennessee. The plateau is characterized by highly weathered hills covered by relatively thin soils and primeval deciduous forests. Cliffs and drainages expose sedimentary rocks. As in the Ozarks, the sedimentary rocks are rich in cherts, although exposures of this economic resource are concentrated, particularly in Union County, Illinois.

The Mississippi Alluvial Plain is pinched between the Ozarks to the southwest, the Central Lowlands to the north and east, and the Shawnee Hills to the southeast. As a physiographic province, the alluvial valley begins at Thebes Gap, where the ancient Ohio and Mississippi rivers used to meet. Only several kilometers south of the Gap, the valley floor already exceeds 80 km in width. Also south of Thebes Gap, bottomland prairies, clayey backwaters, and Pleistocene gravel ridges of the Mississippi Alluvial Plain replace the deciduous forests of the sedimentary and igneous upland interiors (Shelford 1963). At Reelfoot Lake, Tennessee, opposite New Madrid, Missouri, the valley floor is 100 km wide, comprised of several distinctive lowland zones interspersed with Pleistocene gravel ridges (Saucier 1994). The alluvia here mask the famous New Madrid fault. Between December 1811 and March 1812, the New Madrid fault slipped, and the Mississippi valley shook. The quake and its 1800 aftershocks were of such severity that landforms disappeared, sand blows squirted quickened sand into the air, the Mississippi River changed course, wild animals screamed in fear, and people prayed or fled. The worst shock waves rang church bells in Philadelphia and cracked the walls of a building in Savannah, Georgia. In earlier years, such quakes may have shaken both the earthen and the political foundations of Cahokia itself.

North of Thebes Gap, the floodplain of the Mississippi is hemmed in by rock "bluffs," vertical walls of limestone and sandstone up to 60 m high. The intersection of the Missouri and Mississippi rivers and soft rocks exposed at the edge of the Illinois Basin produced the widest expanse of tillable bottomland, located at the northern end of the American Bottom. This pocket of floodplain 16 km wide also marks the northern end of a natural riverine bottleneck formed between the Ozarks, the Central Lowlands, and the unglaciated Shawnee Hills to the south. During the Pleistocene, the Mississippi flowed directly out of the glaciers, draining the meltwater and following a path of least resistance along the edge of the Ozark uplift, carving the northern American Bottom expanse into the softer sedimentary rocks of this edge of the Illinois Basin. The Missouri River flowed into the northern American Bottom, draining the distant Great Plains from the west. The Illinois River met the Mississippi just 30 km upriver from the north; it had been the channel of the ancient Mississippi before the Ice Age. Modest moraines and wide meltwater sluiceways marked the once glaciated upland interiors immediately to the east, the highest hills and interfluves covered with prairie grasses during post-glacial "Holocene" times. The unglaciated hills, rock outcrops, and ancient floodplains to the south of the glacial terminus that skirted the southern American, Bois Brule, and Jackson Bottoms were covered with forests, lakes, marshes, and waterlogged swamps.

Natural resources

In human terms, this convergence of rivers, biomes, and bedrock made for a natural region with a phenomenal diversity of natural resources, landforms, and raw materials (Fig. 2.3). At the point of maximum biotic

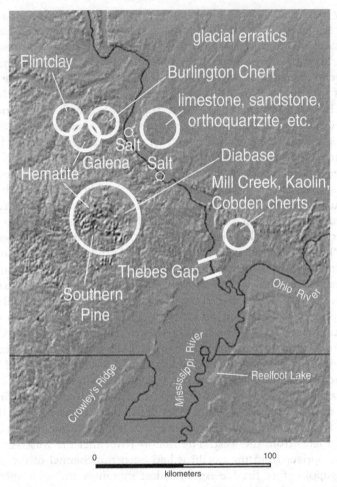

2.3 Select natural resources of the central Mississippi valley

and physiographic convergence was Cahokia. For Cahokians and others, the rugged Precambrian core and the surrounding sedimentary strata of the Ozarks formed a unique environment used for special forays and the extraction of resources during the Mississippian period. From the Ozarks came salt, galena (lead ore), hematite (iron ore), flintclay (red claystone), high-grade chert or flint, and fine-grained igneous rocks (see Box 2). Of these, salt was produced from brackish springs, the most famous of which was near a fortified Mississippian town along the Mississippi. Galena and hematite were metal ores used mostly to produce mineral-based paints, and sometimes to make ornaments and ritual paraphernalia. Flintclay was

Box 2. French colonists in the Illinois Country. The importance of this convergence of mid-latitude climatic potential, rich floodplain soils and interior prairie-edge soils, aquatic resources, the Mississippi flyway, and nearby mineral wealth in the Ozarks produced not only a pre-Columbian centralized society, but also a French Colonial agrarian and mining society that followed the penetration of the region by Père Jacques Marquette and Louis Joliet, Réné-Robert Cavelier de La Salle, Henri de Tonti, and various French Jesuit priests and Canadian *courier de bois* during the late seventeenth century (Walthall and Emerson 1992).

To large extent, the history of the French development of the "Illinois Country" was independent of the pre-Columbian Mississippians. For these reasons, the developmental parallels are striking: the French towns of St. Louis, Ste. Genevieve, and Prairie du Rocher were built on practically the same ground as major Mississippian centers; key river mouths were controlled by French forts and mercantile towns in the seventeenth century just as they were guarded by Mississippian towns in the eleventh through thirteenth centuries; and the French extracted salt, furs, and galena from the Ozark Mountains, as did the Mississippians.

However, to some extent, French Colonial developments were contingent on earlier Mississippian history. Long-established Indian trails became French trails and, much later, major paved roads and highways of the modern United States (e.g., Routes 3, 50, and 66 [see Tanner 1989]). The thirteenth- to fifteenth-century depopulation of southern Illinois and Missouri – owing to events in Mississippian history – permitted the French to set up their colonial foothold in an open landscape, with little to no native resistance. After the French loss of their American colony in the French and Indian (Seven Years) War, and followed by the American Revolution, immigrant revolutionary war soldiers from the United States laid claim to what was still occupied by French descendants. The new Americans now inscribed their own national identity on the "American Bottom" as the French farmers moved to the opposite shore, not yet the soil of the Americans until Jefferson's nearly accidental Louisiana Purchase in 1803.

a soft stone with a distinctive red and white coloration that a Cahokian or Cahokians carved into distinctive figurines and statuettes. Chert and igneous rocks were the raw materials used most often from the Ozarks for the manufacture of chipped-stone tools, expedient flake tools, and groundstone axes and wood-shaping tools.

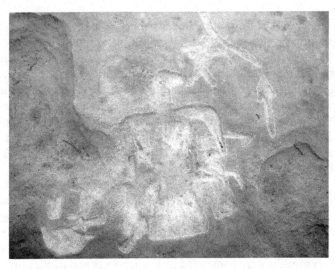

2.4 Raptor petroglyph, Washington State Park, eastern Missouri

Ozark raw materials are found scattered across the eastern United States. The metal ores turn up all over the mid-continent, while finished flintclay figurines are distributed from Wisconsin to Louisiana (e.g., Emerson *et al.* 2002, 2003; Walthall 1981). Even the distinctive white Burlington chert from the Ozarks, 30 km southeast of Cahokia, turns up in Arkansas, Oklahoma, Wisconsin, Tennessee, and Mississippi. The major consumers of Ozark materials, however, were Cahokians. Indeed, Cahokians may have been responsible for much of the secondary dispersal of Ozark raw materials to other parts of the Mississippi valley.

Besides these nonperishable Ozark materials, the Cahokians probably extracted a variety of organic materials from the Ozarks. The pinewood found at Cahokia, for instance, was probably cut and hauled from the nearest known St. François Mountain source, more than 100 km to the southwest. The evidence of the Mississippians' use of and reverence for this Ozark district is perhaps seen in the petroglyphs and pictographs that cover certain interior rock faces and cave interiors of the Ozarks, denoting the liminal position and supernatural associations of the rugged landscape (Fig. 2.4). These are also peripheral to the greater Cahokia region, perhaps delineating a political boundary (see O'Brien 1994; Pauketat 1998b).

The landscape of petroglyphs continues across the weathered and dissected "Shawnee Hills" of the Interior Low Plateau of southern Illinois, extending into Kentucky and Tennessee. In southern Illinois, petroglyphs are associated with specific late Mississippian communities (Wagner and McCorvie 2002). There were earlier ones as well, the best known being located astride the quarries of Mill Creek chert. Raw Mill Creek chert consists of tabular nodules of tough grainy chert, making them natural preforms for the production of large and long-lasting chipped-stone hoe blades, knives, adze blades, and scepters or maces. This chert outcrops in Union County along minor streams that flow into the Mississippi. In the same creeks originates the equally tough and colorful Kaolin chert (not to be confused with the pure white Kaolin clay, which also originated here). Nearby are other cherts whose colors or knapping qualities were sought by Mississippians: Dongola, Cobden, and Fort Payne. The Fort Payne chert was extracted in great quantities at the Dover quarries in Tennessee, where another large-biface industry was centered. Along with Mill Creek and Kaolin cherts, the Dover bifaces were made by local knappers who exported their products in canoes and on the backs of porters to local consumers along the Tennessee, Cumberland, Ohio, Kaskaskia, and Mississippi rivers. Mill Creek chert hoe blades or fragments of them are found as far afield as Wisconsin, Iowa, Alabama, and Oklahoma.

From further afield came a series of other resources. For a brief period of Cahokian history, the Hixton quarry of west-central Wisconsin appears to have been accessed extensively (Green and Rodell 1994; Pauketat 1992). From here was procured sparkling, whitish, quartzite-like "silicified sediment," a silica-rich sandstone that both local people and Cahokians transformed into chipped stone tools and arrowheads. Some archaeologists have also speculated that deerskins and even bison hides may have been procured from the upper Midwest by Cahokians, but those arguments are difficult to support and only one bison bone has ever been reported from Cahokia (Miracle 1998:33; see chapter 6).

Then again, there is plenty of evidence for the long-distance acquisition and use of marine shell from the Gulf of Mexico and copper from the Upper Peninsula of Michigan around Lake Superior. Of course, the people of the middle river had always managed to acquire some Gulf Coast shell and Lake Superior copper, at least since the Archaic period. However, the Mississippians – particularly the Cahokians – laid their hands on significantly more conch, whelk, and bivalve shells. Copper was used sparingly around Cahokia, showing up more at a few well-known southern sites after AD 1200. Both shell and copper may have been acquired through key trading partners or, less likely, by travel to the source itself.

However people were linked, transportation was entirely by foot or dugout canoe. Horses were not introduced into North America until the arrival of the Spaniards in the sixteenth century; the dog was the only domesticated animal in eastern North America. Foot trails established during the Archaic period were probably maintained down through the ages, many of which were used by European colonists and, ultimately, were paved as the modern highways of today. Likewise, dugouts are thought to have been made from felled cypress trees as far back as the beginning of the Holocene in the eighth millennium BC, as possibly evidenced by the wood charcoal residues found embedded in the cutting edges of chipped-stone Dalton adze blades (Yerkes and Gaertner 1997).

Besides the chippable stone, copper, and shell acquired during long-distance excursions, people seem occasionally to have picked up a foreign pottery vessel, although the numbers of actual exotic pots in any one Mississippian settlement is always relatively low. Foreign pots never comprise more than a few percent of a Mississippian pottery refuse assemblage. Unlike other areas of the world (such as certain parts of the American Southwest), suitable clays, tempers, and water were readily available almost everywhere. With the addition of crushed mussel shell for temper, Mississippian potters made especially strong and durable earthenware using the alluvial clays. Potters did not need to trade for pots. That they did acquire the pots of others, at certain times and in certain places, seems to indicate their attendance at central rituals where foods or medicines were distributed to participants in take-home pots.

Likewise, most people probably spun their own threads and yarns and manufactured their own textiles from the plethora of locally available plant fibers and animal hair, perhaps with local redistribution or exchange to acquire necessary raw materials: prairie and marsh grasses, the inner bark of some woods, rabbit and dog hair, and bird down. Certainly, feathers and indeed the entire wings and tail fans of raptors, swans, and songbirds were prized for ritual regalia and costumes (L. Kelly 2000; Pauketat et al. 2002). Besides thigh spinning, there is evidence of the use of spindles in spinning for at least the period AD 900–1200, perhaps correlating with the production of surplus cloth as a social valuable (Alt 1999).

Biotic resources and agriculture

In the southern alluvial valley, the Mississippi River's rich resources help to explain settlement history. Apart from the occasional elk, or the bison in the Great Plains to the west, the most plentiful and meatiest terrestrial game animal of the valley was the white-tailed deer, an animal prone both to serious overpopulation and to overhunting depending on historical circumstances. Fish from the Mississippi's main channel, its tributaries, side channels, and abandoned backwater lakes was potentially a much more reliable resource (Rees 1997). Shellfish also were relatively plentiful, although not available to the same extent everywhere, and not a dietary staple in many places even though their shells were crushed as the temper of choice by most Mississippian potters after AD 1100 or so. More reliable and widely available were millions of waterfowl and shorebirds that migrated north and south through the Mississippi flyway. Ducks, geese, and swans flew south as winter came on, and north in the springtime. The economic potential of the semi-annual event is amply demonstrated by Mississippian food refuse (e.g., Smith 1975).

The biomass of the Midwest and Midsouth had been managed by native peoples since at least the Archaic period, three of the most common practices being the burning of prairies to drive game, the growing of native starchy seed crops, and the tending of nut-bearing tree groves (see Box 3). It is equally likely that ponds, ridgetops, forests, open fields, and waterways were managed near densely occupied settlements to allow easy travel via watercraft and overland trails, and to ensure adequate supplies of construction material, firewood, food, and medicinal plants and animals (e.g., cedar and cypress wood, birds of prey). Given sparse population densities before the Mississippian period, management was probably not coordinated between settlements. However, the population maximum at Cahokia may have strained available wood and thatch supplies unless managed at a regional scale.

Doubtless there were seasonal hunting excursions to provision communal feasts. And there were probably religious or status-based restrictions on who could hunt or collect specific resources. Such management would have offset hypothesized tendencies of people to overexploit wood and food resources, although resource use may have had harmful effects nonetheless, depending on local circumstances (e.g., Lopinot and Woods 1993). Cypress trees probably grew as far north as the northern American Bottom at least up to AD 1200, and their subsequent disappearance north of Thebes Gap may have been due to extensive cutting or the onset of the Little Ice Age (Fig. 2.5). Then again, it makes sense that the use of special aromatic woods, including cypress and cedar, may also have been associated with cultural taboos (Fig. 2.6).

Access to other woodlands may not have been restricted, and the extensive bottomland prairie noted by Henry Brackenridge and other early nineteenth-century Euroamericans as covering the Cahokia and East St. Louis site area was probably not a pristine "natural" zone but a product of several centuries of wood use by thousands of Mississippian residents. In the same way, the sixteenth-century migration of bison herds into the Illinois prairie peninsula probably was not simply a natural

Box 3. Agricultural developments. As early as 5000 BC, the mobile to semi-sedentary people of the main river valleys in the Midwest and upper Midsouth tended crops. Initially, native horticultural practices involved squash and gourds, followed closely in time by an array of starchy and oily seed plants including chenopods (*Chenopodium* spp.), sumpweed (*Iva annua*), sunflower (*Helianthus annuus*), knotweed (*Polygonum erectum*), maygrass (*Phalaris caroliniana*), and little barley (*Hordeum pusillum*) (Fritz 1990). Although certain Early Woodland sites point to a strange hiatus in crop production (other than squash), the preceding Late Archaic and the subsequent Middle Woodland period saw fully domesticated forms of chenopods, sumpweed, sunflower, and squash in Illinois, Kentucky, Missouri, Ohio, and Indiana. The Middle Woodland period also saw the earliest maize (*Zea mays*) in eastern North America, added to the diet "as another starchy grain" and probably originating in the American Southwest (Fritz 1990:397; see Riley *et al.* 1996). At about the same time, tobacco (*Nicotina* sp.) made its appearance, unknown in the Southwest until Spanish contact and presumably originating from eastern Mexico or the Caribbean (Wagner 2000).

Food-plant domestication continued into the Late Woodland period. The intensification of maize, a Mesoamerican cultigen, sometime after AD 800 did not have immediate revolutionary effects on native politics, although it does correlate spatially and temporally with the "Red-Filmed Horizon." Some theorists figure that there were social changes that came first, inducing people to look to the intensification of maize in order to supplement the traditional seed and squash staples. If there was an increased need for a surplus for social uses, then maize may have been a low-effort solution that would not have impinged much on established crop production practices. Part of the reasoning here is that, while it had been known by eastern Woodlands Indians since the time of Christ, many people in the eastern Woodlands were slow to adopt it or intensify their production of it.

outcome of climate change, but a result of the disappearance of central Illinois River Mississippian villages. Up to the mid-fifteenth century, these Indians had blocked bison migrations by their hunting practices (see Conrad 1991). The bison migrations exemplify the long-term dialectical effects of the intercourse between human beings and the natural world. For instance, political no-man's lands allowed for greater concentrations of biomass that, in turn, brought hunters and traders in contact with one

2.5 Cypress swamp, Reelfoot Lake, western Tennessee

2.6 Red cedar tree on the Mississippi River bluffs overlooking the southern American Bottom, Randolph County, Illinois

another and permitted the regeneration of formerly overhunted resource zones. Theoretically, new political or population centers could emerge in the former peripheries of old centers suffering from resource exhaustion or crowding.

Short-term climatic perturbations such as droughts or floods would have had variable effects on different populations of Mississippians depending on the histories of resource management and agricultural practices of a region's population. Droughts and floods did occur, but evaluating the effects on polity and settlement depends very much on local exigencies and historical trajectories (cf. Anderson *et al.* 1995). For instance, the end of the Medieval Warm Period (and the beginning of the Pacific climatic episode) has been blamed for Cahokia's abandonment by AD 1300. At about this time, a huge fourteenth- to sixteenth-century "Vacant Quarter" opened up across the middle-river regions (Cobb and Butler 2002; Williams 1990). Likewise, the overexploitation of wood at AD 1200 is said to have led to region-wide field erosion and a ruined agricultural system (Lopinot and Woods 1993). Then again, population loss and signs of political unrest at Cahokia began shortly after AD 1150, at which time there were ample forests to enable the construction of the 20,000-log palisade wall. It was built and rebuilt four times over a fifty-year period.

Of course, the intensification of agricultural production was the most prominent alteration of the environment in the pre-Columbian Mississippi valley, and would have entailed the reduction of woodlands. In the distant past as in the more recent times, the "great corn region" of eastern North America was "the Mississippi basin, especially that portion lying between Ohio and the plains and north of Tennessee" (Brewer 1883:100, cited by Schroeder 1999:503). Plant and pollen evidence from the vicinity of Cahokia is suggestive of land clearance and the establishment of agricultural fields during the terminal Late Woodland period (e.g., Ollendorf 1993; Simon 2000; Whalley 1990:529). Anecdotal evidence of larger "heavy-duty" groundstone axe heads suggests to Brad Koldehoff (personal communication) that tracts of land were being cleared of trees in and around the American Bottom at the beginning of the Mississippian period. Such clearance would have altered the distribution and numbers of various wild plant and animal species, requiring additional changes in the culinary, textile-manufacturing, and construction practices of people. The numbers of deer would have surged given the broken woodlands and cornfields. Cane breaks probably replaced low-lying groves, cane becoming an increasingly common material for making arrows or for sheathing the walls of buildings.

The crop yields varied and were limited by soil fertility, localized temperature/sunlight variables, and agricultural practices. Families usually cleared and tilled the soil using digging sticks and simple hoes. The easiest soil to cultivate under these conditions, the fine sandy loam of the floodplains, was actually not the most productive soil from a modern agricultural perspective (see Olsen et al. 2000). The most productive soil, the dark and alkaline prairie loams of the Illinois interior, may have been difficult to farm using hand-wielded hoes to cut the thick prairie-grass root mass (Woods and Holley 1991).[8] Certainly, there was little impetus outside the small-scale Late Woodland family- and kin-based work groups to invest in chopping through the prairie grasses. This would change.

In the meantime, the friable soils of floodplains had another thing going for them: they warmed up faster in the springtime, allowing for planting to begin up to two weeks earlier there (see also Phillips *et al.* 1951:21). As in Mexico and elsewhere, certain kin groups and communities would have had greater access to these patches of productive soils than others. The surpluses of Late Woodland peoples could have been used to host meals or to provision those of others (for conservative productivity averages, see Schroeder 1999). Over several generations, such access would have led to differential social standings within any interacting group of communities, with less well-sited families becoming increasingly indebted to better-sited ones. Attempts to level such differentials could have included marginal families relocating themselves nearer the better soils and the well-off communities (Blanton *et al.* 1983, 1999; Pauketat 1994).

The long-term net effect was "caused" not so much by an environmental circumstance as by agricultural practices (i.e., the division of labor, use of stone-bladed hoes or digging sticks, etc.) and by the culture-specific rules of social debt. Then again, the environment established a set of parameters that permitted or denied agricultural intensification or extensification given the particular agricultural practices of that time and place. That Cahokia, for instance, emerged in the middle of a wide patch of Mississippi River floodplain but close to a wedge of upland prairie soils is no accident. That Mississippian farmers were by and large limited to one crop per year, given the climate, is also likely to have set an upper limit to population growth and sociopolitical development.

The Mississippian ethnoscape

The floodplains open to Mississippian agriculture seem endless. However, the net effect of this sea of tillable soils may have been an endless competition between communities and would-be political regimes. Political, cultural, and even linguistic boundaries crosscut the seemingly unbounded floodplains south of Thebes Gap. These boundaries were drawn between hills and gravel ridges, and along waterways (e.g., Morse and Morse 1983).

The productive potential of floodplains doubtless had pulled people into the bottomlands through time over the Late Woodland period, but escaping these floodplains – and the associated cultural geography – also may account for several population intrusions or immigrations into the interior at various points in Mississippian history. Thus, the cultural landscape of the middle-river Mississippians was a field of divisions, possibilities, and limitations. Although the dividing lines are difficult to detect, Mississippians north of Thebes Gap were probably Siouan speakers, known historically in the eastern Plains and upper Midwest. Far to the north were Algonkian speakers and to the south was a mix of Siouan, Muskogean, Tunican, Choctaw, and Caddoan speakers, a fact simultaneously explained by and helping to explain Mississippian cultural history (see Nicklas 1994). Mississippian "culture areas," that is, were real, but permeable and changeable. They were also probably less extensive than first imagined during the late nineteenth century, when Mississippians were, to all intents and purposes, first recognized to be distinct from others (see Holmes 1903; Willoughby 1897). In fact, "cultural regions" were probably defined by the historical relationships of peoples living around specific Mississippian centers (see Pauketat 1994; Rees 1997).

In the early twentieth century, cultural-regional distinctions were explained almost immediately with reference to the environment. "Cultures . . . spread over the whole of the natural area in which their form was worked out" (Kroeber 1953:6). In the spirit of Wissler's (1926) age-area hypothesis, many nineteenth-century archaeologists assumed that there must have existed a Mississippian heartland, or core area, from which ways of life spread (see Smith 1984). Such logic was embedded within the "Midwestern Taxonomic System" of the 1930s in which archaeologists compared lists of traits in order to identify those that may have diffused from one place to another, including far-off Mesoamerica.

By the 1970s, most archaeologists rejected migration and diffusion as explanations even while they retained the belief that cultures were adaptations to local environments (Smith 1978, 1984). Mississippian ways of life were thought to result from the need for a group to level the imbalances that resulted from resource concentrations or annual productive imbalances (Muller 1997; Swanton 1946:253ff). Thus, the proximity of some of the largest Mississippian sites to vast expanses of floodplain soils has been seen by some as a sufficient explanation of the rise and fall of whole polities. However, recent theories suggest that the culture–environment relationship is much more complex than simple adaptationist equations permit.

To begin with, people created the constraints of the environment as part of their ongoing cultural practices and lived traditions (Phillips *et al.* 1951:36). Agriculture and domestication are the perfect examples of this cultural creation process. Clearly, an agricultural landscape is a human creation. So is a monumental landscape, or an urban city. People imbue the environments and landscapes of their experience with meaning merely by the act of living. Thus, cities, pyramids, houses, hills, floodplains, woods, fields – even weather conditions – are meaningful features of the landscape. They are not outside the cultural experience of people. In effect, environments change as meanings change, and vice versa.

Environmental constraints come into play on local scales in decisions concerning where to plant a crop, where to live, or what animals to hunt. These decisions defined settlements, territories, borders, and dangerous zones or "no-man's lands." And they shaped the interregional cultural patterns, languages, ethnicities, and political geography of the Mississippi valley. The overall "ethnoscape" of the Mississippi valley at contact was complex, indicating an equally complex history of local developments, migrations, exchanges, and intermittent encounters of peoples along the Mississippi leading up to AD 1050 (Fig. 2.7; in the sense of Appadurai 1996).

The intermittent travels of people involved trade, pilgrimages, and direct forays for purposes of extracting resources. Information could be shared at such times, and this was probably as important as the objects that are thought to have moved along long-distance down-the-line routes since the Middle Archaic period: Gulf Coast marine shell into Canada, Lake Superior copper into the Deep South. Pacific Coast shells entered the eastern Plains from the northwest and a few Puebloan goods ended up at Caddoan sites (Brown 1996:31; Kozuch 2002). However, middle-river Mississippians' exchange relations do not appear to have involved the people of Mesoamerica, although speculations that Toltec or Maya travelers could have met North American Indians either along the Gulf Coast or inland remain plausible (see chapter 4).

To be sure, earthen pyramids, plazas, and a suite of icons have a long history in the Mississippi valley and may not have been caused by Mexican influences as much as both Mississippian and Mesoamerican cultural phenomena were results of a long-term, two-way sharing of ideas. Then again, Mesoamerican contacts, even if few, indirect, and far between, could have had profound historical impacts on the shape and timing of Mississippianization. Perhaps the intensification of maize (a Mesoamerican cultigen) after AD 800 attests to this.

So we should not discount long-distance pre-Columbian travels and their potential historical impacts, even if those travels were unique or one-time events. The famous Chickasaw map of 1737 is revealing of the likely pre-Columbian knowledge of the interior of North America (Waselkov 1989; see also Lafferty 1994). At contact, there were trade languages, including Plains Indian sign language, which would have facilitated communication across Indian political and linguistic barriers (Drechsel 1994). Certainly, in the seventeenth century, canoe travel carried Iroquoian raiders into the middle Mississippi valley, where they hunted their Illini enemies. It is true that the motivation for this long-distance travel was unique to the seventeenth century (see Dincauze and Hasenstaub 1989; Little 1987; Tanner 1989). Then again, we know there

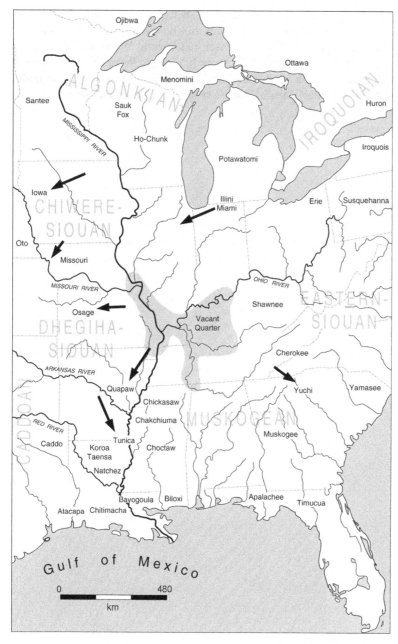

2.7 Major cultural and linguistic groupings, *c.* AD 1500–1700

were instances of similar long-distance travel for other reasons in the distant past: Middle Woodland Indians may have paddled up the Missouri River to present-day Yellowstone National Park in Wyoming in order to obtain raw obsidian and grizzly bear teeth; Poverty Point Indians possibly traveled to the Appalachians and the Ozarks seeking exotica. It is equally likely that the earliest Mississippians traveled as far and as wide.

3   Villages along the Mississippi

Archaeologists have frequently looked to the lower Mississippi valley "heartland" and its ancient "Gulf Coast Tradition" for the origins of Mississippian civilization. After all, platform mounds and plazas had been built in Louisiana since the mid-fourth millennium BC. So were Mississippian mounds and plazas the culmination of a long mound-building tradition? Yes and no.

Of course Mississippian moundbuilders looked to the past when living their present. However, traditions did not cause Mississippian developments and are in general inadequate explanations of history and civilization. Traditions are actively constructed and reconstructed in the present by reconciling one's memories with those of others. Traditions, in other words, are lived. It is also the case that, from tool-making knowledge to ethnic culinary practices, traditions are engrained in people's identities that are, in turn, enacted through group experiences and communal constructions. At one scale of analysis, people who share experiences, traditions, and a sense of identity we might call a community.

Theoretically speaking, communities are always being created and re-created via cultural processes where memories are negotiated through or inscribed in (or on) building, crafting, and sharing common experiences (e.g., Connerton 1989; Rowlands 1993; Van Dyke and Alcock 2003). Communities are in this sense "imagined" and the traditions associated with them "created," sometimes even "invented" to fit a situation (following Anderson 1983; Hobsbawm 1983). They are real enough, but they are generated through this social process involving the negotiation of the past in the present. Community identities and cultural constructions always involve the filtering of individual memories through collective gatherings and performances. Inevitably, the memories of some are given greater weight or emphasis than others. Thus, the construction of social memories and traditions entails the negotiation of social power and is inherently political: Whose memories will define social experience and whose will not?

Practically speaking, there is added reason for avoiding tradition as an explanation. Quite simply, there is no place where mound construction occurred without interruption over the intervening centuries of the Archaic and Woodland periods. In fact, although the construction of mounds is known to date from 3400 BC at Watson Brake, it is arguable that sufficient gaps and divergent developments exist in the occupation history of the Mississippi valley to necessitate the recognition that each instance of regional-cultural development had its own history generated by its own people (Pauketat and Alt 2003). So how can we speak of a mound-building tradition, if by that we mean continuity of form, construction, and meaning? How would that tradition have been handed down, transmitted across space, and reproduced elsewhere? The question is not as simple as it might sound because traditions are embedded in specific places and associated with specific people. Change the time, place, or participants, and one changes the tradition.

One thing is certain: mound construction history, the burgeoning evidence of pilgrimages and migrations, and regional vacancies or abandonments all point to the historical complexity involved in the shaping and transmission of cultural traditions. Tradition building or culture making was (and is) always ongoing, meaning that change should have been the rule. Therefore, apparent continuities require explanations (Pauketat 2001a). Consider the tourist who visits long-abandoned archaeological sites and senses the power of the place without fully comprehending its detailed history. What if that tourist goes home and replicates the shape of what he or she has seen? Or consider a modern potter's recycling of ancient motifs on a potsherd. Such motifs would be meaningful, but not in the same way that they had been (Bunzell 1929:52–7). These are perhaps extreme examples of how architectural or ceramic indicators of presumed cultural continuity actually mask considerable cultural change. Would not the same process have shaped the Mississippian past, if we consider the effects of pilgrimages, long-distance travel, and artisanship that surely existed as early as the Archaic period? To what degree would a similar process explain change even if the builders or artisans were the kin or descendants of the original builders or potters?

Such cultural-creation processes are especially apparent when groups migrate from place to place. Migration seldom sees cultural practices merely transplanted in predictable ways from the place of origin to the new homeland. Things change during the liminal experiences of movement, resettlement, and displacement (Lekson 1999; Nelson and Hegmon 2001). In part, this is because many objects and icons are pieces of larger meaningful landscapes that are meaningless outside that landscape. That is, rather than mere possessions that could be carried from point to point, such things would be "inalienable objects" (Weiner 1994; e.g., Miller 2001; Mills 2000). Good examples of Mississippian inalienable objects are chunkey stones. Of the Choctaw, James Adair wrote in 1765 that the "hurling stones they use at present, were [from] time immemorial rubbed smooth on the rocks, and with prodigious labor; they are kept, with the strictest religious care, from one generation to another, and are exempted from being buried with the dead" (Williams 1930:431).

This is of potentially great significance in understanding the origins of the middle-river Mississippians for whom connections with Cahokia (or other centers) may have been remembered through such objects. To understand the events leading up to the founding and memorializing of a civilization, we must first look outside at the Late Woodland centers and villages to the south and north.

Southern centers, northern villages

Great Woodland period sites with large mounds and enclosures, such as Marksville and Troyville, had been built and abandoned long before AD 900 in the lower Mississippi valley. This is especially impressive given the simple horticultural economies that undergirded the rise and fall of ceremonial centers over the centuries. By AD 900, the "Coles Creek" centers in Louisiana, Mississippi, and Arkansas had taken on distinctive appearances. The platform mounds of Coles Creek centers elevated sacred open spaces and scaffolds (Knight 2001). These would have been stages, literally, for the ceremonial displays watched by the gathered people on formal constructed plazas below, who lived there or gathered there for major annual festivals and important religious events.

Doubtless, the view from the top also afforded a certain kind of power, the power of the "gaze" that belonged to those ritual hosts or actors who could see the entire field of action (*sensu* Said 1978). In so doing, Coles Creek people created collective memories and traditions with each feast, each construction, and each ceremony. The platform mounds and plazas of Coles Creek sites thus look both traditional and novel, harkening back to and yet departing from the ancient Archaic and Woodland period centers (Fig. 3.1).

Although thought to have been the first of the Mississippian agricultural societies until recently, the Coles Creek people are now known to have relied heavily on wild foods to supplement their modest gardens of native starchy-seed cultigens (Fritz and Kidder 1993; Kidder 2002; Kidder and Fritz 1993). Not until AD 1000 or later was maize adopted, after which time buildings were constructed atop the flat-topped pyramids (possibly including some of the first "wall trench" buildings;

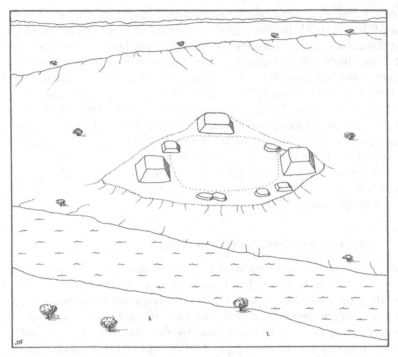

3.1 The Greenhouse site, a Coles Creek center in northeastern Louisiana (drawing by Jack Scott)

Kidder 2002:88). The plazas too were constructions, with soils being carried in to raise and level each public space (Kidder 2003). Archaeologists give these later Mississippianized Coles Creek peoples the name "Plaquemine."

Given the impressive pyramid and plaza constructions, it may seem surprising that many Coles Creek peoples appear "insular," lacking an elaborate iconography and having few external trade contacts (Kidder 1992). The populations around each mound site grew larger through time, but there is no evidence that any Coles Creek group contacted distant peoples until the eleventh century. And this contact was almost always with Cahokians to the north. At least until then, no single center dominated or grew significantly larger than the others (Kidder 2002:87–9). Burials of singularly important community leaders are almost unknown, although interments of bodies processed in various ways, including collections of human crania or mandibles, bespeak a communal concern with the processing and ritual use of the ancestors.[9]

3.2 Mound A at the Toltec site

The northernmost Coles Creek-like mounds and plazas were located at the center of the "Plum Bayou culture" in the central Arkansas River valley (Nassaney 2001; Rolingson 2002). Between about AD 700 and 1000 or so, the Toltec site was built. Like those of their Coles Creek neighbors to the south, the mounds of Toltec were not initially substructural platforms for buildings. However, they did elevate opulent displays, including the use of certain exotic paraphernalia (particularly quartz crystals, novaculite, copper, and marine shell) and the consumption of feast foods, the refuse of which was discarded down the faces of some of the mounds (Rolingson 1998). Surrounding the entire sacred precinct was an earthen embankment, probably erected to shield the precinct from foot traffic or view, if not for actual defense. There is, as yet, no evidence of warfare.

Michael Nassaney (1991, 1992, 1994) has interpreted Toltec to embody the negotiation of an emergent "elite" – those planners and hosts of central rites – with a support population of Plum Bayou people not quite ready for hierarchy. On the other hand, Rolingson (2002) is ready to label this same phenomenon a "simple chiefdom" that had at least two subsidiary centers and a number of farmsteads comprising the hierarchical settlement pattern. From either viewpoint, the large-scale communal construction projects were not so much expressions of absolute elite authority as they were the embodiment of a new kind of centralized corporate authority (Fig. 3.2). These creations reached proportions

Box 4. Late Woodland in the north. Recent excavations of northern Late Woodland sites are revealing the importance of understanding each site in terms of the regional contexts of social life rather than just the "subsistence strategies" of particular localities. Subsequent Mississippian developments are contingent on this regionalization (McElrath *et al.* 2000). Thus, Late Woodland settlements in the southwestern Illinois uplands are described as having a "nested" regional pattern: "The smallest settlement unit during Late Woodland times was a limited-activity camp represented by a single pit, pot-drop, or isolated point... The next settlement level is the pit cluster... [that] might represent the residues of a family... Presumably, the multiple pit cluster was a by-product of the proxemics of camp life involving multiple individuals or families, as the spacings are considered intimate... The next level comprises village segments characterized by a clustering of pits around a structure... The highest level in this settlement hierarchy is the dispersed village, which consists of a string of village segments across the land... Village size was based largely on landform, and something about 100–200 m in any dimension appears to have been appropriate" (Holley 2000:155–6).

In eastern Iowa, the settlement data have been interpreted with respect to gender. David Benn and William Green note "the instrumental role that Native women played in determining the mode of production in Late Woodland societies. Their most sophisticated craft, spinning and twining, prominently displays women's symbols on the necks of pottery vessels, which are also the symbols of reproductive success for the kin group... Women also must have been responsible for introducing the maize crop into their gardens after AD 700, a technical achievement that would have been feasible and likely if maize had already been adapted to the northern hemisphere (Fritz 1992:29). Add in other Late Woodland characteristics, such as the use of expedient flake technology, the bow and arrow, and the building of less labor-intensive mounds, and we have a basis for arguing that there was a profound shift in the allocation of labor time from the surplus-producing corporate structure of the Middle Woodland period to subsistence production by smaller kin-based units of the Late Woodland period... Furthermore, it can be argued that women played a pivotal role in the persistence of the Woodland tradition even as the Mississippian lifestyle was emerging to the south. Resistance to the intensification of maize agriculture, and promotion of the mound-building tradition, which played on the balance of the upper (sky) and lower (earth/water) divisions of society (see Hall 1993:44), can be cited as examples of behaviors that produced the traditional roles of women in kin-based organizations" (Benn and Green 2000:480).

exceeding the Coles Creek mounds and plazas to the south, and far exceeded the modest and usually moundless terminal Late Woodland "Baytown" settlements nearer the confluence of the Ohio and Mississippi rivers.

Then again, even these minimally centralized terminal Late Woodland peoples to the north could have constituted small-scale chiefdoms, depending on one's definitions. Thus, whatever the history of governance at Toltec, the more significant dimension of its history, and perhaps the reasons for the scale of the monumental constructions, may well have been the particular and still ill-understood politicization of traditions or the resistance to such politicization and to the authority of presumed emergent elites (Nassaney 2001). Such resistance was probably not overt defiance by people, but an unwillingness to change whether they fully understood it or not. Resistance of this sort, subtle and deeply engrained in people's daily lives, may have had its roots in a culinary tradition; the Plum Bayou people did not intensively farm maize.

At the same time, up the Mississippi River north of Thebes Gap, Late Woodland communities did not coalesce via the types of massive coordinated labor projects seen at Toltec or at the Coles Creek centers farther south. Only the Late Woodland peoples of northern Illinois, Wisconsin, and Iowa built earthen mounds, some small and conical, and others made to look like bears, birds, and underworld creatures or water spirits. Such "Effigy Mound culture" sites seem to have been frequented for periodic ritual events that included the burial of the dead. Repeated use of some locations led to entire hilltops being covered with the small mounds (Birmingham and Eisenberg 2000; Mallam 1976).

Late Woodland people who lived south of the Effigy Mound culture and north of Thebes Gap built few to no mounds. Especially notable is the absence of mound constructions in and around the American Bottom between AD 400 and 1000. The many Late Woodland settlements before AD 900, in fact, were scattered about the wooded hills and marshy floodplains of the Midwest. Here and elsewhere across the Midwest was a patchwork of modest-sized settlements, seldom more than a few families living in a few houses per site (see Box 4). The houses were usually small semi-subterranean huts, often with keyhole-shaped entranceways, occupied during the cold winter months. One would have to step or crawl down into these buildings, the floors of which originally would have been half a meter or more below the ground surface. Larger aboveground buildings may have been warm weather houses for larger residential groups or special communal buildings (e.g., Fortier and Jackson 2000; Fortier et al. 1984). Regardless of housing practices, all Late Woodland people stored considerable quantities of foodstuffs on a seasonal basis, as the

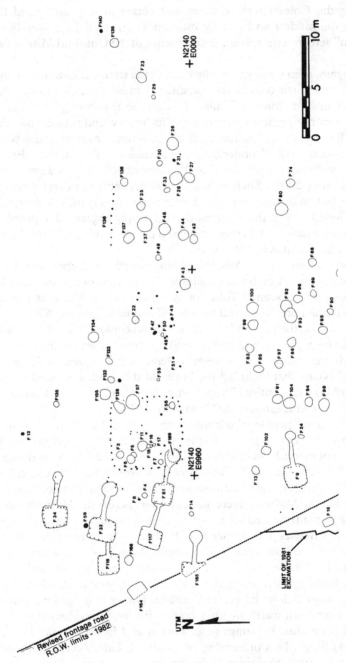

3.3 Plan view of a portion of the Late Woodland Fish Lake Site, St. Clair County, Illinois (courtesy Illinois Transportation Archaeological Research Program)

pit-to-building ratio is characteristically high (Fig. 3.3). In addition, with the ever-increasing reliance on starchy seeds as a dietary staple, and with the addition of maize during the ninth century AD, the earthenware dishes of Late Woodland groups were diversified to accommodate the parching and boiling of seeds and, possibly, the increasing social use of foods.

In places, Late Woodland people lived a fully sedentary village life; in others, they moved within a restricted territory from season to season (Koldehoff 2002). There is little evidence before AD 900 of the increased pan-regional "information exchange" and social homogenization once hypothesized (Braun and Plog 1982). Before that time, Late Woodland peoples everywhere, it seems, were rather insular. However, insularity is another way of saying that the processes of change were entirely local. Dale McElrath, Thomas Emerson, and Andrew Fortier (2000:17) have recently argued for a social-demographic shift that followed on the heels of the adoption of the bow and arrow at about AD 600. Around the American Bottom, habitation sites became much more visible on the landscape.

Visibility in this instance seems less a matter of permanence of individual settlements – whether people lived at one site or several within a territory over the course of a year – and more a creation of a landscape of storage that transcended individual sites. Late Woodland horticulturalists dug pits and stored foodstuffs all over the place, with certain landforms being little more than special extraction and storage sites (Fortier 1998; Fortier and Jackson 2000:138; e.g., Holley 2000; Koldehoff 2002). Storage pits vastly outnumber houses at such sites, if indeed there were any houses at all! Here and at regular domestic settlements, pits included huge bell-shaped containers reaching sizes of up to 2.5 m^3.

Perhaps the storage revolution helped proliferate social divisions according to age, gender, or kinship, thereby creating increasingly complex if still unranked social relations between kin groups and settlements (i.e., "heterarchies" [see Crumley 1995]). Modeled clay effigies of people and creatures occur at some sites, the representations of tattooing on some of these further suggesting the relationship between human bodies and social identity (Fig. 3.4). Given that relationship, it might seem odd that cemeteries are almost unknown in the vicinity of the American Bottom. Perhaps the dead were laid out on scaffolds and the bones kept or disposed of elsewhere. In any case, despite a lack of formal cemeteries, we know that there were plenty of people alive at the time. In fact, population densities pretty clearly exceeded those of Middle Woodland times (McElrath et al. 2000).

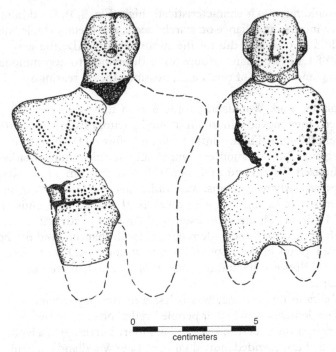

3.4 Clay objects from Late Woodland sites in St. Clair County, Illinois (adapted from Holley *et al.* 2001:figs. 9.27–9.28)

We also know that, unlike the Coles Creek peoples down south, villagers north of the confluence of the Mississippi and Ohio rivers relied on cultivated squash and native seed crops. By AD 900, maize was to be found in the gardens of most Indians living along major waterways of the central valley. Perhaps associated with the increasingly maize-centered horticulture were the minimally centralized settlement patterns of the tenth century. For example, in the "Big Bottom" north of Reelfoot Lake, Tennessee, settlements appear clustered, each village surrounded by "ten to fifteen smaller hamlets that are separated by unoccupied areas" (Mainfort 1996:84, citing Kreisa 1987). The Hoecake site, across the river in Missouri, could have been an especially large local center at this time (see Box 5). This village pattern continues up to Cahokia, which was also an unusually large village along the Mississippi surrounded by lesser hamlet-sized settlements during terminal Late Woodland times. There were other large villages in the American Bottom too, probably indicating that Cahokians were first among equals at this time.

Box 5. The Hoecake and Rich Woods sites. The largest site in the Ohio–Mississippi confluence area is named after a particular kind of cornbread cake that African-American slaves in the Mississippi Alluvial Valley used to cook on the metal blades of their hoes in the morning before going to the field. Richard Marshall and J. Raymond Williams conducted excavations here at the "Hoecake" site (Marshall 1987; Marshall and Hopgood 1964; Williams 1974). The village excavations in combination with a surface collection pointed to a very large residential occupation during the terminal Late Woodland or early Mississippian period. The semi-subterranean houses with single-set-post walls are approximately the same size and style as those seen in the American Bottom at the same time. The mound excavations, however, have confused the issue. The mounds themselves appear to cover mortuary tombs, and may even date to the Middle Woodland period. Marshall and Hopgood (1964) and Morse and Morse (1983) considered the tombs to date to the terminal Late Woodland "Baytown" component, on the strength of four shell-tempered sherds in the tomb fill. Williams (1974) and Lewis (1991) conclude that the sherds are incidental mixture in the later fill of one of the tombs, and that pieces of deteriorated copper artifacts suggest an earlier date. It should also be noted, of course, that log-lined tombs are known from the eleventh and twelfth centuries at the Shiloh, Spiro, Cahokia, and (probably) Kincaid sites. Whatever the construction history of the mounds at Hoecake, the residential evidence minimally indicates a large village center that spanned the Red-Filmed Horizon.

"The only other contender is the Rich Woods site, located 65 km to the west, at the edge of the terrace defining the Malden Plain. Both sites would fit Fowler's (1969) 'second-line' Cahokia community definition. Rich Woods consisted of 33 mounds stretching over a space of 1450 m. Hoecake was credited with 54 mounds, ranging up to 7.5 m in height at the beginning of the century... It may have been a planned community similar to Cahokia... [but] Robert Adams and Winslow Walker in 1942... did not think it had a plaza or square associated with the large central mound group" (Morse and Morse 1983:215).

The Red-Filmed Horizon

As first among equals, Cahokians tapped the regional exchange network that Rolingson (2002) notes that the Plum Bayou folks also tapped. Exotic raw materials, including Lake Superior trade copper, moved along watercourses connecting, intermittently at least, the Plum Bayou people with the northern terminal Late Woodland groups. Those linkages can be seen in the American Bottom as well in the form of foreign ceramic styles, such as "French Fork Incised." The effects of such historical connections may account for the widespread adoption of red filming as a ceramic practice at about AD 900. At that time, potters at sites between Reelfoot Lake and the American Bottom began routinely applying a thin film or slip of untempered clay to the interiors or exteriors of certain bowls, pans, bottles, seed jars (or "tecomates"), and cooking jars. As a practice, red filming on pots was especially prevalent in southeast Missouri and adjacent portions of Arkansas, Tennessee, Kentucky, and Illinois. For instance, at the Zebree site in northeastern Arkansas, the "Varney Red Films" were distinctive and coated the interior walls of jars, bowls, and pans (P. Morse and D. Morse 1990, after Williams 1954).

A fortification ditch surrounded Zebree and, possibly, the nearby Kersey site, a contemporary small village whose potters practiced less red filming. Owing to the possibility of fortifications, Morse (1974) suggested that these people intruded into the region from Missouri, to the north. Perino (1971) and Porter (1974) had also suggested southerners had intruded into the American Bottom, explaining why, they thought, red-filmed traditions may have appeared there. More recently, Mainfort (1996:89) suggested that an anomalous occurrence of check-stamped pottery in the alluvial valley at Reelfoot Lake, Tennessee, indicates an intrusive population from the east, since most Reelfoot area people made plain-surfaced, grog-tempered pottery.

At the pre-Mississippian site of Cahokia, potsherds in refuse dating to the tenth and early eleventh centuries reveal a remarkable diversity of paste composition, surface finish, and vessel shape. Among the varieties are actual or emulated "foreign" types from the south: shell-tempered Varney Red-Filmed jars, grog-tempered Baytown Plain, Kersey Incised, and Larto Red-Filmed jars and bowls, grit-tempered Yankeetown appliqué jars, and fine-grog-tempered Coles Creek Incised bowls. Until recently, this diversity suggested to some a lively trade in earthenware pots by people who themselves did not migrate, locally referred to as members of the "Late Bluff culture" (Kelly 1993). However, this view is currently unsupported by petrographic and chemical studies. Even to the naked eye, the pastes of the supposed "trade" wares often appear to be derived from sources local to the American Bottom. Thus, we have a situation where nominally "non-local" pots were being made locally.

Perhaps, like the situation south of the Ohio–Mississippi confluence, the diversity of ceramic styles in the American Bottom may also have resulted, in part, from the migrations of small groups into the American

3.5 Terminal Late Woodland pottery assemblage in the central American Bottom (from Kelly *et al.* 1990, courtesy Illinois Transportation Archaeological Research Program)

Bottom, co-residing with the local villagers who lived there during the tenth and early eleventh centuries. Based on the frequency of foreign ceramic stylistic attributes, most of these foreign potters probably relocated primarily to Cahokia or to one of several of the larger villages in the area (Pauketat 1998a). Such exotic potters seem to have continued using the styles of their natal communities, or at least certain attributes of those styles, sometimes producing a bewildering diversity of hybridized construction techniques and paste recipes.

At the same time as exotic potters may have immigrated into the American Bottom, there is evidence of intensive between-village intercourse in that same stretch of floodplain. As petrographic analyses have shown, varieties of ceramic pastes from various corners of the American Bottom are found in the refuse of most villages, although in varying proportions. Pottery tempered with crushed sherds ("grog") was made at Cahokia and other points around the American Bottom; pottery tempered with crushed rock ("grit," from burned glacial cobbles) was made at villages marginal to the northern end of the American Bottom; pottery tempered with burned and crushed limestone (procured from the bluffs in the central bottom) was produced at and around large villages called the Washausen and Pulcher sites (perhaps already with platform mounds at this time; see Porter 1974). Yet all of these varieties, and more, can be found in the refuse of these and any number of tenth- and early eleventh-century settlements (Fig. 3.5).

It seems reasonable to suspect that the ceramic hybridization and pot distribution patterns were produced because food from one place was transported to and cooked at a second place. In other words, that the pots of one's neighbors ended up in the refuse of one's own village probably indicates periodic inter-village feasting, with hosts and guests alternating between villages from event to event (Pauketat 2000a). The practice of adding a red slip to pots then coincides with the likely use of those pots during public preparation and consumption of foods. Perhaps the pots themselves helped to create a new sense of what potters, cooks, and the hosts of feasts meant to each other. Historically, of course, the color red was an extremely potent symbol that evoked broad cultural themes of life, longevity, blood, and violence. During pre-Columbian times too, the wood found in special contexts is often the rot-resistant red cedar, used in ceremonies, for marker posts, and to create special ritual brooms, mound-top buildings, and monumental constructions (such as Cahokia's "woodhenge").

In the tenth and eleventh centuries, red pigments could have been used for body paints or for dyeing cloth. Between northeast Arkansas and southwestern Illinois, the horizon sees the appearance or increase in the numbers of perforated circular potsherds, sometimes thought to be gaming pieces but most likely spindle whorls used for the production of textiles (Alt 1999). At about this same time, and presumably owing to the adoption of the spindle whorl technology, "Z" twist cordage replaced the old "S" twist variety formerly used to make fabric. This may signal larger-scale cloth production, and hence the use of clothing for public display.

In sum, between AD 900 and 1050, the public domain became enlarged and politicized. The Red-Filmed Horizon seems to have been a time of increased interaction along the river, seeing the physical movement of peoples – at least some potters – over distances of up to 200 to 300 km. In the American Bottom, this same period was marked by a high degree of inter-village feasting, at a minimum indicating a disappearance of the sort of insularity that had reigned for centuries prior to this terminal Late Woodland period. The color red was synonymous with that domain if not also with the painting and clothing of the human body in ways intended to be seen. How did this come about?

By AD 900, the social changes already set in motion by Late Woodland horticulturalists had produced a population nucleation immediately prior to or coeval with the intensification of maize. The intensification of maize, in fact, may have become the means reliably to secure the surplus needed for the feasts that seem to have become a routine part of social life during the terminal Late Woodland period in the American Bottom. In any event, several villages on the floodplain of the Mississippi had grown large by the tenth century. There may have been several hundred people at a handful of villages. The Cahokia village itself may have had a thousand or more at the time.

Besides a possible increase in local birthrates, population nucleation in the American Bottom proper appears accompanied by a draining of population from the adjoining interior uplands and stream valleys. Presumably the advantages of floodplain farming accrued to the families that lived in the floodplain, producing a multiplier effect, as outlying families increasingly were drawn into the floodplain sphere of influence. Perhaps the floodplain families could support more children, or perhaps an established floodplain family might have seen some short-term gain by having more children. Ultimately, regional social life began revolving around the burgeoning bottomland settlements.

If the earlier Late Woodland people had been semi-sedentary, the terminal Late Woodland residents now occupied their villages year-round. Huts were enlarged, more than doubling in size over a century-long period so that floor areas covered 10 m^2 or more by end of the tenth century. Like the earlier keyhole huts, these were semi-subterranean, with floors dug as much as a meter below the surface and with walls partially buried by heaped up earth. The interiors would have been dark. Entering them doubtless involved ducking one's head and stepping down onto a wooden stump or step on the floor. From the floors, the bent-pole walls extended up beyond the surface, and were tied off along a ridge-line to create arbor roofs that were, in turn, covered with bundles of grass or mat shingles.

The effect may have been to produce a hut that looked like an elaborate animal den from the outside. Such huts were arranged in clusters at small settlements (Fig. 3.6). After AD 900, we know that these were arranged around courtyards at two larger villages (and probably others), each open space of 150–300 m^2 in area surrounded by a few to a dozen huts (Kelly 1990a; Kelly et al. 1990; Pauketat 1998a). Courtyard size did not vary much from this norm, so the largest villages were composed of several contiguous courtyards and house clusters. In each courtyard was a post or a set of pits marking the center. Houses were built in succession, sometimes superimposed on earlier ones and sometimes placed alongside the former one. Excavations at the Cahokia and Range sites point either to short-term occupational hiatuses or, more likely, a courtyard-wide construction cycle. Sometimes, all of the houses of a courtyard were built at once, rebuilt at once, or abandoned at once (Pauketat 2003b:28fn). Each construction was probably a meaningful communal experience (compare Gose 1991). When rebuilt, the courtyard's new houses were built either directly over or, conversely, alongside the old courtyard group (Kelly et al. 1990; Pauketat 1994).

3.6 Oblique view of excavated village courtyard, Range site, St. Clair County, Illinois (from Kelly *et al.* 1990:plate 10.1, courtesy Illinois Transportation Archaeological Research Program)

Gaming, smoking, praying

A 10 m^2 hut is hardly large enough for many activities besides sleeping and procreation. Indeed, house floors seldom produce the bits of primary refuse or even the slightly burned spots indicative of hearths. Daily routines, including cooking, were conducted outdoors, probably in backyards. Courtyards were often devoid of refuse.

Careful examination of building floors at the eleventh-century Halliday site indicates that most houses did not open toward the courtyards. Thus, entering and exiting one's house, working in the backyard, and a good deal of socializing probably did not happen in the courtyard. In fact, the courtyards may have been reserved for special uses associated with the central post or pits. At the Cahokia village, the central posts were sometimes placed and replaced several times. At the Halliday site, one courtyard was riddled with a dozen postmolds owing to the central post having been reset as many times. Clearly, the modest 10 to 20 cm diameter posts in the courtyards were marking the centerpoint of the courtyard space. What the pits in the centers of some Range site courtyards were for is less certain, although John Kelly has observed that they come in fours, essentially partitioning the courtyard into fourfold space. The same quadripartitioning of horizontal space is found on red-filmed tecomates of this period. These "seed jars" may have been made by a restricted number of potters at a few sites, such as Pulcher, and subsequently used for non-cooking tasks or for public rituals.

If the horizontal space of courtyards and pots was divided into four fields, then other realms were segmented into two divisions. For instance, the courtyard space acted like a central inner (revered) ground, while the outer yard space may have been used for ordinary activities. The court-yards were fully exposed to the sky, the central post projecting into the air, while the domestic quarters were below the ground. Indeed, the act of entrance or exit could have evoked a sense of vertical movement be-tween the upper and lower realms, or between light and dark (or even life and death), even as the horizontal movement across a courtyard entailed traversing both ordinary and revered zones.

Played in the courtyards of these terminal Late Woodland villages would have been an all-important game, a version of the "hoop and pole game" centuries later called "chungke" by the Choctaw in northern Mississippi, "chenco" in North Carolina, or "tchung-kee" by the Mandan on the Plains (Culin 1992, citing Adair, Brackenridge, Catlin, Lawson, Lewis and Clark, Long, and others). James Adair translated the term to mean "running hard labor." The rules of the game varied across the mid-continent and Southeast by the time of European contact. In most variations, a small disk was rolled across a playing field – usually a town plaza – while two teams ran alongside and attempted to stop the roll or score points by throwing special wooden poles near its final resting point. Members of opposing sides would wager their possessions, even their families, on the roll of the chunkey disk. The loser was even known to commit suicide. Among the Muskogees, William Bartram recorded the association of the game with the execution of captives. In 1734, Le Page du Pratz witnessed a game that consisted "in rolling a flat round stone, about 3 inches in diameter and an inch thick, with the edge somewhat sloping, and throwing the pole at the same time in such a manner that when the stone rests the pole may touch it or be near it. Both antagonists throw their poles at the same time, and he whose pole is nearest the stone counts 1 and has the right of rolling the stone" (Culin 1992:488).

This high-stakes chunkey contest can be traced to more modest Late Woodland beginnings in the central Mississippi valley near the American Bottom. The earliest certain modeled-clay and carved-stone chunkey disks (also known as discoidals) are dated to about AD 600 and are found at sites in southwestern Illinois and in adjacent parts of eastern Missouri. These Late Woodland chunkey stones are small, averaging 5 cm in diameter, and sometimes feature a cross (or an "X") scratched into one

3.7 Late Woodland chunkey stone, Randolph County, Illinois

or both of their cupped sides (Fig. 3.7). Their size and ubiquity here, and at other contemporary sites, point to a game routinely played by adults and children alike, even if restricted to certain occasions.

Such was not the case with another item found in lower numbers at Late Woodland village sites. Smoking pipes were modeled from clay or carved from stone and were used to smoke tobacco, among other things. While known since the Late Archaic period, smoking pipes had almost always been left behind within the monuments or tombs of communities or prominent community representatives, suggesting that they were inalienable objects – their meaning and value was wedded to the people or places with which they had been associated. Even chunkey stones may well have had such inalienable properties, accruing event biographies or owner histories as they were used in winning or losing games. There are hints that pipes and chunkey stones were the property of particular kin groups within communities. For instance, "nearly 60 percent of all discoidals found [at Range] were recovered from features located adjacent to one of the large [high-status or public] structures" (Fortier and Jackson 2000:138, citing Kelly et al. 1987:423). By AD 900, both items were being left behind in certain courtyards.

In effect, a set of inalienable properties may have characterized certain courtyard groups: smoking pipes, discoidal stones, and central posts or pits (Pauketat 2000a:27, citing Kelly 1990b:79ff). To this list, we must add one more. At the large Range site, the central courtyards are also associated with large, square single-set post buildings. These buildings, either in the center of the courtyard or, in several cases, off to the western side of a courtyard, were typically 6 to 8 m on a side, making them several times larger than a dwelling hut. In addition, they were not built in semi-subterranean basins, but were constructed on the surface. John Kelly has further noted that this pattern may have a counterpart in the tenth- or early eleventh-century site of Pulcher, where flat-topped earthen platforms – probably topped by public buildings – seem to have been located off to the western side of habitation areas. It is unclear whether the mounds themselves were constructed at this time, or later in the eleventh century, perhaps over the top of former pre-Mississippian public buildings.

In any event, the above-ground public buildings provide the symbolic link between the enclosed semi-subterranean realm of dwellings and the inner open-air realm of the courtyard. Perhaps the communal objects – chunkey stones and smoking pipes – were curated within the public buildings, making them the terminal Late Woodland precursor to a Mississippian "temple" (DePratter 1983; Knight 1986). Bits of human remains were found scattered about the village midden of the ninth- and tenth-century village of Range, and may be indicative of the processing of the deceased within the settlement, if not within the temple. A similar argument has been made for the eleventh-century settlement of Halliday (Hargrave and Hedman 2001).

Thus, these early public buildings may have further bridged the living with the dead through the rites and supplications connected with a courtyard temple. If so, then these buildings were virtual "portals" between the past and the future in more than one sense. The earthen pyramids that would soon elevate these buildings to heights not previously known were considered as portals or "earth navels" by various southeastern Indians (Knight 1986, 1989). Mississippian platform mounds, according to V. James Knight, embodied the connections between upper and lower supernatural realms, central and peripheral cosmographic districts, past and present, sacred and mundane, and pure and profane.

But this was not yet the case in the years before what has come to be known as Cahokia's "Big Bang" (Pauketat 1997a, 1998b, 2002). Leading up to that explosive development, we have seen that a storage revolution had generated outward-looking northern Late Woodland peoples who were transcending the societal insularity of the past. By the tenth century AD, crops were grown for social uses, including maize from the American Bottom south to Reelfoot Lake and Plum Bayou (e.g., House 1996:145). Cloth production was stepped up as part of the new sociality of the times. New communication routes had opened up, spreading the exotic media and practices of a Red-Filmed Horizon throughout the central valley. Limited movements of people generated a degree of cultural pluralism in some quarters, building up to prominent levels at a few sites such as Cahokia village.

By AD 1000, the Coles Creek people of the southern centers and the Late Woodland horticulturalists of northern villages were very much aware of one another. Within the American Bottom, awareness gave way to competition, played out through feasts and localized exchange. The lived traditions of these terminal Late Woodland peoples generated large central villages, competitive village-based feasts, local resettlements, and long-distance migrations of some people who, subsequently, made foreign-style pots. The productive capacity and storage potential of the northern peoples had grown great, and the seeds of the events to come were ready to germinate.

All of these changes were necessary antecedents to subsequent events, but none can be claimed as sufficient to explain those changes. Pre-Mississippian developments did not, strictly speaking, cause Cahokia to happen. The traditions of these people were the media of the generation of Cahokia at about AD 1050. The memories and stories of the Plum Bayou, Varney, Coles Creek, and Late Bluff peoples would be retold in novel ways, within a locally pluralistic setting, to invent a new tradition and to build a new place for which there were no precedents and from which there was no turning back. Something big was about to happen in the American Bottom.

4   Early Cahokia

Many have considered the development of Mississippian cultures a gradual evolutionary process that occurred everywhere across the mid-continent and Coastal Plain simultaneously. They envisioned a two-century-long Emergent Mississippian period that culminated in mature Mississippian. The earlier people, the story goes, must have been pre-adapted to become "Mississippian" owing to some combination of pan-eastern changes that took place between the ninth and the early eleventh centuries AD: the medieval warming, technological innovation, or the introduction of maize and the universal human tendency to minimize crop-production risks. In any number of scenarios, archaeologists have imagined that autonomous Woodland horticulturalists gradually attached themselves to managerial-style leaders who, subsequently, inherited their authority just as one inherits a family name. In the process, these Emergent Mississippians would have communicated or traded with their neighbors, spreading the burgeoning culture all across the eastern United States (cf. Smith 1990).

In some versions of this explanation, Mississippian cultural changes were inevitable. Had you been a sedentary horticulturalist who grew maize in the Mississippi valley, you too would have evolved into a Mississippian (see Box 6). However, there is ample evidence generated since the mid-1990s to argue that such a seamless, spontaneous development *never happened!* That evidence tells instead of a *historical disjuncture.* The evidentiary centerpiece is the grand, new political-administrative capital constructed atop the former village of Cahokia. For this reason, the Emergent Mississippian concept is deceptive, and is avoided here in favor of the hopefully less loaded notion of a terminal Late Woodland period (see Fortier and McElrath 2002).

The central political-administrative complex

By itself, Cahokia is today the largest archaeological site in North America. The heart of this archaeological behemoth is Monks Mound,

Box 6. Alternative views of Cahokia. Competing claims concerning Cahokia's complexity and historical significance have coalesced since the 1990s. The present volume could be said to represent the "historical-processual perspective." Another perspective casts Cahokia as the center of a mercantile polity based in the control of Mississippi River commerce (e.g., Dincauze and Hasenstaub 1989; Kelly 1991a; Peregrine 1992). A third promotes a sense that Cahokia was a communal or ceremonial site that serviced the ritual needs of kin groups (J. Kelly 2002; L. Kelly 2000; Saitta 1994). We might label this the "rituality" explanation, following Yoffee *et al.* (1999). A fourth has been tagged as a "lesser Cahokia," "minimalist," or "adaptationist" perspective. The advocates of this fourth position, steeped in the neo-evolutionism and processualism of 1970s archaeology, remain dubious of claims that Cahokia was anything more than one of many regional manifestations of a general evolutionary development – Mississippian culture. As best represented in the writings of George Milner (1998), the lesser Cahokia advocates envision Cahokia as the *result* of environmental or behavioral causes; they generally do not see political centralization as a process that caused environmental or behavioral change. Since the carrying capacity of the floodplain could not support a dense population on its own, one line of reasoning goes, a dense population could not have existed.

While there remain areas of agreement between all competing positions, there are also disagreements profound enough to make one wonder how such dissimilar "alternative views" of Cahokia could possibly be supported by what seem, on the surface, to be the same archaeological data! The short answer is that, despite *access* to the same data, the *alternative views are not actually based on these same data.* In part, this is because the different perspectives and biases of researchers lead some to gloss over certain evidence while amplifying other evidence. There is also an obvious correlation between those who base arguments on new field data and those who have never conducted their own archaeological fieldwork at Cahokia. Fortunately, archaeological evidence can and does "constrain" interpretations of the past in the long run. The result over time is that certain ideas are *gradually* eliminated from the realm of plausibility (Brumfiel 1996; Trigger 1991). The gradual reconciliation of perspectives means that disagreements will reign until sufficient data exist to make one alternative not only the most plausible but also the undisputed champion. In the meantime, disputes continue until everyone weighs all of the evidence equally.

4.1 Oblique aerial view of Cahokia's central precinct (2002)

the tallest and widest pre-Columbian construction in North America and the third or fourth largest ancient pyramid in the New World (Fig. 4.1). In its final form, it was 30 m high with a fill volume of about 731,000 m^3. It had three major flat terraces and covered an area at its base of just under 7 ha, a larger area than covered by the Pyramid of Khufu in Egypt (which of course exceeds Monks Mound in height). It looms over what are today two modern highways, unincorporated residential neighborhoods, and the Cahokia Mounds State Historic Site.

Monks Mound fronts the northern end of one of the largest pre-Columbian plazas in North America, the 19 ha Grand Plaza, and is situated in the middle of other large 9 ha plazas to the north, west, and east (Pauketat and Emerson 1997). Scattered in an 8 km^2 site catchment around it are remains of some 120 lesser pyramids, each known today by its mound number and its association with one of a series of major pyramid-and-plaza groups or "sub-communities" (Fowler 1997). Thousands of wooden pole-and-thatch buildings, as well as palatial-sized temples, upright marker posts, compound walls, bastioned palisades, and at least one "woodhenge," flanked the various mound groups. Today only the eroded pyramids remain, the stains of thousands of decayed

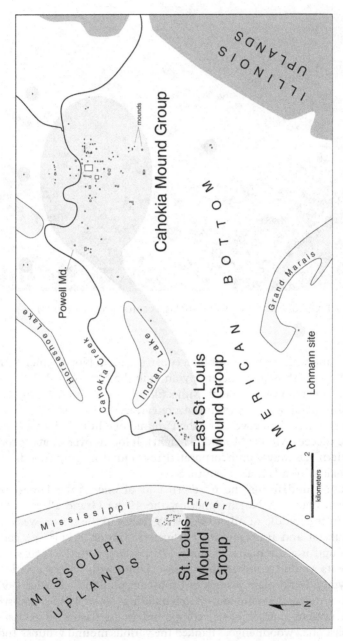

4.2 Plan map of the central political-administrative complex

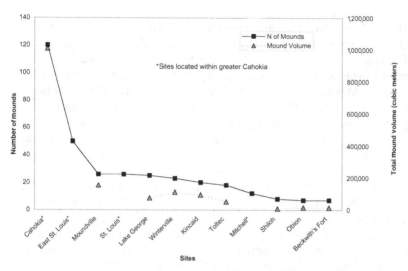

4.3 Graph showing Midsouthern and southeastern Mississippian sites by volume and number of mounds (adapted from Muller 1997)

wooden thatched buildings, walls, and posts remaining unseen beneath the present-day sod. Monks Mound itself has slumped repeatedly, with major damage probably caused by one or more great New Madrid earthquakes in the past (Emerson and Woods 1993; Woods 2001).

However, Cahokia was not alone. It was actually just one of three not-so-discrete archaeological sites within an even larger "central political-administrative complex" that sprawled along an ancient riverbed and hopped across the Mississippi River (Fig. 4.2). To the south was the East St. Louis site, with its fifty earthen pyramids and associated temples, storage huts, and walled compounds (J. Kelly 1997; Pauketat 2004). Immediately across the Mississippi from East St. Louis, occupying the western end of the political-administrative sprawl, was the St. Louis or "Mound City" site, with its twenty-six pyramids and 2 ha plaza. Unfortunately, the pyramids of both the East St. Louis and the St. Louis groups were leveled during the nineteenth century. Perhaps for this reason, few written descriptions of greater Cahokia do justice to the scale of the entire central political-administrative complex. For instance, seldom appreciated is the fact that, at least in terms of numbers of pyramids (and excluding the uncertain Hoecake and Rich Woods mounds), the East St. Louis and St. Louis sites are number 2 and 4 in a list of the top-ten largest Mississippian sites! Both sites featured large pyramids (Fig. 4.3).

Box 7. Cahokia–Mesoamerica connections? Anyone familiar with the civilizations of Mesoamerica will recognize some features of Cahokia: a planned symmetrical center, large four-sided pyramids built in stages, and pole-and-thatch houses. Thus, many have wondered if Mexicans, namely the Toltecs, inspired Cahokians to build their great center. The Toltec case may be reasonable in some people's minds given the supposed expansionistic qualities of Toltecan culture – as seen not only in central Mexico but also at sites such as Chichen Itzá in the Yucatan Peninsula – and given that the Mexicans and Maya were known on occasion to take to the ocean in boats. Why not sail up the Mississippi? What would have been the impact of some Toltec wayfarers contacting some North American terminal Late Woodland people?

However, for most just-the-facts-please North American archaeologists, Mesoamerican arguments strain credulity. Never mind the vexing question of why any self-respecting Toltec trader would care about the backwoods Woodland dwellers of the Mississippi valley; there is no direct evidence of Mexican contact anywhere in the eastern United States save a single Mexican obsidian scraper at the Caddoan region Spiro site in Oklahoma (Barker *et al.* 2002). To conjure up Mexicans in North America seems to many North Americanists wild speculation not founded in fact. It might also be construed as yet one more Moundbuilder denial that North American Indians could have created the Mississippian centers.

On the other hand, acknowledging that there may have been intermittent contacts of a sort across the Texas–Mexico borderlands over the Archaic-through-Woodland period is perfectly reasonable. During the Mississippian period, the Huastecan peoples of northeastern Mexico were building modest pyramid-and-plaza centers 400 km south of Brownsville, Texas, while the Mississippians occupied the mid-continental United States and shared certain material-cultural similarities with the Caddoan groups, namely engraved shell (e.g., Willey 1966:169–71). And there are similarities between certain religious beliefs, legends, origin stories, and symbols of the eastern Woodlands and Mesoamerica (Hall 1989, 1991, 1997). Some of these similarities stem from shared historical-linguistic origins.

The likelihood of intermittent contacts and the arguments for cultural or linguistic similarities remain of uncertain relevance to the founding of Cahokia. Robert Hall and Melvin Fowler see the four executed men in Cahokia's Mound 72 and various female sacrifices as reminiscent of the central Mexican practice of sacrifices having to do with the corn goddess Xilonen (see Hall 2000; Young and Fowler 2000:269). In addition, Hall (1991:31) has compared the Mexican diety "Xolotl" and the Mayan hero "Hunhau" to the Long-Nosed God represented in early Mississippian ear ornaments (see chapter 5). At one time, James Porter (1977:156–7) wondered if Mississippian culture spread up the Mississippi floodplain carried on the backs of "southern traders" who moved along a riverine "highway" that might even have seen travelers from Mesoamerica. Certainly there are many known instances in other parts of the world of dramatic political events and the founding of dynasties associated with the arrival of foreign lords or "stranger-kings" who immigrated to new lands and super-imposed their wills and sense of order over those already there (e.g., Frazer 1947; Sahlins 1985).

In 1811, Henry Marie Brackenridge described them all. To him, and to others today, they seemed like something out of ancient Egypt or Mexico (see Box 7). They suggested the existence of a once-great population center.

I have frequently examined the mounds at St. Louis: they are situated on the second bank just above [north of] the town ... About six hundred yards above [the 25 other pyramids] there is a single mound, with a broad stage on the river side; it is thirty feet in height, and one hundred and fifty in length; the top is a mere ridge of five or six feet wide. (Brackenridge 1814:189)

I crossed the Mississippi at St. Louis, and after passing through the wood which borders the river, about half a mile in width, entered an extensive open plain. In 15 minutes, I found myself in the midst of a group of mounds, mostly of a circular shape, and at a distance, resembling enormous haystacks scattered through a meadow. One of the largest which I ascended, was about two hundred paces in circumference at the bottom, the form nearly square ... [and the] top was level, with an area sufficient to contain several hundred men ... Around me I counted forty-five mounds, or pyramids, besides a great number of small artificial elevations; these mounds form something more than a semicircle, about a mile in extent ... Pursuing my walk along the bank of the Cahokia [Creek], I passed eight others in the distance of three miles before I arrived at the largest assemblage. When I reached the foot of the principal mound, I was struck with a degree of astonishment, not unlike that which is experienced in contemplating the Egyptian pyramids. What a stupendous pile of earth! ... As the sward had been burnt, the earth was perfectly naked, and I could trace with ease, any unevenness of surface, so as to discover ... a great number of small elevations of earth, to the height of a few feet, at regular distances from each other, and which appeared to observe some order. (Brackenridge 1814:187–8)

As Brackenridge noted, the pyramids of Cahokia merge with those of East St. Louis via a corridor of earthen pyramids and residential

4.4 Oblique aerial view of the Powell Mound, *c.* 1930 (courtesy of the Illinois Transportation Archaeological Research Program)

development that followed the bank of an ancient Mississippi River channel, locally called "Indian Lake." Along the way was Powell Mound, the second-largest pyramid at Cahokia up until its destruction in 1930. Witnesses on hand as it was steam shoveled away observed two large mortuary features, scores of human interments, and an associated mollusk-shell-studded garment (Ahler and DePuydt 1987). Apparently, human bodies and bundles of human bones had been laid out on the flat top of an earthen pyramid and then covered over with more dirt, giving the final mound a distinctive "ridge-top" roof shape not unlike the hipped roofs of buildings (Fig. 4.4). Like others of its kind, the Powell Mound was placed in a visually prominent location removed from the central precinct of Cahokia. Other such ridge-top mounds include the large "Cemetery Mound" in the center of East St. Louis and the "Big Mound" at the northern end of the St. Louis site (Fig. 1.4).

With one possible exception (at the Shiloh site in Tennessee), such ridge-top tumuli are unknown outside of the greater Cahokia region. Yet, there were at least ten such ridge-top mounds within the greater Cahokia region, including Mounds 49, 66, 72, and two others at Cahokia, two or three smaller tumuli near Powell Mound, the largest East St. Louis and St. Louis mounds, and the Great Mound at the Mitchell site (10 km north of Monks Mound). Based on the surviving accounts of trenches full of skeletons adorned with shell and copper ornaments, we know that all were mortuary mounds. We also know from descriptions of their dimensions that four of them were among the ten largest earthen constructions in the greater Cahokia region, with fill volume estimates ranging from less than 10,000 m³ to some 200,000 m³ of earth!

Given their shapes, sizes, and mortuary contents, and because they are unique in the Mississippian world, it is reasonable to suspect that the ridge-top mounds are key to interpreting the central political-administrative complex. That is, if the enormous sizes and prominent locations of the mounds bespeak the exceptional importance of the people buried there, then perhaps these were the mortuary tombs of the apical families, retinues, and sacrificial victims of a short-lived late eleventh- and early twelfth-century social experiment unique to greater Cahokia: a dynasty of administrators and officials drawn from succeeding lineages commemorated with the earthen roof covering each mortuary tomb complex. Alternatively, the placement of ridge-top mounds at various points around the central political-administrative complex may hint at a horizontally complex and potentially "group-oriented" form of Cahokian governance. In this case, some of the ten tomb mounds could be contemporary, and indicative of an unusually elaborate elite "heterarchy" (à la Crumley 1995).

Whereas some may conclude that a heterarchical or "corporate" form of governance indicates the absence of a strongly centralized administration, new regional-scale evidence says otherwise.[10] Indeed, the impressive death pits of Mound 72 may affirm that early Cahokia constituted a unique, short-lived episode of corporate "state-making" in native North America (see chapter 8). Cahokia's status as a veritable founding city hastened the formation of other polities and, ultimately, mid-continental ethnicities. The linchpin in such an argument is found in the construction of early Cahokia.

The construction of early Cahokia

By the early 1990s, archaeologists had begun to appreciate more fully the scale and internal complexity of the political-administrative complex of Cahokia and East St. Louis. Remote sensing, archaeological excavations, and a topographic survey had been used to identify a likely palisade wall, a monumental circle of posts (also known as the woodhenge), walled compounds, specially constructed and oversized buildings (usually but not always on pyramids), unusual mortuary tombs, and enormous central plazas (Fig. 4.5). Excavations also discovered that large portions of the East St. Louis site remained intact beneath the nineteenth-century streets and buildings. Those excavations appeared to affirm the idea that

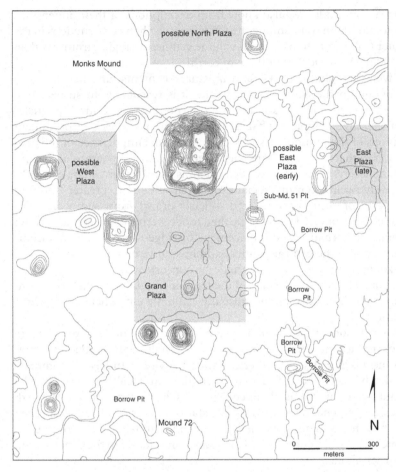

4.5 A topographic map of downtown Cahokia (original base map courtesy of Melvin Fowler)

the founding moments of Mississippian civilization in the region involved
large-scale public-works projects that transformed space by moving
earth.

Indeed, by the late 1980s Rinita Dalan's non-invasive electro-magnetic
survey of the large open space at the center of "downtown" Cahokia led
her to surmise that this 19 ha rectangular ground was a constructed
feature (see Dalan 1997). She suspected that pre-Columbian people had
graded down the naturally undulating topography of this area, truncating
ridge tops and filling in the intervening low swales. Excavations targeting

4.6 An excavated profile of Grand Plaza at Cahokia showing pre-Mississippian surface, plaza fill, and upper plow-churned surface zone (1997)

the apparent plaza verified that most if not all of it was built in one massive labor project, marking the end of the terminal Late Woodland period and the beginning of the Mississippian period Lohmann phase (see Holley *et al.* 1993; Pauketat and Rees 1996). A sandy loam plaza fill is visible atop the original pre-Mississippian ground surface in profile (Fig. 4.6). The plaza seems to possess a slight grade, being several centimeters higher at the north end than the south. Combined with the fine sandy fill, the grade helps explain why even today rainwater does not pond on the Grand Plaza.

On the basis of extensive coring, it appears that the initial stage of the largest pyramid, Monks Mound, was a single massive construction 6.5 m high, built simultaneously with the Grand Plaza (Dalan 1997:93, citing Reed *et al.* 1968). Excavations into a small "ridge-top" Mound 49 in the middle of the plaza also revealed an initial meter-high clay mound built simultaneously with the Grand Plaza. Plaza fill is not present underneath Mound 49 in the plaza, which is surrounded by "lateral borrow areas" stripped of ancient topsoil and mined for dirt, presumably to build the mounds (Holley *et al.* 1993; Pauketat *et al.* 2002; Pauketat and Rees 1996). Thus, those who have worked in the inner pyramid-and-plaza precinct of Cahokia – the very core of the Cahokian landscape – conclude that it was planned and executed in a massive construction phase dating to about AD 1050 (Dalan 1997).

The planned central space was considerably more than simply a large rectangular open ground intended to hold a certain-sized social gathering. The positioning and heights of the pyramids were also probably intended for more than visual impression. These spaces were to be experienced, possibly intended to generate certain physical sensations if not emotional responses. First, they constrained or freed-up the movement of human bodies within them. Walking through the Grand Plaza takes time. Climbing Monks Mound similarly takes time and some exertion. Along the way, the movement itself engenders an appreciation of the proportions and re-lationships between the pyramids and the plaza. In the past, considerably more upright posts, thatch-roof buildings, and gathered peoples would have been part of the experience of movement and changing perspectives. One's sensibilities and dispositions would have been defined in relation to this experience.

In the Mississippian past, the visual sense would have been just one of the senses affected by the pyramid-and-plaza experience. During our excavations in the middle of the Grand Plaza in 1997, we observed that conversations of people ascending or descending Monks Mound were perfectly audible (in the early morning quiet of the plaza). In the past, pro-nouncements, chants, songs, and the beating of drums probably would have carried across the entire space, just as did the early morning mound-top calls of the contact-era Mississippian chiefs (e.g., Du Pratz 1975). The plaza's sights and sounds would have been accentuated by the scents and flavors of feast foods and fires.

Residential neighborhoods

The social and demographic significance of the initial pyramid-and-plaza construction is amplified by evidence from excavated residential areas beyond the central precinct. These include areas designated by archaeol-ogists as Tract 15A, Tract 15B, the Dunham and Powell Tracts, and the Interpretive Center Tract II, also known as ICT-II (Bareis, notes on file, University of Illinois; Collins 1990, 1997; O'Brien 1972; Pauketat 1994, 1998a). These tracts of land, covering a combined excavated area in ex-cess of 3 ha, also point to an abrupt transformation of population density, residential space, and daily domestic practices that marked the end of the terminal Late Woodland period. As indicated by a doubling of numbers of houses and a more than threefold increase in the average floor space per phase, the human population of the Cahokia site is thought to have

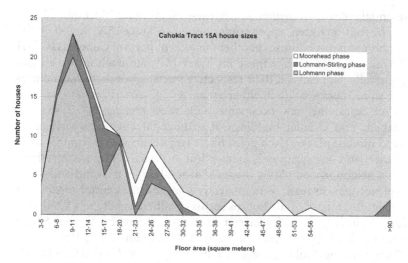

4.7 Graph showing house size modes, Tract 15A, Cahokia (data from Pauketat 1998a)

more than quadrupled over a fifty-year period (Fig. 4.7). The precise rate of increase is difficult to know, given the ambiguities in precisely dating house abandonment relative to the fifty-year phases currently in use. However, over a period of one to two generations, Cahokia's population swelled from approximately 1400–2800 pre-Mississippian people to 10,200–15,300 Mississippians in a 1.8 km² area (Pauketat 2003b; Pauketat and Lopinot 1997:table 6.3). This rate of increase is suggestive of the relocation of people from the surrounding floodplain and beyond to new lodgings at Cahokia.

One tract (15B) featured a pre-Mississippian residential occupation that, possibly in one fell swoop, was replaced by large Lohmann phase public buildings or oversized homes. A second excavation (15A) revealed pre-Mississippian houses around village courtyards that were replaced abruptly by a new Lohmann phase neighborhood with larger storage pits and more houses, now segregated by size and shape. There were rectangular houses, a few of which had special entrances or storage rooms giving them an "L" or a "T" shape in plan. There were also the unprecedented circular buildings, some of which have central hearths, around which other domestic buildings appear to cluster. And the larger domestic buildings were separated from at least one cluster of smaller ones, possibly indicating groups of higher- and lower-status families. The residential remains from another extensive excavation of the Powell Tract, yet to be fully analyzed, appear quite similar to Tract 15A. So too do the first Lohmann phase houses in other (southern) parts of Cahokia (ICT-II and Dunham) appear like those on Tract 15A, although in these cases they literally "appear" on their respective tracts, since there was no pre-Mississippian occupation in either area.

In all cases, the new occupants built their rectangular, T-shaped, L-shaped, and circular buildings at orthogonal angles to each other around modest plazas. Each plaza had a large central post (up to 1 m in diameter) and one (or more?) storage hut or granary. Presumably, these modest neighborhood plazas clustered around larger pyramid-and-plaza complexes that, in turn, were all arrayed around the central precinct of Cahokia. Alignment of the houses seems to adhere rigidly to a Cahokian grid, presumably part of a master plan first noticed by Harriet Smith during her 1941 mound excavations (see also Collins 1990, 1997).

Wherever one looks among the excavations at Cahokia, evidence abounds that the new houses built during the urban renewal events of AD 1050 were assembled in a new architectural style characterized by "wall trenches." The wall posts of pre-Mississippian buildings were set in individually dug postholes, with the center of each wall usually having the largest or deepest posts. The finished rectangular huts could sleep five or so people side-by-side on their semi-subterranean dirt floors. More than likely, the wall posts were saplings bent over and tied off in the center to fashion an arbor-shaped roof. To keep the rainwater out of the house, it is likely that earth was heaped up against the wall exterior and the roof was brought down low to the ground.

Contrast these to new wall trench domiciles built to house Cahokia's booming population. While these retained the rectangular semi-subterranean look, the use of trenches (dug using the stone-bladed hoes) rather than individual postholes makes it possible that walls were prefabricated on the ground and then set into place at once. For a rectangular house, this means that the roof would probably have been a separate construction and, as supported by interior post supports, of a thatched hipped roof variety. The floors of most houses were still dug below the ground surface like the single-post precursors. And like those pre-Mississippian buildings, the absence of any evidence of mud-daubed walls from a variety of documented burned houses makes it likely that earth was heaped up against the wall exteriors both for added wall stability and for protection against the weather (Fig. 4.8). For circular buildings, lightweight pliable walls may have been prefabricated and then bent into the trenches before the wall members were tied off in wigwam fashion or a separate roof structure was added.

4.8 Mississippian style, hipped-roof, semi-subterranean buildings: top, excavated house at the Grossmann site, St. Clair County, Illinois (2002); bottom, reconstructed example on the campus of the University of Illinois (2001)

Artifact assemblages and technological styles

The analyzed remains of the domestic occupation from Cahokia's excavated tracts indicate significant shifts in the artifact assemblages associated with the people living in the new wall trench houses after AD 1050
(Pauketat 1994, 1998a:341). There are surges in the amounts of most
lithic and ceramic refuse in domestic garbage and there are new artifact
styles introduced at this time (Fig. 4.9). As opposed to the years preceding AD 1050, there are three to four times as many lithic artifacts (discarded in double the volume of domestic midden) in and around Tract
15A's Lohmann phase houses. Of particular note are increased densities

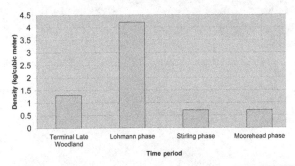

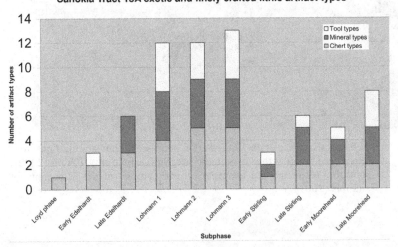

4.9 Select artifact assemblage time-series data from Tract 15A, Cahokia
(adapted from Pauketat 1994, 1998a)

of chipped-stone projectile points (made in a new triangular "Cahokia" style), spindle whorls, large exotic chipped-stone knives, cherts used for expedient tools and projectile points, the debitage and broken pieces of groundstone and chipped-stone woodworking tools and hoe blades, bits of copper, mica, and quartz crystal, and the sherds of well-made cooking pots and decorated fineware serving containers.

Brad Koldehoff (1987, 1990a, 1995) has suggested that pre-Mississippian stone tool technologies became more formalized, some requiring considerable skill (large-biface production) and some requiring less skill (expedient tool industry). Probably this same thing applies to other production tasks. There can be no doubt that large-biface reduction did not take place in the American Bottom as a rule. This was done by skilled knappers at or near the Burlington quarries in Missouri and the Mill Creek quarries in southern Illinois, and at lesser chert outcrop sites.

The same selectivity of raw materials, localization of production, and likely segmentation of labor appears to characterize the groundstone industry. For instance, igneous rocks for axe heads were probably acquired from the St. François Mountains, south of the Burlington quarries, made into blanks nearby and then finished at and around Cahokia (Pauketat and Alt 2004). Expert axe head makers at Cahokia finished some of these, while rural farmers seem to have finished others.

Certainly, the production of earthenware pots became increasingly formalized and segmented. The diverse tempers and pottery manufacturing treatments once employed by many people within a potting community before AD 1050 became progressively more restricted or segmented after AD 1050. For instance, all pre-Mississippian potters in the vicinity of the Pulcher and Washausen sites south of Cahokia had made limestone-tempered cooking jars, bowls, and tecomates before AD 1050. By the Lohmann phase, however, potters at these same sites, at Cahokia, and even at distant upland villages used limestone-tempered pastes almost exclusively for bowls and tecomates, while they made jars using other tempers, especially shell (e.g., Pauketat 1994:57).

At the same time, those jars were increasingly made using a more sophisticated construction process than had been the case during the terminal Late Woodland period: a one-step coiling technique gave way to a multi-stepped process sometimes involving slabbing or molding techniques (Pauketat 1998a, 2004). For instance, the typical Stirling phase "Ramey Incised" jar was made as follows: (1) the lower body was formed using a slab or large coil construction with the aid of a simple bowl mold; (2) its interior was heavily scraped to thin the wall when the lower portion was sufficiently dry; (3) an upper inward-angled portion was constructed using slabs or large coils and, unscraped, was welded onto the lower body; (4) a lip coil or bead was added and any external decorated carvings were made; (5) the entire vessel exterior was slipped and then heavily burnished; and (6) the pot was fired, often in a reducing atmosphere to smudge and darken its appearance.

Along with the earlier lithic industries, such a complex ceramic "technological style" (i.e., the cultural routine in which things were produced) and the production of distinctive wares by specific people or for specific reasons is suggestive of socially specialized or segmented manufacturing processes (see Dobres 2000). Indeed, this pattern is probably related to the production of certain material goods by talented individuals or by neighborhood, sub-community, or rural district. There is reason to suspect that certain kinds or quantities of axe heads, cloth, pots, and beads were both temporally restricted and spatially localized (see Alt 1999, 2001; Pauketat 1987c, 1993b, 1997b). Thus, at Cahokia's Tract 15A, there are high densities of axe-head-making debris and spindle whorls but scant evidence of the microlithic tools indicative of shell working. This contrasts with evidence from small-scale excavations and surface collections on another part of the Cahokia site, the so-called "Kunnemann Tract." There it seems likely that marine-shell bead making and necklace production was a neighborhood-specific craft activity during the Lohmann and early Stirling phases (Holley 1995; Mason and Perino 1961; Pauketat 1993b; Yerkes 1983, 1991). In the vicinity of the Powell Tract, evidence of both axe-head and shell-bead making is known (C. Bareis, personal communication, 1991; Kelly and Koldehoff 1996). At the ICT-II, there is no evidence of any of this (DeMott et al. 1993; Gums 1993).

Creating a Cahokian ethos

It is possible that craft and cloth production may have been inalienable practices associated with central persons or social groups. It is equally plausible that making beads, axe heads, finewares, and cloth was inseparable from certain events, as seems indicated by finds from the sub-Mound 51 pit (Pauketat et al. 2002). In 1965, a massive refilled borrow pit was discovered 150 m southeast of Monks Mound, partially buried beneath Mound 51. Perhaps in order to fill in a portion of the Grand Plaza or to construct the core stage of Monks Mound, it seems that Cahokians had excavated natural sediments from what would become a gouged-out hole more than 56 m long, 19 m wide, and 3 m deep at the edge of the new Grand Plaza. After sitting open for at least a year (attested by preserved marsh grass at the pit's bottom), Lohmann phase Cahokians began refilling the borrow pit in a series of massive debris-dumping episodes.

Each of seven major strata in this remarkable feature appears through-out the length and breadth of what would have been a treacherous gaping hole. The uniform strata indicate that each zone was a single, large-scale event or a series of tightly spaced events that included several fires. Given the buried ants, fly pupae exuvia, and various flesh-eating and plant-eating beetles sealed in the layers, it is certain that each layer was a rich, rotting compost of filleted animal remains, decaying pumpkins and squashes, and other cooked and uncooked plant and animal food wastes. The filling of the borrow pit was rapid, probably happening over the course of a few years. Each layer rotted and compressed for a season, a year, or more, and was then buried completely by the next. At least one of the burned layers appears to have involved the spontaneous combustion of a huge amount of shallowly buried roof thatch.

Two other layers contained a restricted array of animal taxa (deer parts, swans, prairie chicken, large fish, etc.), fruits and porridge remains, craft production debris, broken dishware, ritual or sumptuary paraphernalia, tobacco seeds, scattered human bones, cypress and cedar wood chips, and burned firewood and roof thatch – all of these in some of the best-preserved conditions and concentrated in some of the highest densities known from Cahokia. The interpretation of the pit's layers as the residues of large-scale public ritual events centered on feasts appears warranted both by the contents and the pit's location alongside the Grand Plaza. The association of production debris suggests that crafting of the many new objects of Cahokia was a meaningful part of these gargantuan gatherings. At each public event several hundred to several thousand deer were consumed, several hundred to several thousand pots were broken (intentionally or accidentally), and several thousand to hundreds of thousands of tobacco seeds were dropped and left behind (Pauketat *et al.* 2002).

Hundreds to thousands of people, crowds worthy of the Grand Plaza, probably attended these rites. Doubtless many of them were rural farmers or visitors who did not reside at Cahokia proper. Presumably, while at Cahokia they either were fed from communal stores or came with their own provisions. In either case, a thin line may have separated their own provisions from the tribute due to Cahokians. Their own perceptions, in this case, may have been critical (cf. Sahlins 1972). Perhaps those perceptions were influenced by what they smoked while at Cahokia. It is noteworthy that native tobacco's "ß-carbolines could act psychoactively as hallucinogens," and for various North American Indians it did involve "the ingestion and at times inhalation of a significant amount of tobacco smoke or tobacco plants, often accompanied by fasting" (Adair 2000:183). This is all the more reason to appreciate the significance of Gail Wagner's (2000:198) observation that although "tobacco in the American Bottom rarely occurs in contexts that suggest ritual use, it is striking that so far nearly all contexts with tobacco that do suggest ritual use occur in the American Bottom." Indeed, she continues: "All special contexts for tobacco that have been identified date between AD 900 and 1200."[11]

Perhaps the perceptions of the crowds attending central rites also were influenced by what they took home with them afterwards. There is indirect evidence in the form of widely dispersed, centrally made "Ramey Incised" pots from the early twelfth century that visitors did not leave empty handed, even if they left with less than what they brought (Pauketat and Emerson 1991). Perhaps Cahokians "redistributed" the surplus provisions, giving away ritual medicines, blessings, or foods from storehouses (Emerson 1989).

It is also possible that the provisioning and redistribution of surplus may have been linked to the chunkey game. Warren DeBoer (1993) has argued that the chunkey game fell into the hands of the Cahokian elite during the Lohmann phase. The evidence for this is distributional: Cahokians and the people of major floodplain towns had chunkey stones but, after AD 1050, floodplain farmers did not.[12] As this game involved competing teams and gambling, it is then significant with respect to the outcome of the game that Cahokians always had a home-team advantage. Perhaps visiting teams did not even expect to win, the transfer of winnings being a ceremonious but foregone conclusion. Then again, the game may have been a principal attraction of Cahokia, perhaps even generating a common home-team mentality and loyalty. If nothing else, the chunkey game may have placed a whole new spin on one's perceptions of the possibilities and rewards attendant to the new Cahokian order.

During a Cahokian chunkey game, a well-attended religious rite, or a gargantuan feast, gathered throngs at Cahokia would have had considerable public-works potential. We have already examined the scale of the initial construction of the Grand Plaza. Earth-moving projects of a similar sort are now also known in the Lohmann and early Stirling phase infilling of ancient natural depressions – swales – in the eastern portion of Cahokia and at the East St. Louis site, the latter in fact associated with a shallow midden of ritual food refuse and the construction of elite buildings and pyramids (J. Kelly 1997; Koldehoff et al. 2000; Pauketat 2004). In all likelihood, other portions of Cahokia, East St. Louis, and St. Louis – along with outlying towns – were also landscaped as part of large-scale public-works projects. Perhaps the best examples of such public-works efforts are the pyramids themselves. Importantly, the mound-construction evidence from Cahokia's Mounds 10, 11, 31, 33, 34, 38, 39, 49–51, 72, and 86, from the Horseshoe Lake, Mitchell, and Emerald site mounds, and from East St. Louis's Mounds E6 and E11 shows what Preston Holder recognized in 1955: pyramid building was never a one-time effort but a continuously prosecuted social act by many participants (see Pauketat 1993b, 2000b).

While it is clear that there were massive clay cores to the first pyramids of Cahokia's central precinct, it is equally obvious that there was a highly ritualized construction cycle materialized as the alternating light and dark "blanket" mantles of the mounds (Fig. 4.10). In many instances, the blanketing of the pyramid with pure sands and dark clays clearly entailed the removal of the surmounting pole-and-thatch buildings and the subsequent reconstruction of these elite homes, storage buildings, council houses, or temples. In historic periods in the southeastern United States, the idea was to purify and renew the inner sancta of the community, especially the "temple" (DePratter 1983; Knight 1986, 1989). At Cahokia and nearby towns, such a temple-renewal cycle appears to have extended to other monuments and public buildings as well, and involved the use of red pigments, red cedar, paints, fire, and special white and yellow sand and clay linings to hearths, floors, and pit bottoms (Alt 2003; Booth et al. 2001; Emerson 1997c; Jackson et al. 1992; Kruchten 2000; Pauketat 1996). The burning of the old temple thatch and the rethatching of the temple – if not all domestic buildings – was doubtless a highly charged act. The ritual significance probably is embodied in the roof-shaped ridge-top mounds that may be virtual mortuary temples in an earthen medium.

Temples, of course, were the repositories of the remains of ancestors, along with the inalienable objects of that ancestry. Given the evidence of human remains in the sub-Mound 51 pit, perhaps there was also an ancestor veneration and mortuary ritual component to the celebrations, craft productions, and public-works projects embodied in the sub-Mound 51 garbage. In fact, a series of Lohmann phase death rituals may have constituted a bizarre kind of inclusive ritual performance associated with the public-works and feasting events. Recall that the trench and platform-summit burials associated with the ridge-top mounds reveal "group-oriented" mortuary ritual. A small mound, number 72 at Cahokia, best exemplifies this.

Besides various single-person interments, the Mound 72 mortuaries include eight excavated group mortuary tombs or platforms. One of

4.10 Close-up of excavated Horseshoe Lake mound profile showing Lohmann phase blanket mantles (1993)

these contains the famous "beaded burial" of two men, one atop a shell-bead cape and one below it, with their attendees nearby (Fig. 4.11). Four of the other mortuaries are the mass graves of killed women, at least some of whom were selected from distinct non-Cahokian populations, as indicated by their dental traits, the isotopic traces in their bones, and their stature and skeletal features (Ambrose *et al.* 2001; Rose 2000:81–2). Like the beaded burial, and like other groups within the mound, the four female mortuary pits reveal to the present-day analyst an unambiguous

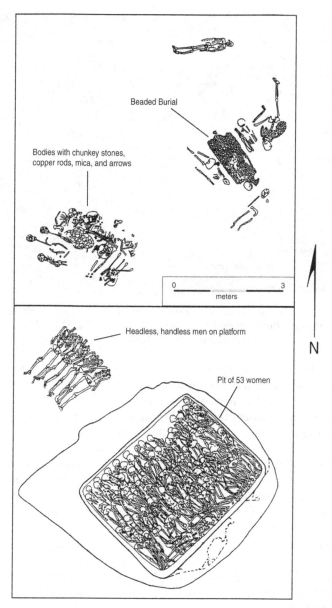

4.11 Plan view of Mound 72 burials: top, Beaded Burial complex; bottom, executed men on platform and women in pit (adapted from Fowler *et al.* 1999, courtesy Illinois State Museum)

4.12 Chipped-stone tips of one cache of bundled arrow offerings with Beaded Burial complex in Mound 72 (Cahokia Mounds Interpretive Center, used with permission of Melvin Fowler)

dualism (Fig. 4.12). In death, they were divided into two groups, the orientation of their bodies appearing to reference the Cahokia master plan and, later, the beaded burial (see Box 8).

Among other things, the burial program and mortuary history of Mound 72 may be argued to represent two related phenomena: (1) major life-cycle events such as the death of singularly important individuals, and (2) periodic commemorations possibly tied to a ritual calendar, evidenced by episodic sacrifices and by the inclusion of dead individuals brought to the site in various states of decay and disarticulation (see Goldstein 2000; Porubcan 2000). Some of the dead were important leaders or representatives from outside the Cahokian community carried to Mound 72 with great ceremony. Others were probably expendable individuals (mostly women) from outlier communities. In any case, some of the death rituals were probably public spectacles, if only owing to the numbers of people killed and the manner of some of the executions (Fig. 4.13). Thus, while we might call some of the Mound 72 mortuary events "commemorations," it also seems that Cahokians were materializing their power over groups of laborers if not over the very idea of labor in general.

The calendrical possibilities and possible theatrical aspect of the dark events of Mound 72 should remind us of the cyclical feasts and

Box 8. Mound 72 depositional history. At the beginning of the Lohmann phase, mortuary temples or "charnel houses" were built and huge marker posts were emplaced as part of the founding events associated with the new planned center of Cahokia. One charnel house and a post stood a few hundred meters south of the Grand Plaza (Fowler *et al.* 1999). Nearby were newly built wall trench houses and residential neighborhoods, all oriented – like this mortuary temple – a few degrees east of north. Just a few years later (based on the lack of rebuilding), this particular temple was abandoned and dismantled and the huge post nearby may have been pulled. A series of disarticulated skeletons, perhaps originally inside the building, were piled on the dismantled building floor. In addition, four recently dead people in two pairs were laid out over the dismantled charnel house. The body of one man, face down, was laid alongside that of a woman, face-up, both wearing shell-bead chokers. The bodies of two other men, face down, were nearby. One wore a shell-bead hairpiece.

At about the same time or shortly thereafter, two pits full of executed women, placed in two layers of nineteen and twenty-two individuals respectively, were buried a few meters away. The small, low platform mound was extended over them as well, with the mound edges and the women's bodies oriented a few degrees east of north. That orientation, aligned to the Cahokia master grid, was about to change following the most significant mortuary event in this sequence of events. Just 10 m to the southeast of the first burials, two adult men were buried together, their bodies laid one atop the other at about 20 degrees east of north. The first man's corpse – apparently laid face down – was covered with a falcon-shaped shell-bead cape 2 m long while the second was laid atop it and over the first man (Young and Fowler 2000:267). With them were interred two groups of twelve more individuals, mostly young adults, buried at a similar orientation. One of them wore a shell-bead choker. Included were the bones of someone long dead and the body of another who seems to have been "thrown down or not completely dead when positioned" (Rose 2000:64). These two were among four people interpreted as "retainers" by the excavators, while another group of seven laid nearby were lavished with the wealth of early Cahokia: a 7 liter pile of mica crystals (from the Appalachian Mountains), three bundled meter-long copper tubes (probable chunkey sticks), a dozen chunkey stones, strands of large mussel-shell beads, and two separate groups of about 800 arrows, each group bundled into quivers according to the type of chipped-stone and carved-antler projectile points made in a number of serrated and barbed varieties.

Another large pit was possibly dug at the same time into the northwestern platform directly over an earlier pit containing nineteen women. In it were placed two deposits of artifacts: one small pile of 451 chipped-stone arrowheads and another heap of artifacts that included traces of a few copper sheets or "tablets," a few dozen antler projectile points, and 36,000 whelk-columella beads strung together and studded with nine whelk-shell pendants and ten copper beads. Like most subsequent burial pits in this mound, this dedicatory pit was oriented at an angle paralleling the beaded burial. Indeed, a series of burials, including two more mass graves of women, were interred just meters northeast of the beaded burial and, like the orientation of the enlarged ridge-top mound itself, appear to reference the 20 degree beaded burial orientation. In fact, one of these pits was covered with a mound of earth in such a way as to mark unmistakably the location of the death pit below. The Cahokians appear to have sought to remember precisely where this pit's two layers of twenty-four women were. On the basis of the dedicatory pit and the various alignments with the beaded burial, we can be relatively certain that they did.

The continued execution of women may have been another kind of commemoration event. Shortly after the rituals above, another pit was filled with the bodies of fifty-three women, laid out in two rows and in two layers. Associated with this burial of the fifty-three women were four beheaded and behanded men laid on the low mound summit overlooking the women; all were buried by more mound fill that covered both the men and the women in the pit (Fowler *et al.* 1999). Among other later interments were two trenches filled with more bodies, this time including adult men and women and at least one child, their bodies wrapped and carefully laid into a trench on wooden-pole litters. In one of these trenches, beneath an upper layer of fourteen skeletons, were the bodies of thirty-nine more people, probably executed on the spot and "thrown into the pit with little regard to aesthetic appearance" (Rose 2000:70). Three people had been decapitated, one incompletely, and another with sufficient force to fracture and separate the mandible. Arrow points were found lodged in the rib cage of one person and stuck in the lumbar vertebra of another.

public-works projects in and around the Grand Plaza. Besides being public, highly religious, and inherently political affairs, the death rituals and celebratory feasts share an even more salient characteristic: the paramount importance of human labor and the ability to coordinate,

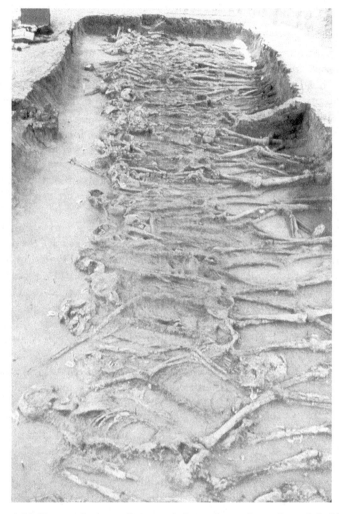

4.13 Executed men and women in lower layer of trench tomb in Mound 72 (Cahokia Mounds Interpretive Center, used with permission of Melvin Fowler)

control, and sacrifice it. One might even propose that labor *was* value and the human body the unit of value in early Cahokian society (Emerson and Pauketat 2002). If correct, then the mechanisms and media of the Cahokian economy are much more complicated than simple western economic notions of commodity, exchange value, and wealth allow.

Conclusion

There is little evidence that a gradually evolving chiefly economy led to the construction of Cahokia. Instead, Cahokia appears as a historical disjuncture in the Mississippi valley. Large-scale public works, inclusive feasts, theatrical deaths, and stratified and segmented social spaces and cultural practices were all parts of a construction process that generated the disjuncture (Pauketat 2002). From the available evidence, we may surmise that part of this process entailed the creation of a new "spatiality" – a whole new relational environment where people remade traditions. So, after AD 1050 private and public social life was being played out in new space and according to new constraints of locality (who and what was where) and orthagonality (houses sited and oriented to the central precinct).

The new place, Cahokia, superimposed and transcended the old pre-Mississippian village pattern. The historical effect may have been to "disembed" cultural practice and governance from a pre-Mississippian sense of space (Blanton *et al.* 1993; Kus 1983). Old houses, old ways of arranging courtyards, and old domestic practices were "co-opted" and altered – if not eliminated and replaced – in ways that changed the scale and character of the place and helped to create a new kind of social and political order (Pauketat 2000a, 2000b; Pauketat and Emerson 1999). In a sense, the result was the founding of a new political-administrative capital and a remarkably pervasive transformation of people, their cultural practices, and even the meanings of their bodies (Fig. 4.14). It involved all aspects of life, death, domesticity, religion, bodily movement, and sensuous experience. In other words, Cahokia's founding seems played out in multiple dimensions simultaneously – material, spatial, corporeal, and temporal.

The new capital seems to have been a hierarchically nested place of segregated and rigidly oriented houses or kin groups around circular buildings and small plazas. These were arrayed, in turn, around local pyramid-and-plaza complexes, and finally clustered around the Grand Plaza and

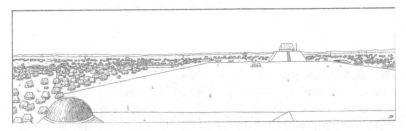

4.14 Artist's reconstruction of Cahokia, *c.* AD 1100 (rescaled from a Lloyd Townsend mural, drawing by Jack Scott)

Monks Mound. Perhaps such spatial nesting went hand in hand with the mode by which immigrants attached themselves to the new capital. Perhaps it also makes sense of the emergent sub-communities evidenced by neighborhood craft production.

In any event, that Cahokia was an integrated whole is indicated by the simultaneity and pervasive character of the locational, residential, architectural, and artifactual shifts, all kicked off by a series of monumental public-works projects. The leveling of the Grand Plaza alone must have entailed great central coordination. Likewise, a total shift to a new style of house, potentially one that could be rapidly constructed by a work crew, would have entailed new organization that must have transcended the labor-coordination capacities of earlier pre-Mississippian courtyard groups (Pauketat 1994). Understanding that organization, it turns out, requires us to look outside the capital city of Cahokia.

5   Greater Cahokia

If the Cahokia site is the evidentiary centerpiece of a Mississippian *historical disjuncture*, the greater Cahokian phenomenon is considerably more than just that centerpiece. True enough, the "urban renewal" projects of *c.* AD 1050 completely altered residential space, monumentality, and the sensuous experiences of the Cahokians who moved through the spaces and contemplated the monuments. However, the new reality of Cahokia was not restricted to the pyramids and plazas of the central political-administrative complex. Greater Cahokia subsumed the American Bottom, the lower portions of the Missouri and Illinois river floodplains, and the adjacent hilly uplands and feeder streams on both sides of the river (Pauketat 1998b).

It was a cultural region formed by a suite of objective and subjective changes to social life. These changes are immediately apparent by comparing the settlement patterns in the American Bottom and surrounding upland environs between AD 1000 and 1100 (Fig. 5.1).[13] At the edge of this radius is rock art that Patricia O'Brien (1994) has suggested corresponds to a political boundary. Likewise, at the southern end of the American Bottom there may be a ceramic style zone boundary at about this same distance from Cahokia (Milner 1993, 1998).

Prior to AD 1050, a two-tiered settlement hierarchy probably existed in certain localities at the heart of this region on the Mississippi floodplain. The villages of Cahokia and Pulcher would have been dominant settlements or local centers of minimally centralized political units. In other localities, pre-Mississippian settlements in either the floodplain or the adjacent uplands were unevenly distributed. Single-home "farmsteads" were few and far between in any locale while upland villages were clustered along the bluff edge of the American Bottom (e.g., Emerson and Jackson 1984; Milner 1984; Pauketat *et al.* 1998).

This pattern changes noticeably and in short order at AD 1050, when the Cahokia, East St. Louis, and St. Louis complex was the apex of a minimally three-tiered settlement hierarchy in the northern American Bottom. This central complex was surrounded by an array of lesser towns or outliers. These include several modest single-mound towns, the oddly elongate Lunsford-Pulcher site, the hilltop and multi-pyramid Emerald site, and the compact Mitchell site, with twelve pyramids and a plaza of at least 4 ha. The subsidiary status of several of the lesser towns remains uncertain since their occupational histories have yet to be outlined by archaeologists. However, salvage excavations at the Mitchell site led Porter (1974) to conclude that Cahokia-related people had founded a small town center there sometime in the eleventh century, expanding it considerably during the late twelfth century. More recent excavations at the Pfeffer, Emerald, Lohmann, and Horseshoe Lake sites indicate construction histories that all began around the middle of the eleventh century (Esarey and Pauketat 1992; Kruchten 2000; Pauketat *et al.* 1998).

At the same time, excavation and survey evidence indicates that people abandoned a whole series of pre-Mississippian villages or hamlets on the northern floodplain at about AD 1050. Doubtless, many moved to Cahokia or to one of the new secondary towns. However, some of the people who left their home villages probably moved to one of a series of *new floodplain farmsteads* and *upland villages* founded at this time. Archaeologists have excavated scores of such floodplain farmsteads and large portions of several upland villages, a sufficient sample comprised of hundreds of domestic buildings and thousands of midden-filled pits to understand the generalities of the occupation history of the rural landscape.

Given this database, Thomas Emerson (1997a, 1997b) has characterized the initiation of farmstead settlement as a "replacement" process, a resettlement of farmers that accompanied the Cahokia-centric restructuring of the regional landscape at AD 1050. The replacement process completely altered some localities. In one area, a Lohmann phase farmstead population of between forty and eighty persons/km^2 filled up an area where previously there had been few to no pre-Mississippian farmsteads (Milner 1986). Within that particular floodplain area, all of the farmers had been living at one large village, the Range site (Kelly 1990b; Kelly *et al.* 1987). In another locality around Horseshoe Lake adjacent to Cahokia, a series of multi-family pre-Mississippian villages or hamlets seem to have been abandoned and replaced by single-family Lohmann phase farmsteads, presumably each with one or two houses (Lopinot *et al.* 1998; Pauketat *et al.* 1998).

Given the evidence for Emerson's replacement hypothesis, it is intriguing that, between AD 1050 and 1200, floodplain farmers living at isolated home sites appear to have fed themselves off the wild and cultivated resources of the land. Even more intriguing and informative, then, is the evidence that these farmers were tethered in some way to one of the local

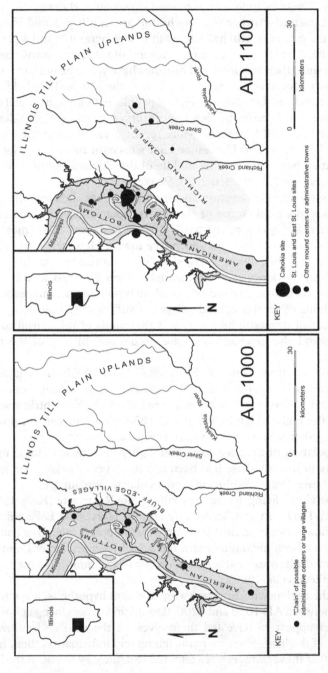

5.1 Major settlements in greater Cahokia's core at AD 1000 (left) and AD 1100 (right)

floodplain towns, if not Cahokia itself. The evidence for this again has been mustered by Thomas Emerson (1997a, 1997b) and consists of a series of "nodal farmsteads." Nodal farmsteads appear to have been home to important families who acted as religious, social, and economic "nodes" in the dispersed rural landscape. Such nodal farmsteads are denoted by special non-domestic architecture – large buildings or circular sweat lodges – and by greater amounts of precious materials – crystals, pigment stones, red cedar, and medicinal plants – found at Cahokia but rare at ordinary rural sites (see Emerson 1997a). Notably, this laterally complex or heterarchical array of farming settlements characterized *only* the Lohmann and Stirling phase in the floodplain. The non-domestic architecture and special artifacts at these farmsteads disappeared by the Moorehead phase along with the presumed breakdown of Cahokia's regional political economy.

The transformation of the rural countryside that accompanied the AD 1050 flashpoint is even more apparent in the upland perimeter surrounding the American Bottom to the east. Survey and extensive excavations now indicate a series of towns, villages, hamlets, and farmsteads along the Richland and Silver creeks where none had been previously (Alt 2001; Koldehoff 1989; Pauketat 2003b). Ballpark estimates of population density in one portion of this upland district range from ten to twenty-five persons/km^2. In this 300 km^2 locality – dubbed the "Richland complex" – there were at least eight contemporary villages and possibly several more, each with scores to hundreds of residents. There are scores more smaller Richland hamlets and uncounted farmsteads, all of which appear to have been founded at or shortly after AD 1050. Two of them have earthen pyramids and one is an oddly compact hilltop "outpost" of some sort, thought by Susan Alt (2003) to have administered the immediate surrounding farmers.

Although the Missouri and Mississippi floodplains dominate the central portion of the greater Cahokia region, there is much more upland area that could have been settled outside the Richland complex. In Illinois, there are a few thousand square kilometers of habitable uplands within a 50 km radius of Cahokia. This is nearly doubled with the addition of Missouri's uplands. Unfortunately, there is next to no systematic archaeological survey of this region – in part owing to the modern urban sprawl – despite the indications of other settlements comparable to the Richland villages. To the east is the Kaskaskia River drainage, a vast drainage basin with known Lohmann and Stirling phase settlements (e.g., Hargrave *et al.* 1983; Kuttruff 1972). To the west, in the floodplain and adjacent uplands of the lower Missouri River, there are more terminal Late Woodland, Lohmann, Stirling, and Moorehead phase sites

(Blake 1955; Harl 1991; Hunt 1974). To the southwest, along the rivers flowing out of the Ozarks, there are even more such sites. In 1939–40, Robert McCormack Adams (1949) investigated a two-mound center, the Long site, located along the Big River near the galena source. The Cahokia style pottery from this site dates to the late Stirling and Moorehead phases. Adams (1941, 1949) also excavated portions of villages at the Boyce and Herrell sites, finding semi-subterranean houses and early wall trench houses just like those in the Richland complex. James Collins and Dale Henning (1996) excavated similar houses and terminal Late Woodland and early Mississippian refuse from the Bonaker site.

Rural surplus production and storage

As particularly evident in the Richland complex, each outlying settlement has unique spatial, architectural, storage, or artifactual qualities and settlement histories. Alt (2001) concludes that this inter-settlement diversity indicates that Cahokia's hinterlands were characterized by a village-based cultural pluralism. That pluralism, in turn, seems related to the facts of mid-eleventh-century resettlement. There is even some pottery evidence of immigrants from southeastern Missouri or their descendants among the likely settlers of one of the larger villages, Halliday (Pauketat 2003b). Other settlers probably came from the nearby American Bottom or from more distant points in Illinois or Missouri, coalescing into a series of daughter communities that appear advantageously positioned with respect both to the rich prairie soils of this district and to major overland Indian trails. That positioning, especially given the AD 1050 date of the founding of these villages, indicates a potentially close association with the construction of Cahokia itself.

Artifactual, depositional, and architectural evidence suggests that this new rural landscape of diverse settlements and peoples was part and parcel of the creation of a centralized economy that further segmented the rural labor force based on age, gender, or cultural identity. It is noteworthy that Cahokian valuables or craft debris at the upland farming villages occur in the lowest densities of any place in the region (Fig. 5.2). For instance, the only marine-shell beads found among the more than 260 houses and associated domestic middens at fifteen excavated sites were the eight whelk-shell disk beads and seven *marginella* gastropod beads of a single broken necklace at the Halliday site (see Pauketat 2003b:table 1). Yet there are indications that textiles, marine-shell beads, and groundstone axe heads were produced at several of the upland sites by these upland farmers, possibly for extra-local (i.e., Cahokian) consumption. Alt (1999) argues for the intensive production of yarn, rope,

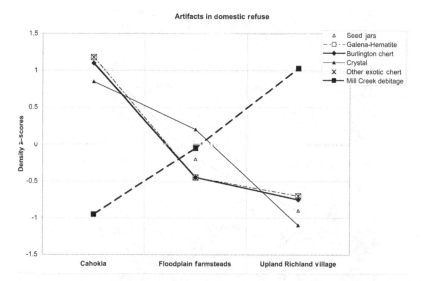

5.2 Density z-scores of select artifacts in the greater Cahokia region (adapted from data in Pauketat 1998b)

and cloth by upland farmers based on the high densities of spindle whorls, large and small, some with multiple holes (Fig. 5.3). These are known from many upland sites but are found at some upland sites in concentrations matched only by the densities at Cahokia's residential Tract 15A (Alt 1999). Likewise, finds of microdrills and microblade cores at the upland sites are restricted in the fifteen site sample to single-house concentrations at three village sites and one farmstead. Finally, the debris from axe-head making is known from only four houses at or adjacent to one upland village in the fifteen site sample. Of these, each house produced fewer than twenty percussion flakes of igneous rock imported from the St. François Mountain district of the Missouri Ozarks.

This modest rural craft production pattern parallels that known from floodplain farmsteads and indicates a localization or temporalization of labor that many would gloss as "part-time specialization" (Pauketat 1997b; cf. Muller 1997). It also complements the more intensive concentrations of microliths and axe-head-making debris from portions of Cahokia. At the Kunnemann Tract, for instance, there are significantly higher densities of microlithic remains and, unlike rural sites, evidence of the manufacture of a variety of columnar beads, non-shell beads, and mollusk-shell pendants (Holley 1995; Pauketat 1993b; Yerkes 1983, 1991). Likewise, there are concentrations of axe-head-making debitage and broken

5.3 Upland Mississippian spindle whorls (top) and Mill Creek chert hoe blades (bottom) from the Halliday site, St. Clair County, Illinois

preforms around Cahokia, sometimes found unfinished in cache pits, the largest of which was from Cahokia's Kunnemann Tract and included 100 or more oversized and unfinished axe heads (Pauketat 1997b).

Like the axe heads, chipped Mill Creek chert hoe blades were occasionally cached at both rural and central sites. A cache of some fifty tool blades was found with unfinished axe heads at the East St. Louis site, while rural caches tend to involve one to several blades (Fig. 5.3). In the latter case, cached hoe blades may simply constitute reserves kept on hand to replace worn-out tools. Hoe blades were common at the upland farming villages (see Box 9). In fact, upland Richland complex village sites produce the highest densities of hoe blade resharpening and recycling debitage known from the region (Fig. 5.2).

Since the remains of Cahokian craft production decrease with distance from Cahokia while the bits of worn Mill Creek hoe blades increase with distance, the greater Cahokia region easily fits Renfrew's (1975) "central-place redistributive" pattern. The logical conclusion to draw is that low-status farmers using hoe blades were producing a surplus of crops ultimately to provision Cahokians. Definitive plant-food evidence of tribute does not exist, however, even if suggestive, anecdotal, and ultimately equivocal maize data could be used to argue for it (compare Johannessen 1984, 1993; Lopinot 1994; Pauketat 1994:61, 2004). However, there is a wealth of faunal evidence that supports the proposition that meat was brought into Cahokia on a regular basis (Kelly 1979, 1997, 2000; Pauketat et al. 2002).[14]

There were also changes in storage technology that suggest appropriation of domestic produce, or attempts by some producers to avoid such appropriation. There are two known types of storage facilities: subterranean pits and above-ground storage buildings or warehouses (Fig. 5.4). Grains and other plant foods were especially suited for seasonal storage in cylindrical or bell-shaped pits that usually ranged in depth below the surface from about an arm's length to a person's height (see Wilson 1917 for an ethnographic example). Interestingly, the numbers of such pits increased over the terminal Late Woodland to Mississippian continuum. By the Lohmann phase, Cahokians possessed considerable pit storage potential. In addition, the location of some storage pits changed during the late eleventh to twelfth centuries. Initially outdoor facilities, pits were moved indoors by families perhaps concerned that they control their own stores (see DeBoer 1988; Holley et al. 1989; Mehrer and Collins 1995; Pauketat 1998a).

Importantly, pits may not best indicate the full potential or centrality of the bulk of communal stores. Putative communal stores supervised by central administrators were more likely kept in granaries or warehouses,

Box 9. Mill Creek hoe blade production. Mill Creek hoe blades were not the "prestige good" equivalents of shell-bead necklaces or cloth, but may have been procured by farmers via lateral exchanges with kin or via the centralized redistributions from communal storehouses. Charles Cobb (2000) and Brad Koldehoff (1987, 1990a, 1990b, 1995) have analyzed the technological and social aspects of the production of large Mill Creek chert bifaces, which include elongate ("Ramey") knives, adze blades, and hoe blades. Koldehoff (1990a:70) states that "Mississippian large bifaces were manufactured by direct percussion with hard (stone) and soft (antler or wood) hammers . . . [L]arge-biface production can entail little more than detaching a series of large flakes from both faces. Yet, a great deal of expertise is needed to detach these large flakes successfully, without snapping the biface in the process . . . The use polish that developed on digging and woodworking tools allows hoe and adze maintenance and recycling to be traced. Hoes and adzes were recycled into an array of other tools: cores, flake tools, hammers, arrow points, microliths, and possible smaller bifaces . . . The centralized production and the regional consumption of large bifaces appear to indicate some level of specialized production."

From a Mill Creek valley perspective, Cobb (2000:191) concludes that "the available evidence from the Mill Creek locale suggests the presence of part-time specialists working within a production system that was dispersed yet encompassed a few mound sites. The wide spatial distribution of communities, workshops, and source areas . . . [indicates that] this region does not appear to have undergone the sort of transformation that some have argued for Mississippian regions elsewhere . . . Yet labor relations in the Mill Creek locale were not necessarily like those in other small-scale Mississippian polities, either."

Although these researchers have opinions as to the organization of labor and the relations between Mill Creek knappers, Cahokians, and other peoples, the reality is that the local political-administrative centers of the Mill Creek valley – namely the Hale, Linn-Helig, and Ware sites – have yet to be properly investigated, even though first mapped by Cyrus Thomas during his BAE survey (see Milner 1998). Likewise, another large-biface production center in the Crescent Hills Burlington chert quarries of the northeastern Ozarks has received scant archaeological attention (Ives 1975, 1984; Koldehoff 1990a).

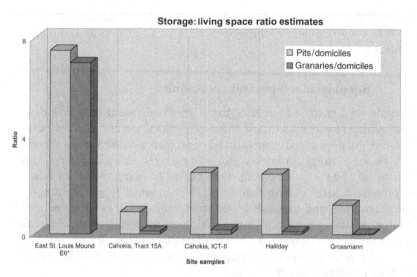

5.4 Graph showing estimated storage pit and granary potential

for which we have mostly anecdotal evidence owing to the difficulty in identifying these facilities. For instance, one out of every 7.5 buildings or attached rooms at the extensively excavated upland Halliday and Knoebel sites was a small square hut or attached room probably used for storage (see Alt 2002). These huts are comparable in size and shape to an isolated, small square hut or "granary" in the middle of a Lohmann phase plaza, adjacent to the plaza's post, on the Interpretive Center Tract II (Collins 1990). Likewise, a modest wall trench house (H91) in the interior of a small plaza on Tract 15A may also have been used for storage, like other buildings of its size (Pauketat 1998a). Both houses in both plazas would have been visible to the entire neighborhood and presumably were filled with communal stores.

By comparison, a partially excavated elite residential compound at the East St. Louis site consisted of a sequence of houses or temples atop a small pyramid, Mound E6. Also found on the summit and off to one side of Mound E6 were at least fourteen contemporary storage huts, most virtually identical to the ICT-II plaza granary. However, a modest compound or palisade wall surrounded the East St. Louis buildings and the rest of the Mound E6 complex, meaning that the contents of the huts were not necessarily communal. In this particular case, the storage buildings were all incinerated during a conflagration of some larger portion of this site at or after about AD 1160 (based on the recovered late Stirling phase pottery, mound stratigraphy, and a suite of radiocarbon dates). Inside the buildings were smashed pots, some full of shelled maize, and a variety of intact groundstone, chipped-stone, and wooden tools and utensils (Pauketat 2004).

Surplus, ideology, and community

It would be a mistake to assume that Cahokians would only seek to extract sufficient surplus to meet their own caloric needs. This is because Cahokia's various social events and labor projects would have been funded by Cahokians using communal stores in turn requiring surplus production to fill. That is, Cahokians were probably doing much more with surplus food than feeding themselves. Presumably, they hosted elaborate ceremonies and they subsidized work projects, all of which required feeding visitors or workers. Thus, multiplying the total population by the amount of farmland needed to feed a farm family would underestimate the food resources needed to support Cahokia. So, how much food was necessary to feed *and fund* Cahokia?

Merely asking the question is an important step, made even more important by recent suggestions that Cahokians may not even have been able to feed themselves (see Pauketat 2003b). By contrasting Cahokia's estimated Lohmann phase population of 10,200–15,300 people (not counting those thousands more who lived at East St. Louis and St. Louis) with Milner's (1998:74) estimated carrying capacity of 8000 people for the Cahokia environs, we may understand that farmers necessarily provisioned the central political-administrative complex (see Pauketat 2003b). Population estimates of Cahokia and two rural districts also provide some sense of the potential magnitude of food production and consumption in the region (Fig. 5.5). Thus, the Cahokian motivation for upland resettlement or the replacement of floodplain villages with farmsteads is relatively transparent.

However, farmers' reasons for abandoning pre-Mississippian settlements and either moving into the interior uplands or moving to isolated farmsteads are not as easily discerned, but were probably weighed against the perceived drudgery of surplus production. Perhaps there was minimal drudgery involved, with sufficient surplus easily accumulated as part of the large-scale Cahokian feasts so well represented in the sub-Mound 51 feasting pit. Or perhaps the "rewards" given to farmers who collaborated with Cahokians may have transcended any negative associations that they might have perceived to accompany the new Cahokian order.

Certainly there may have been a movement among farmers to join with Cahokians in the strange new endeavors of AD 1050. Why? Consider Mary Lucas Powell's (1992) studies of Mississippian health in the

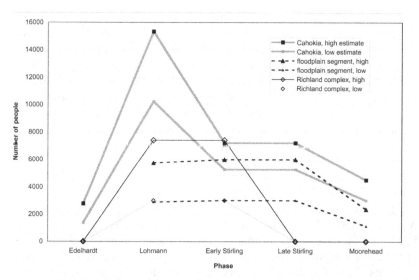

5.5 Population estimates for three localities within greater Cahokia through time: Cahokia proper (1.8 km²), southern floodplain farmsteads (48 km²), and the upland Richland complex (300 km²) (compiled from Milner 1986; Pauketat 2003; Pauketat and Lopinot 1997)

Midsouth. She found that a better diet and improved health may have been a perceptible outcome of the formation of regional-scale polities. As compared to smaller-scale regimes, the large organizations presumably better managed the uncertainties of food production, not an unattractive prospect to farmers concerned with the occasional lean year. Certainly, there were no noticeable adverse effects to the health of Cahokians as a result of political consolidation (Milner 1992). Hence, pre-Mississippian farmers may have readily joined in support of political consolidation, perhaps owing to the recognizable benefits! In any case, the social histories of farmer–Cahokian "negotiations" were probably critical in shaping political history (Pauketat 2000b, 2003b).

Of course, Cahokia would have mainly benefited Cahokians. This is evident even within the greater Cahokia region by the lack of Cahokian finery in the hands of upland farmers, the better diet of Cahokians relative to those farmers, and the obvious executions of non-Cahokian women in Mound 72. This observation, that there were Cahokians and there were others, permits us to consider two components to the process of how Cahokia developed. First, Cahokia must necessarily have been constructed as a community identity or ideology. Through such a means, Cahokia may have brought more and more people into the fold even as it essentially "co-opted" the traditional associations of community (Emerson and Pauketat 2002; Pauketat 2000a, 2000b; Pauketat and Emerson 1999). Second, this kind of "community ideology" would have undergirded social stratification at a regional scale. Presumably, members of the Cahokian community actually built Cahokia, moved to Cahokia, or collaborated with Cahokians, while communities of "others" in the region, or outsiders beyond, may have tolerated, emulated, or even resisted Cahokia. In other words, the net effect of greater and greater community or corporate cohesiveness at one scale was probably greater and greater distancing and disenfranchisement at another.

With the disparities in life and death evident across greater Cahokia, it seems unlikely that all farmers may have been similarly motivated to support the objective challenges to peoples' varied understandings of pre-Mississippian traditions. Perhaps the public executions of people buried in Mound 72 were sufficient to suppress resistance to the Cahokian economy before it could coalesce into a political force (Pauketat 1997a). But few data are definitive with respect to resistance. (What would constitute such data?) Some farmers may have happily contributed to the construction of Cahokia, envied Cahokia, or believed fervently in Cahokia. Ideology should not be underestimated.

Others may have accommodated it in the hopes of maintaining their own traditional sense of social life and cosmological balance. Still other farmers may have intentionally defied certain aspects of Cahokian labor and surplus demands (e.g., Sahlins 1972). In fact, all of the above could have coexisted at certain times and places in eleventh- and twelfth-century greater Cahokia. The accommodative, collaborative, or defiant dispositions of farmers would have been inculcated during their living in certain landscapes under certain conditions. Their sense of social identity would have been instilled during the social gatherings in villages, in plazas, or during other encounters. Their kinship, village, or larger community (or ethnic) identities would also have been lived on a daily basis both in and out of their houses via the most quotidian and routine of practices.

Culinary practices embody the essence of the fluidity of identity formation and its susceptibility to politicization in the sense advocated here. People who eat together not only stay together, they negotiate their familial, age-related, and gendered relationships *vis-à-vis* larger social contexts, political realities, cosmological principles, and religious beliefs. Other private or domestic-level practices, ranging from tool making to farming to sexual intercourse, reference these same extra-local cultural, political, and religious meanings and are thus situated within the lived experiences of individuals. Thus, the extent to which such practices and contexts are inextricably wedded to a political order is the extent to which a "cultural hegemony" is lived and, thus, constitutive of political history (e.g., Kus 1983; Kus and Raharigaona 2001; Pauketat 1994, 2000a).

The consensus, accommodation, collaboration, or defiance resident in cultural practices shapes the contours of public-works projects, collective rituals, and political centralization. Given this, it is equally crucial to recognize that any major population center cannot emerge without marginalizing somebody, without engendering some kind of subjective or objective opposition, and without accommodating the interests and dispositions of the masses of participants. Any cultural hegemony, by definition, is shot through with negotiation, syncretism, and compromise (e.g., Pauketat 1994). Hegemony may be centered in the village or the political capital, and the marginalized may be inside or outside the community, but both necessarily exist.

In the case of Cahokia's upland villages, we may gauge that process by observing that each settlement was different in some respects from the others and, collectively, from Cahokia proper (Alt 2001). For instance, pre-Mississippian style courtyards with their central posts seem to have organized the space of at least one upland village, while they were missing or de-emphasized at others. At some places there were also pre-Mississippian style single-set-post buildings and oddly composite or "faux wall trench" houses built after AD 1050 (Alt 2001, 2002). Some potters mixed old-fashioned traits with new. Community cemeteries and community smoking pipes were kept in the village, and the chunkey game was still played at the village level at a time when it was absent from the farmsteads of floodplain farmers.

When compared with the material evidence of orthodoxy at Lohmann phase Cahokia, these lines of evidence indicate cultural diversity, persistence, hybridity, and creolization. What does this mean? If one ignores other regional-contextual data, one could interpret diversity and persistence to indicate political autonomy for the upland villages. However, both theory and empirical evidence – the central-place redistributive pattern and the facts of resettlement noted earlier – do not support such an argument. The rural villages in question were all within 10–30 km of Cahokia and the rapid rate and large scale of resettlement did not allow sufficient time for cultural homogeneity to have been created (Pauketat 2003b). Furthermore, Alt (2001) has argued that there is little reason to assume that outlying farmers would automatically adopt Cahokian practices regardless of the degree to which they had bought into a Cahokian ideology. Instead, there are any number of historical cases where administrators tolerated if not encouraged cultural diversity and producer autonomy or self-governance in order to reduce the costs of administration (see Wright 1984). Indeed, village-level cultural diversity through resettlement could have been a political tactic intended to foster reliance on Cahokia – what Marshall Sahlins (1985) has called "hierarchical solidarity" (as opposed to the organic kind) – and inhibit the political resistance that might result from cooperating farming villages (Pauketat 2003b).

Engendering a Cahokian ideology

Among the pervasive social changes attendant to resettlement and the rise of Cahokia may have been the polarization and politicization of gender. That which constituted femininity and masculinity at early Cahokia was probably different from that which characterized the preceding Woodland period. The evidence for this is circumstantial, but logically follows the direct evidence for a greater Cahokian division of labor by kin group, subcommunity, or settlement after AD 1050. For instance, in the Richland district, the concentrated spinning of fibers, the intensification of hoe agriculture, and the persistence (if not amplification) of pre-Mississippian domestic and culinary practices may have engendered village life in ways previously unknown.

So too may the manufacturing and use of cooking and storage pots have engendered village life in unanticipated ways. Consider again the Ramey Incised jar. Beginning at about AD 1100, the motifs of sky deities and fertility – especially falconoid or thunderbird eyes, wings, and tails – were placed on the rims of these probably centrally made pots, many subsequently dispersed out from centers to farmers (Pauketat and Emerson 1991). The iconography has been interpreted as just one component of the meaning of the pots, decorating a design field that acted to delineate the symbolic accessing of pots' contents (Pauketat and Emerson 1991). The contents, especially agricultural grains and foodstuffs, were probably associated with feminine life forces (see below). Thus, whether they were made by women or not, the use of the Ramey Incised pots may have held divergent implications for men and women, the very act of using the pot affirming the order of the cosmos: the relationship of earth to sky, nature to culture, and women to men (Fig. 5.6). Perhaps the somewhat discrete symbol sets associated with other kinds of material culture did the same.[15]

It is potentially significant, in fact, that hoe agriculture (and perhaps spinning) is depicted with feminine characters on a suite of carved flintclay figurines made early in the twelfth century (Emerson 1982, 1997c). Some carvings regularly show feminine body forms associated with agricultural tools, crops, earth-monster serpents, or baskets thought to represent containers for the bones of ancestors. Other characters are

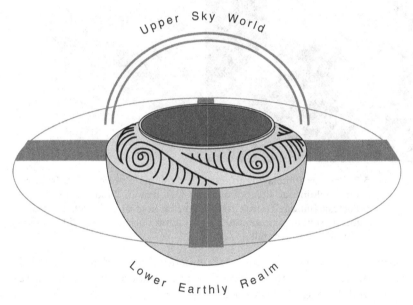

5.6 Lohmann phase imagery excised on potsherds (top) and Stirling phase Ramey Incised "Pot-as-Cosmos" (bottom; adapted from Pauketat and Emerson 1991)

masculine, represented by phalluses, and routinely depicted as warriors, chunkey players, or priests (Fig. 5.7). One male character on a Cahokian flintclay pipe from Spiro, Oklahoma, wears an apparent feathered cape and human-head ear ornaments evocative of the falcon symbolism of the central beaded burial of men in Mound 72. It is also significant with respect to the engendering of Mississippianism in general that, although originating at or near Cahokia, many – notably almost exclusively

5.7 Cahokia flintclay figurines: left, feminine representation from red cedar building at the Sponemann site near Cahokia, >15 cm tall (courtesy Illinois Transportation Archaeological Research Program); right, masculine representation from tomb burial in Mound C, Shiloh, Tennessee, 24.5 cm tall

masculine representations – were subsequently dispersed across the Midsouth (Emerson *et al.* 2003). Female representations, by and large, remained in the greater Cahokia region.

A Cahokian cult?

Doubtless, Cahokian symbolism memorialized "traditional" pre-Mississippian notions of the cosmos as partitioned into horizontal and vertical fields inhabited by supernatural beings and people. However, traditions are also the media of social life and social change, and the contexts of memorialization – who did what, where, and how – create new memories and associations even as they seem to commemorate the past. Ramey Incised pots are ideal examples: as centrally made products of Cahokia, they embodied someone's sense of cosmological order that – to the extent Cahokia and Cahokians occupied the cosmological center – served political ends most assuredly *not* known in Woodland times.

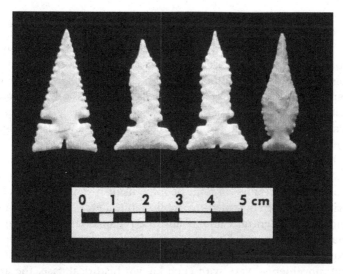

5.8 Hybrid projectile points from Mound 72 cache (center) compared to individual Cahokia and Bayogoula points from Mound 72 (left) and the Grossmann site (right)

The invention of tradition at Cahokia is no more evident than in the unprecedented construction of the pyramids and Grand Plaza of the central precinct, perhaps an import from Toltec or other Coles Creek places to the south. Certainly other forms and meanings were co-opted from distant sources and hybridized with local ones, nicely embodied in an array of projectile points from Mound 72 made by someone who mixed Cahokia style attributes with those of Bayogoula and Hayes styles from the Coles Creek-Plaquemine region of Louisiana and southern Arkansas (Fig. 5.8; see Bell 1958; Justice 1987; Perino 1968).

Yet co-optation, hybridization, and the invention of tradition do not simply happen without people *doing* the co-opting, hybridizing, and invention. The question remains, whose political ends were being served? Why thunderbirds or falcon-warriors? Why earth-monsters and fertility symbolism? Why the particular mode of mound-building or the character of sub-Mound 51 feasts? The answers of course may be as varied as the people etching motifs, adding earth to pyramids, or feasting in the plaza. How was the idea of Cahokia reconciled by thousands of ordinary farmers? Thus, the question really is: *How* were political ends being served? Or, how were Cahokian ideas if not a Cahokian identity created?

The answers to these questions may seem contingent on recovering the actual central figure, the great charismatic leader, or the group of movers and shakers who were the organizing forces behind a rapid expansion of ideas (Pauketat 1994). Can archaeologists actually recover this degree of archaeological detail? Given the controlled regional-scale archaeology of greater Cahokia, I think that the answer may be "yes" but is, nonetheless, beside the point. Do archaeologists need to recover the actual individuals behind the development of Cahokia? Not really, since the Mississippianization process we seek to explain was necessarily a region-wide *collective* negotiation of social interests, beliefs, practices, and memories. Such a regional-scale negotiation is precisely what Cahokia archaeologists have recovered.

In the greater Cahokia region, the apparent co-optation of traditional practices – the new or revalued practices of building temples and mounds, venerating the ancestors (of some people), using meaning-laden color and material symbolism in scaled-up public venues, etc. – and even the rapid restructuring of central Cahokia and the regional landscape may all be the material and spatial dimensions of a dramatic, participatory political-religious movement. Indeed, while the shapes and scales of "cults" and "social movements" vary with each known historical case, the array of material symbols and the abrupt region-wide transformation of the pre-Mississippian American Bottom into the integrated greater Cahokia region around AD 1050 suggests central figures with followers who collaborated to create an entirely new society (Pauketat 1994). This society was, to all intents and purposes, first inscribed into the landscape as a founding city to which local farmers and distant outsiders might travel in homage to certain new ideas, a group of persons, or even an entire community of people. Presumably, foreign visitors to Cahokia went home and, to the degree that they aspired to replicate what they had seen, overlaid to varying degrees the new Cahokian principles and cultural practices on to their local "traditional" ones. They would have become, hence, the proselytizers for or missionaries of some new anomalous Cahokianism visibly emanating from the American Bottom.

The possibility of such an unusual sociological phenomenon a thousand years ago in the Mississippi valley may seem more or less compelling to the reader, and is certainly not commonly accepted by your average midwestern or southeastern archaeologist. So, is there a smoking gun that might prove the veracity of such an archaeological story? Perhaps, but to find it we must leave archaeology and delve into the oral histories and legends of contemporary Indian peoples.

In 1956, Stephen Williams and John Goggin proposed the existence of a Long-Nosed God Horizon for the early phases of middle-river Mississippian culture history. They based this suggestion on the distribution of a series of mollusk-shell and copper earrings shaped like human heads with exceptionally long noses (Fig. 5.9; see Hall 1997 for a chronological

5.9 Long-Nosed God ear ornaments: left, two marine-shell ornaments (adapted from Hall 1991, originals about 7 cm tall); right, depicted as worn on Cahokia style flintclay pipe, Spiro, Oklahoma, 26 cm tall (courtesy The University Museum, University of Arkansas)

summary). Robert Hall (1991) first linked these earrings to the story of Red Horn, a legendary culture hero whose story was relayed in the oral histories of the First Nations (see also Duncan and Diaz-Grandos 2000; Salzer and Rajnovich 2000).

In versions of the story, Red Horn – a legendary man with a long braid painted red and wearing "human heads as earrings" – plays a ball game with bears or giants of the underworld, and is killed along with his friends: Turtle and Thunderbird. Later, Red Horn and friends are resurrected by two sons – the "children of the sun" or the thunderers (and one of whom was a "bead spitter") – to conquer the giants (see Box 10). It is not a stretch to substitute chunkey for the kind of stick ball game (lacrosse) played during their historic period, and to imagine the beaded burial in Mound 72 as a Red Horn impersonator or one of the thunderer sons, perhaps buried with his legendary brother, beads, and a thunderer cape. A similar argument has recently been made that men buried in Mound C at Etowah, Georgia, had co-opted in the thirteenth century the imagery of Red Horn for political effect (King 2002).

Box 10. The legend of Red Horn. Drawing on the oral history of the Ho-Chunk (Winnebago) people of Wisconsin (especially Radin 1990), Robert Hall (1997:149) explains that the character Red Horn (also known as "He-who-wears-human-heads-as-earrings") is one of a pair of brothers who defeats giants in a ballgame, places them "in four circles, each of which is destroyed in their turn by lightning bolts from the war club of Red Horn's companion Storms-as-he-walks, a thunderbird." One giantess survives to become the second wife of Red Horn. Both wives give birth to "boys, half-brothers," but only after the men were killed during yet another encounter with giants in some underworld context. One of the sons had "long red hair but with human heads attached to his nipples rather than to his ears." The sons "seek out the giants, kill them, and return with the heads" of Red Horn, Storms-as-he-walks, and the turtle, "and magically return them to life." The son or sons, in fact, seem(s) represented in rock art at Gottschall and Picture Cave, and seem(s) signified in the enlarged breasts of certain falcon–human images of the Southeastern Ceremonial Complex and in the pairs of Long-Nosed God ear ornaments (Duncan and Diaz-Granados 2000). According to Hall (1997:151), "the Long-Nosed God maskettes may have functioned in the Early Mississippi Period of the eastern United States within an adoption ritual much like that of the Calumet ceremony of the Historic period. The difference I see is that the Calumet ceremony served to create bonds of kinship between persons of roughly equal social status, while the maskettes could have functioned within a ritual to create fictions of kinship between the powerful leader of a large polity and his political clients in outlying areas."

Carrying the historical logic further, Robert Salzer and Grace Rajnovich (2000:65–6) suggest "that there may be some historical fact imbedded in the Red Horn legend," especially important given "increasingly convincing evidence that people from Cahokia... actually moved into southern Wisconsin (Green 1997) . . . [T]hese intruders set up towns in territory formerly occupied by Effigy Mound peoples . . . *The timing of the painting of the Red Horn Composition and these historical and cultural events is simply too close to allow us to dismiss the possibility that the aggression described in the Red Horn legend may, in reality, be a commentary on actual historical events*" (emphasis original).

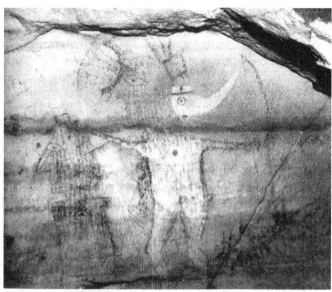

5.10 Red Horn pictographs: top, Picture Cave, Missouri (used with permission, from Diaz-Granados and Duncan 2001); bottom, Gottschall Rockshelter, Wisconsin (used with permission, from Salzer and Rajnovich 2000)

In fact, the rock art in two caves in the Midwestern United States seems to link this tale of a legendary man, his brother, a race of giants, and an encounter with death and the underworld to the tenth or eleventh century through radiocarbon dating of organic paints and residual floor debris. In Picture Cave, about 100 km east of Cahokia, red, white, and black paintings show an image interpreted to be the son of Red Horn, wearing Long-Nosed God maskettes, with an arrow headdress and a bow (Fig. 5.10; Diaz-Granados and Duncan 2000). Depictions of Red Horn and his supernatural friends also appear in the Gottschall Rock Shelter in southeastern Wisconsin (Salzer and Rajnovich 2000).

According to Robert Hall (1989, 1991, 1997) and Duncan and Diaz-Granados (2000), the Red Horn and sons story was the metaphor for a widespread ritual adoption ceremony, where one group accepted others into their fold. This was not unlike the historically known calumet ceremony (smoking the peace pipe), and has overlapping imagery and thematic qualities. In any case, the net effect seems to have been a mechanism for the transference of ideas if not also the construction of fictive kin ties and alliances between distant peoples (Hall 1991:33, citing Gibbon 1974). The archaeological evidence for such a unique pan-regional sociological phenomenon bears further consideration.

6   Mississippianization

For reasons of Cahokia's large size and precocious emergence, various archaeologists have concluded that Cahokia's historical impact on the Indian peoples of the mid-continent may have far exceeded that of smaller Mississippian polities or tribes. After all, there was nothing else that could rival Cahokia's size and internal complexity in the eleventh century (see Emerson 2002). The nearest potential rivals were either very small or were hundreds of kilometers away. Places such as Kincaid and Obion in southern Illinois and western Tennessee may have coalesced at or shortly after AD 1050, but those pyramid-and-plaza sites were distant runners-up to the behemoth in the American Bottom, as were an array of lesser sites in western Kentucky, southeast Missouri, and southern Illinois about which not much is known. Not until AD 1200 did the large regional centers of Moundville, Winterville, and Lake George emerge far to the south in Alabama and Mississippi. In fact, many small-scale political centers in the central Mississippi valley did not rise to prominence until the beginning of the thirteenth century, leaving some to wonder if Lohmann and Stirling phase Cahokians suppressed their competitors until the Moorehead phase (Anderson 1997).

However, if Cahokia suppressed significant competition, it may also have been the cause of competition. Bearing in mind the possibility of a Cahokian cult, we might envision Cahokia as the founding archetype that would-be Mississippians in the middle valley could emulate. There are widespread indications that non-Cahokian peoples were to variable extent connected to, aware of, or directly affected by Cahokia. The evidence of emulation of Cahokia by foreigners, if not the existence of a Cahokian diaspora in lands as distant as Wisconsin or Louisiana, is at once provocative and equivocal. For this reason, archaeologists have produced a number of conflicting accounts of this unique pan-regional phenomenon that range from trading colonies to dissident emigrants. Depending on the place and time, there may have been one or more direct and indirect "contact" experiences or mechanisms by which Cahokian or middle Mississippian ideas were transmitted (Emerson 1991; Stoltman 1991, 2000).

Cahokia's calling cards

We may understand Cahokian contacts and the historical development of Mississippian peoples by examining, first, the distribution of specific objects or raw materials with restricted origins and, second, the specific site histories up and down the Mississippi valley. Northern Mississippian places include a series of "intrusions" and developmental discontinuities that stand out against the local terminal Late Woodland landscapes, while southern places founded in vastly different contexts are less obviously intrusive and discontinuous. We are only at the threshold of understanding the intricate historical relationships between peoples, things, and places, but we know enough to assert that Mississippianization was not a simple phenomenon that can be attributed solely to trade, migration, or technological change, although all of these things are implicated in part.

Trade is the most usual of suspects identified in attempted explanations of Mississippianization. Certainly, finished objects and raw materials were imported to Cahokia from far away (Kelly 1991a, 1991b). Among the most common of these are arrowheads and the occasional decorated pot from south of the Ohio–Mississippi river confluence (e.g., Koldehoff 1982; Pauketat 1984; Pauketat and Koldehoff 2002). There are also several elongate and highly stylized axe heads ("spuds") that seem to originate in Tennessee (Pauketat 1983). Other *finished* foreign valuables, however, are quite rare – too rare to conclude that trade or "prestige goods exchange" was the driving force of Cahokia's rise and fall (Muller 1995, 1997).

For instance, large bifacial hoe blades, knives, and woodworking adze blades *were* imported in large numbers from the Mill Creek valley villages or Burlington quarries. It is likely that there were at least as many hoe blades as there were adults in greater Cahokia. While some hoe blades were doubtless imported via the lateral ties of the many farming families of upland villages and bottomland farmsteads, the numbers of them at Cahokia and the restricted production centers in southern Illinois or the northern Ozarks argue for some kind of centralized redistributive mechanism (see Brown *et al.* 1990).[16] Yet, few consider these tool blades themselves as wealth items or "prestige goods" comparable to beads, crystals, or arrows. Instead their importation may suggest the great value of the labor associated with the farming of land or the shaping of wood embodied by these objects.

Like hoe and adze blades, there is an obvious use value to utilitarian groundstone axe heads. Like hoe blades, these tools are occasionally cached in groups of up to 100 objects at special sites like Cahokia, Lohmann, and Grossmann. And like the chipped-stone bifaces, many axe heads, we now realize, were made from blocks of St. François Mountain rock (i.e., diabase). This rock it seems was paddled 100 km up the Mississippi River for final production, much (but not all) of which probably occurred at and around Cahokia (Pauketat and Alt 2004). Then, the finished axe heads were distributed locally, some perhaps being traded long distances, even ending up as far away as the middle Missouri River (see Tiffany 1991a, 1991b, below). Some degree of centralized control over production and distribution seems likely. An inalienable pedigree probably traveled with the objects.

Debris from the manufacture of other objects made using a variety of exotic raw materials is commonly found in Cahokia's domestic refuse, especially during the Lohmann phase. However, like southern Illinois cherts and St. François Mountain rock, the sources for most of this fall within 150 km of Cahokia (Emerson and Hughes 2000; Pauketat 1998b; Pauketat and Emerson 1997). There are exceptions. Marine shell, mica, quartz crystal, Hixton sandstone, and copper were procured from the Gulf of Mexico, the Appalachian Mountains, the Ouachitas, western Wisconsin and Lake Superior, respectively. For these materials, intermediaries or down-the-line trading partners may have facilitated the transport or exchange. Then again, Cahokia has produced far more marine shell per cubic meter of excavated earth than any site between it and the Gulf (Morse and Morse 2000:352, citing Parmalee 1958). The same goes for the chippable Hixton sandstone from western Wisconsin. Thus, Cahokians themselves may have traversed great distances in canoes or along trails to obtain the raw materials they sought, which was not without historical precedent (see chapter 2). Such travel, of course, probably would have necessitated a trade language, such as Plains sign language, to traverse safely the varied ethnoscape.

If Cahokians did travel to the sources, or if they established long-term trading partnerships and maybe even extractive outposts, would they have left calling cards? Possible Cahokia-made Ramey Incised pots, Long-Nosed God earpieces, and flintclay figurines are found over much of the Mississippi valley (Fig. 6.1). There are also possibly Cahokia made axe heads, arrowheads, microliths, mollusk-shell beads, and Cahokia style chunkey stones from Mississippi to western Iowa. The chunkey stones are made from colorful quartzites and sandstones and have been found at places such as Aztalan, Kincaid, Shiloh, Lake George, and Obion (Fig. 6.2; see Barrett 1933; Cole et al. 1951; Garland 1992; Tiffany

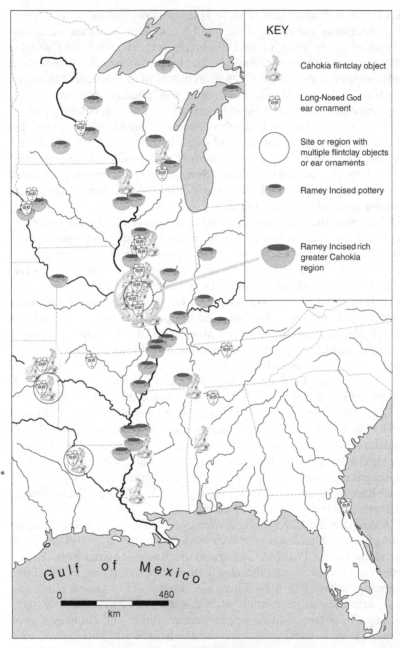

KEY

Cahokia flintclay object

Long-Nosed God
ear ornament

Site or region with
multiple flintclay objects
or ear ornaments

Ramey Incised pottery

Ramey Incised rich
greater Cahokia
region

Gulf   of   Mexico

0   480
km

6.1 The distribution of Ramey Incised pots, Long-Nosed God ear ornaments, and Cahokia flintclay figurines (adapted from Emerson *et al.* 2002, 2003; Hall 1991; Kelly 1991)

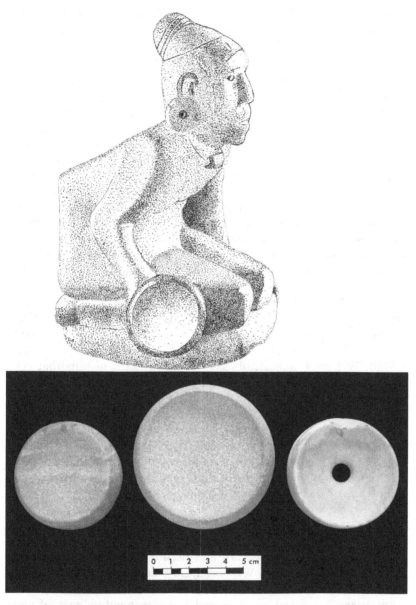

6.2 Cahokia style chunkey stones: top, as depicted on Cahokia style flintclay pipe, Hughes site, Oklahoma (height 21.5 cm); bottom, from the Wilson Mound mortuary (center) and upland villages (right and left)

1991a; Welch 2001; Williams and Brain 1983).[17] One heavily worn Cahokia-style chunkey stone even turned up in South Carolina (Culin 1992:fig. 675b).

The Cahokia form of chunkey stone appears to comprise a minority of the discoidal stones in these other places but their presence corresponds with the possible introduction of the game to these distant peoples. The same is true of Cahokia-style triangular projectile points and the Cahokia microlithic technology, both made from the Burlington chert that outcrops 30 km away from Cahokia (see Justice 1987; Perino 1968). The Burlington microliths and microblade cores are found as far afield as the Yazoo Basin of Mississippi, western Kentucky, and northeast Arkansas (Johnson 1987; Koldehoff and Carr 2001; Morse and Morse 1983, 2000). In the case of the microlithic industry, there is no known technological reason for the exclusive use of the Burlington chert. However, if we understand technology as cultural know-how, and know-how to have involved inalienable qualities and biographical information, then the microlithic technology may be understood as inextricably tethered to Burlington chert, if not also to the idea of Cahokia.

The pan-Mississippian distributions of possible Cahokian material culture and technologies may also be explained either by Cahokians immigrating to new lands or by non-Cahokian pilgrims who took Cahokian souvenirs or technological know-how home with them (see Pauketat 1998b). Perhaps Cahokian objects were distributed as gifts that conveyed something more than "prestige" and in return required something more than a portable token. Saying this does not diminish the importance of exotica in the manufacture of valuables. Instead it should deflect our attention away from vaguely uninformative notions of trade or prestige goods and toward a nuanced appreciation of the materiality of migrations, extractive expeditions, outposts, pilgrimages, and a possible political-religious cult that might have brought a kind of "peace" and order – a *pax Cahokiana* – to the Mississippi valley.

Northern intrusions

Sites dating to the late eleventh and twelfth centuries in central and northern Illinois, southern Wisconsin, northeastern Iowa, southeastern Minnesota, western Missouri, western Iowa, northeastern Nebraska and southeastern South Dakota show evidence, direct and indirect, of some kind of contact with Cahokia or its intermediaries. For instance, Red Wing sites in southeastern Minnesota reveal evidence of profound historical change already in the early eleventh century, the beginning of the "Silvernale phase" (Rodell 1991). The Silvernale people lived in "large,

fortified villages often surrounded by numerous conical mounds" concentrated in this the northernmost of Mississippian settlement complexes
(Green 1997:215–16). Guy Gibbon and Clark Dobbs (1991:303) specu-
late that southern Mississippian women may have been incorporated into
these northern communities, generating profound cultural change.

Mississippian-inspired settlements and cultural change continued to
the west and even on to the Plains. Great Oasis, Mill Creek (no relation to the southern Illinois chert), and Cambria phase sites in Nebraska,
western Iowa, and southern Minnesota contain evidence of contacts most
probably resulting from sporadic (although potentially momentous) encounters with Mississippian travelers or with Mississippian places down-
river (Johnson 1991; Tiffany 1991a, 1991b). Small earthen platforms in
the Cambria region mimic Mississippian mounds. Joseph Tiffany (1991a)
and John Ludwickson and coworkers (1993) illustrate columnar and disk-
shaped marine-shell beads, Mississippian axe heads, Ramey Incised pottery, a Long-Nosed God maskette, Cahokia style chunkeys, and Cahokia
arrowheads from discrete cultural regions in Iowa, Minnesota, Nebraska,
and South Dakota. Between the Great Oasis and Mill Creek peoples
and Cahokia were the Glenwood and Steed-Kisker complexes, whose
Cahokia-like pottery is further evidence of contacts along the Missouri
River (O'Brien 1978; Tiffany 1991b). Between Red Wing and Cahokia
was a series of other likely outposts, Cahokianized settlers, or local converts who may have made their own pilgrimages south to witness the great
happenings at Cahokia (see Pauketat 1998b).

In addition to the possibility of pilgrimages, Thomas Emerson (1991b)
has argued that political tensions within early Cahokia may have pre-
cipitated small-scale emigrations of politicos and their families from the
American Bottom outward. Such movements, common to chiefdoms and
kingdoms known from historic accounts in the Old and New Worlds,
are plausible given the evidence at some sites that contacts were single
events followed by prolonged periods of cultural hybridizations between
the intruders, local Cahokian converts, and local Woodland populations
(Emerson 1991a). Such one-off contacts may have sometimes involved
third parties or other Mississippian(ized) peoples in addition to or instead
of Cahokians. Already in the early twelfth century, northern Mississippian
people and places could have served as ideologues and archetypes one or
two steps removed from Cahokia itself.

Local would-be leaders and religious specialists may have gained legiti-
macy by publicly using their Cahokian material culture and their esoteric
Cahokian knowledge, perhaps engendering the pan-regional spread of
Cahokianism. An early example of such a site is found in east-central
Illinois. The Collins site is a modest local mortuary center and village,

with several mounds and at least one mortuary platform made from red cedar dating to the late eleventh century (Douglas 1976). Here, no more than three or four decades after Cahokia's Big Bang, local people used or copied Cahokia's Lohmann phase pottery in conjunction with their own terminal Late Woodland varieties. Although less than 10 percent of the domestic pottery is Cahokian or Cahokia style, the red-slipped pottery vessels nonetheless may have constituted the principal ceremonial or high-status ware, perhaps materializing Cahokianism, potentially almost as a religious movement, amidst local non-ranked horticulturalists.

Perhaps the best arguments that Cahokian contacts led to profound social change are based on finds from central and northern Illinois, southeastern Iowa, and southern Wisconsin. Beginning in the late eleventh century, the central Illinois River valley was home to several "Spoon River" and "La Moine River" Mississippian polities, each with a large town center arrayed around large public architecture (Conrad 1989, 1991). The beginning of this Mississippian occupation, not surprisingly, dates to a moment of "Late Late Woodland/Mississippian contact" at or shortly after AD 1050 (McConaughy 1993). At the Rench site, about 37 percent of the broken pottery consists of shell-tempered wares that look like those of greater Cahokia's Lohmann phase, while the remainder are local "Mossville" Late Woodland types (McConaughy 1991:108). Both of the excavated buildings at Rench, a small homestead or hamlet possibly comprised of several more homes, had burned to the ground.

The Lohmann phase horizon as represented by the Rench site merges with the "Eveland" phase, a late Lohmann and early Stirling phase cognate in the central Illinois River valley (Harn 1991). Alan Harn (1991:130) believes that the type site and its associated cemetery, Eveland and Dickson Mounds, were "[c]lose enough to Cahokia to invite frequent contact" and yet "sufficiently isolated to ensure their own individuality." At least a dozen large public and small domestic wall trench style buildings, several of which had been incinerated, were spread over a 2 ha habitation site. A charnel house surmounted a truncated mound on the nearby Dickson cemetery ridge-top. One burial pit in the cemetery contained four beheaded men reminiscent of Cahokia's Mound 72.

Perhaps like Eveland and Dickson Mounds, there are other places readily termed "outposts." These outposts are presumably settlements of emigrant Cahokians or other non-local intruders who kept lines of communication open with their homelands for years, possibly decades. Such sites north of Cahokia may have served in the limited extraction of lithic resources, galena deposits, and animal hides, or in the control of copper exchange routes (e.g., Finney and Stoltman 1991; Tiffany 1991a).[18] A good example of such an extractive outpost may be the Trempealeau site

in western Wisconsin, situated less than 50 km from the Hixton silicified sandstone quarries at the north end of the unglaciated Driftless Area
(Green and Rodell 1994:353). The Trempealeau site features a terraced
bluff-top, creating the appearance of a multi-staged platform mound
seemingly intended to enhance its visual effect. While little is known
about the residential habitation of Trempealeau, there is Lohmann phase
pottery at the site, including red-slipped tecomates and jars. Platform
mounds are unknown in this region prior to this, although local peoples
had earlier built the nearby effigy mounds. Thus, the significance of the
Cahokia-like platform mound at this site lies precisely in its existence
during the fifty-year phase during which almost all Hixton seems to have
been imported into the American Bottom (Pauketat 1992).

Likewise, along the Apple River in the rolling unglaciated hills at the
southern end of the Driftless Area in extreme northwestern Illinois, a series of settlements were occupied around a mound at the John Chapman
site (Emerson 1991a). As with other sites just to the north, Chapman
seems to have been built in the vicinity of or as part of terminal Late
Woodland conical (and at least one effigy) mound constructions. This
site and others in the surrounding valley have produced early Cahokian
Ramey Incised pottery alongside local grit-tempered and shell-tempered
wares (Emerson 1991a). University of Illinois excavations at Chapman in
2003 revealed small semi-subterranean huts surrounded by storage pits
at one of two or three occupation areas along the large terrace overlooking Apple River. Following its abandonment sometime in the mid to late
twelfth century, the focus of activities presumably shifted to the Mills
site, also with a platform mound, other conical mounds, and a probable
palisade wall, presumably the local administrative center of a simple two-
tiered settlement hierarchy. This settlement hierarchy may have remained
hypothetical even in the minds of some Apple River people, however, and
Cahokian contact did not necessarily engender political stability. Rather,
the opposite was probably the case.

There is a growing realization that the terminal Late Woodland or
the Effigy Mound peoples of southern Wisconsin, northern Illinois, and
eastern Iowa experienced a veritable "intrusion" of foreigners (Theler
and Boszhardt 2000). This moment of culture contact looks to have
put an end to Effigy Mound construction at AD 1050 (Stoltman and
Christiansen 2000:514). However, it is clear that important early Mississippian sites all across this portion of the upper Mississippi valley
are located astride effigy and conical mounds of the terminal Late
Woodland period. There is also a series of possibly palisaded villages
in southern Wisconsin, some hidden along the courses of small feeder
streams to the Mississippi River (see Salkin 2000). The well-known but

underinvestigated Hartley Fort site in eastern Iowa appears to have been a fortified village occupied by people who made or used both Late Woodland ceramics and Cahokia pots: Ramey Incised and Powell Plain (Tiffany 1982). Recent excavations at the small Union Bench site near Dubuque, Iowa, revealed the entire plan of a short-term palisaded settlement of some ten houses and one public building occupied by local people who made and used local cord-impressed terminal Late Woodland pottery dating to about AD 1050. This site is thought by David Benn to have been occupied for only a few years – given the lack of accumulated domestic refuse – when it was burned and abandoned (Benn and Powell 2002).

At yet another single-component palisaded village in southeastern Wisconsin, Fred Edwards, terminal Late Woodland residents made cord-impressed pottery and built small single-set-post houses around a village plaza during the late eleventh and early twelfth centuries. Possibly similar to the settlement(s) at Chapman, this unburned village produced "unequivocal" evidence of sustained Mississippian contact, primarily in the form of "a wide range of exotic" southern artifacts including Cahokian "Ramey Incised and Powell Plain jars, Mill Creek chert, Dongola chert, Kaolin chert, Burlington chert, marine shell (both beads and larger fragments), and polished stone earspools, all of which presumably originated from a source or sources well to the south of Wisconsin" (Finney and Stoltman 1991:229). Importantly, there are also "a number of additional non-local items, such as Hartley Fort ceramic types, Aztalan Collared jars, copper, Hixton silicified sandstone . . . Knife River flint" and pieces of Missouri flintclay (used in the making of carved redstone figurines at Cahokia; see Emerson *et al.* 2002). For excavators Fred Finney and James Stoltman (1991:248), this indicated "an extraordinary amount of cultural interaction" among the many Late Woodland peoples of the northern frontier. Elsewhere there is more evidence of the interactions between the Cambria, Apple River, and Mill Creek regions (Tiffany 1991b:187). Places such as Chapman or Trempealeau may have been powerful centers, or the homes of local power brokers. Cahokia, if not directly involved in some way, presumably was a stimulus to local development or perhaps aided in the legitimization of these northern powers.

This kind of pan-northern interaction was not a uniform feature of all northern peoples in the upper Mississippi valley. To wit, scarcely a Mississippian or Mississippianized artifact is known from northeastern Missouri (Chapman 1980:161; O'Brien and Wood 1998:274). Instead, the pan-northern interaction seems somehow related to certain language groups or to instances of migrations of peoples evident across northern Illinois, southern Wisconsin, and Iowa. One likely migration of

Illinoisans – possibly including some Cahokians – north into Wisconsin is thought to have led to the transformation of the Aztalan site sometime in the late eleventh century (Goldstein 1991; Goldstein and Richards 1991; Hall 1986; Richards 1992).

Researchers are uncertain whether foreigners were invited in or took over the location without an invitation. However, it is clear that before AD 1050, Aztalan was an important place of effigy mounds, conical mounds, an earthen embankment, and a residential settlement along the Crawfish River (Goldstein 1991:215; Richards 1992). Sometime shortly after AD 1050, a new 9 ha fortified village was superimposed over this sacred landscape (Fig. 6.3). Interior to a new palisade wall, complete with protruding bastions, the Aztalan people built two modest earthen pyramids overlooking a 3 ha plaza, using the hillside to accentuate the size of the mound terraces as at Trempealeau.[19] Beyond the plaza were the residences of Aztalan inhabitants, built using wall trenches as at early Cahokia.

Given the mix of intrusive Mississippian and local Late Woodland material culture, we can be sure that Aztalan was not a gradual evolutionary development, but an abrupt historical moment of culture contact. The effects on the people of the surrounding region were equally profound. Some people, perhaps the enemies of the local Aztalan folk, were displaced northward (Overstreet 2000). The migration may have contributed to the ethnogenesis of these emergent "Oneota" people.

Meanwhile, the Mississippianized Aztalan people continued to make local pottery styles, but also possessed Cahokian style pots, hybrid pots, Cahokia arrowpoints and chunkey stones, Mill Creek hoe blades, and marine-shell beads. One tecomate variety from the site, called Crawfish White-on-Red, is almost certainly an import from Cahokia itself where almost all of them have been found (Richards 1992, personal communication, 2001; see Pauketat et al. 2002). Samuel Barrett's (1933) finding of burned human body parts – portions of at least six human crania, a burned articulated human hand, four isolated mandibles, three articulated human legs, and one articulated arm – discarded in pits along with ordinary food refuse suggested to him cannibalism. Whether or not Aztalan people actually ate human flesh, the delimbing and beheading of people and the subsequent burning and discard of the parts is a most unusual mortuary practice in this most unusual of places, and remains to be satisfactorily explained.

Aztalan is a particularly vivid example of the social changes taking place in the upper Mississippi, Illinois, and Missouri river drainages simultaneous with the construction of Cahokia and its apparent consolidation of control between AD 1050 and 1150 over the place where these three

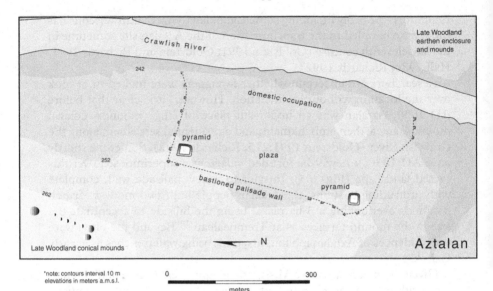

Crawfish River

Late Woodland earthen enclosure and mounds

242

domestic occupation

pyramid

252

plaza

bastioned palisade wall

pyramid

262

Late Woodland conical mounds

N

Aztalan

*note: contours interval 10 m
elevations in meters a.m.s.l.

0   300

meters

6.3 Aztalan: top, plan view (adapted from Goldstein and Richards 1991); bottom, view to south

rivers converge. The evidence in the north is varied but compelling in that it is suggestive of effects as profound as whole-group migrations, sporadic violence, settlement conflagrations, and a significant increase in interregional exchanges. Cahokia most certainly did not cause all of this directly.[20] However, it is difficult not to conclude that developments at Cahokia had profound effects, even if indirectly. Cahokians provided unprecedented opportunities that, in turn, may have inspired unprecedented political competition in the north. Add to this the possibility of a religious cult, as inscribed in the Gottschall Rock Shelter or embodied by the Cahokia chunkey stones, Long-Nosed God earpieces, and falconoid icons of the Ramey Incised pottery: a *pax Cahokiana* moves into the realm of the explicable.

Undoubtedly there were limits to the Mississippianization of the north (see Emerson 1999). The most distant complexes of the Red Wing, Cambria, and Upper Republican regions do not show the sustained contacts or possible outposts seen in central and northwestern Illinois, southern Wisconsin, and eastern Iowa. The peoples of these most distant of places did not adopt the novel wall trench construction of Cahokia, as did the peoples of central Illinois or Aztalan, at least not until much later (e.g., Barrett 1933:164; Claflin 1991; Green 1997; Harn 1991). Yet the historical effects of contact, the possible ritual adoption of outsiders if not also the spread of some sort of religious cult(s), would have varied widely. It is even likely that archaeologists have overlooked the signatures of resistance to the ideas, people, or accouterments embodied by Cahokia, perhaps seen as the absence of Mississippian material culture in northeast Missouri, as the migrations of Late Woodland peoples laterally across the northern frontier, or as the conflagration of some northern settlements.

The view from the South

If Aztalan-like intrusions occurred south of the American Bottom, identifying them would be tricky. Partly, this is because of the difficulty in distinguishing pre-Mississippian mound centers from Mississippian ones in the Midsouth, or the pre-Mississippian Red-Filmed Horizon ceramic assemblages from Mississippian ones. However, it is also the case that we have only a modicum of excavated data from many southern sites, despite the New Deal archaeology's emphasis on large-scale horizontal exposures of habitation remains.[21] Add to these few data the interpretative biases of Midsouthern researchers and the view from the South looks very different from that of the upper Midwest.

In some quarters, there has always been a sense of Cahokia's historical priority in the development of later Mississippian iconography, also called the "Southeastern Ceremonial Complex" (Anderson 1997; Brown and Kelly 2000; Emerson 1989; Emerson *et al.* 2003). However, whereas northern archaeologists often prostrate themselves to Cahokia, many Midsouthern Mississippianists would rather be struck dumb than knowingly attribute any aspect of Mississippianization to Cahokia (see Box 11). In fact, some past syntheses of "the Mississippian Southeast"

Box 11. Cahokia defines Mississippianism, 900 years later.
Thanks to a non-destructive technique perfected by Thomas Emerson and his colleagues (Emerson and Hughes 2000; Emerson *et al.* 2002, 2003), we now know that the finest three-dimensional statuette and fig-urine carvings known from pre-Columbian North America were made from a carvable, red Ozark pipestone, called "flintclay," by an artisan or school of artisans associated with Cahokia. In these widely dis-persed images, Cahokians are shown playing chunkey, smoking pipes, practicing shamanic ritual, tending to the ancestors, beheading en-emies, protecting themselves in battle, wearing beads and earrings, cultivating the earth, and communing with deities. What would have been the effects of such Cahokian representations when carried off to Oklahoma, Louisiana, Alabama, Tennessee, Wisconsin, Illinois, and Missouri?

One of the effects has been to confuse archaeologists 900 years later. Prior to the study by Thomas Emerson and his coworkers (2002, 2003), Cahokian figurines had been used as the hallmarks of famous places or as the representations of the archaeology of a region, a state, or a phenomenon. Thus, the famous Shiloh kneeling pipe, featured on every fourth postcard from the Shiloh National Military Park, was almost certainly made by Cahokians. The chunkey player pipe from Muskogee County, Oklahoma, has been used as the stereotypical Mis-sissippian chunkey player – but Cahokians made it too. Also known to be "Made in Cahokia" were the figurines on the covers of *The Ar-chaeology of Wisconsin* (Ritzenthaler 1985), *The Prehistory of Oklahoma* (Bell 1984b), *The Prehistoric Indians of the Southeast* (Walthall 1980 [the original hardback edition]), and *American Bottom Archaeology* (Bareis and Porter 1984). In 2002, *Archaeology* magazine featured a story by Alex Barker about "decoding" the Southeastern Ceremonial Com-plex. The cover art was a representation of Red Horn found at Spiro but made at or near Cahokia from Missouri flintclay (see also Fig. 5.9)! Even today, it seems, that which constitutes Mississippian is being de-fined by ancient Cahokians.

have actually omitted Cahokia entirely! It was too large, too far north, and too different (Knight 1997:229).

There are indications of a Midsouthern historical disjuncture more or less coeval with Cahokia's rise to the north. Barry Lewis (1991) has noted that Late Woodland mound centers across the Midsouth appear qualitatively dissimilar from subsequent Mississippian towns. Clearly, some Late Woodland mound sites, such as the Hoecake site and the Toltec site were abandoned by the eleventh century. John House (1996:145) describes as "vexing" the "inability to identify any occupation in the Arkansas River Lowland in the several centuries after AD 1000."

Where there was occupational continuity to the north, south, and west of the vacant central Arkansas region, there are both indications of Cahokian contacts and possible absences of Cahokian contacts. To wit, Cahokian flintclay figurines, copper Long-Nosed God earpieces, or both are found at the southern Caddoan site of Gahagan in Louisiana, in contemporary deposits at the early Caddoan Harlan site in northeastern Oklahoma, and of course at Spiro (see Bell 1984; Brown 1996; Emerson *et al.* 2003; Griffin 1952b; Webb and Dodd 1939). In Louisiana, recent excavation at the late Coles Creek site of Lake Providence has produced a suite of non-local Ramey Incised and Powell Plain jar fragments that, based on their appearance, were probably imported directly from Stirling phase Cahokia (Richard Weinstein, personal communication, 2002).

In Arkansas and western Tennessee, the Red-Filmed Horizon of AD 900–1050 gave way to an early Mississippian phase where the angled-shoulder jars are reminiscent of Lohmann and Stirling phase pots. Around Reelfoot Lake, Tennessee, there were two mounded sites just 2 km apart, one of which was an 8 ha town with two platform mounds 3 and 6 m high. Atop the nearby bluff, the dead were buried in an associated accretional burial mound, some with pots that closely resemble the bottles, bowls, and jars of the American Bottom's Lohmann phase (Mainfort 1996:85). Meanwhile, just across the river in eastern Arkansas, the contemporary early Mississippian "Barrett complex" has been defined on the basis of "red-slipped jars with recurved rims" and "Burlington or Crescent Quarry chert from the St. Louis area" (House 1996:147).

In addition, here in eastern Arkansas and southeast into Mississippi are found Cahokia microliths made from this same imported Burlington chert along with the occasional Ramey Incised jar fragment (Buchner 1998; Johnson 1987; Morse and Morse 1983). So-called "Cherry Valley phase" sites in Tennessee and Arkansas produce locally made ceramic assemblages strikingly similar to Cahokia's Stirling phase pots (Mainfort 1996; Morse and Morse 1983; Perino 1967). Cherry Valley sites appear to have included outlying settlements arrayed around "a vacant ceremonial center, consisting of two to five mounds and often no obvious residential debris" (Morse and Morse 2000:354). The mounds covered earlier buildings, probably charnel houses, and included a variety of burials.

However, at Beckwith's Fort and the Lilbourn site, near the Ohio–Mississippi river confluence on the Missouri side, there is no evidence to date of Cahokian things or influence. The seven-pyramid, 7 ha fortified Beckwith's Fort site and the ten-mound, 18-plus ha fortified site of Lilbourn supposedly may have been built during terminal Late Woodland period, a tenuous inference based only on the distribution of Late Woodland potsherds on their surface (Fig. 6.4; Cottier 1977a; O'Brien and Wood 1998:292). It is possible that fortified complexes at both sites actually post-date AD 1200.

There may be less evidence of Cahokian contacts at other early Mississippian towns in the Big Bottoms and on the bluff crests north along the Mississippi River in western Tennessee and Kentucky (see Lewis 1991). Unfortunately, most of these have not seen anything but preliminary archaeological investigation. This is not the case with the Wickliffe site, located on a bluff overlooking the Ohio-Mississippi river confluence from the Kentucky side. Based on Cahokian ceramic and lithic artifacts, Kit Wesler (2000:131–2, emphasis original) states that the

possibility must be raised that Wickliffe indeed was part of Cahokia's rural hinterlands and that Wickliffe was affiliated *at some level* with a Cahokian sphere of influence.... (The Early Wickliffe period corresponds temporally with the Stirling phase in the American Bottom, when that area's population was greatest [Milner 1986] and Cahokia arguably at its strongest.) This may have happened as a Cahokian representative with a large retinue appeared at the gate, calling forth the sort of diplomatic response presented by Smith and Hally (1992) whereby a chief of lesser stature established fictive kinship as an alternative to conflict; or it may have happened as an ambitious Wickliffe chief made an expedition to Cahokia to gain the anointment of a spiritually powerful leader (bringing back a Ramey Incised vessel much like bringing back a bust of Elvis to commemorate a pilgrimage to Graceland).

Of course, Wickliffe is just one of several towns on the Kentucky side of the river. These were spaced out to maximize the control over a locality rather than each other. The same may be true of the numerous Mississippian centers of southeastern Missouri and northeastern Arkansas that fill the landscape and occupy the time between AD 1200 and 1400 (see Chapman 1980; Morse and Morse 1983). Like most of the early Mississippian places to the south of Cahokia, two- or three-tiered settlement hierarchies consist of single fortified towns surrounded by outlying farming settlements and homesteads (Smith 1978, 1995). This may be true

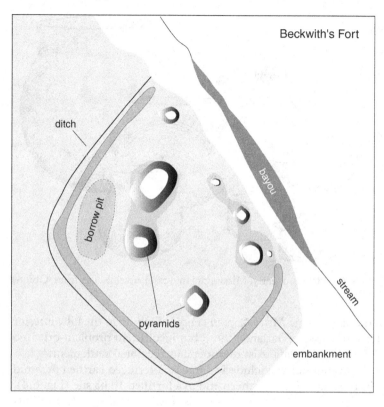

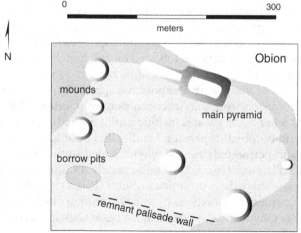

6.4 Plans of two Mississippian towns: top, Beckwith's Fort (adapted from Lewis 1991 and Williams 1954); bottom, Obion (adapted from Garland 1992)

6.5 An idealized early Mississippian vessel assemblage from Obion, Tennessee

even of the single large Mississippian center of Obion in the hilly interior of western Tennessee (Garland 1992), but insufficient problem-oriented survey or excavation data exist to understand regional settlement.

Obion's seven mounds included a large two-terraced earthen pyramid 8 m high. It occupied the northern end of a fortified 10 ha site (Fig. 6.4). The actual extent of the site's palisade is uncertain, and early accounts describe a walled precinct in excess of 10 ha (Garland 1992:37). Excavations into the various pyramids revealed a series of ancient surfaces within the structures, each associated with large buildings. The earliest buildings had single-set-post foundations, followed by wall trench foundations. Near the base of one of the smaller pyramids, Mound 3, was a burned building on the floor of which were four pots that appear shaped much like early Powell Plain vessels from the American Bottom (Garland 1992:11, fig. 36). Obion's other pottery wares include distinctive red-slipped grog-tempered jars with bi-lobed suspension handles and hooded bottles with small, squared and perforated "ear" appliqués added to the sides of the open "blank-faced" mouth (Fig. 6.5). Similar vessels at Cahokia dating to the Lohmann phase share these ceramic attributes (Pauketat 1998a:184). In the few petrographic examinations by James Stoltman (1992) to date, the Powell ware at Obion and the Obion-like ware at Cahokia seem to be local copies of exotic styles.

Obion's outliers and farmers remain to be located by archaeologists. One might propose that Obion squelched competitors, this perhaps explaining the empty interior of Tennessee, an area known for its "excellent agricultural soils . . . abundant along the major river valleys" (Mainfort 1996:91). Other early Mississippian villages and possible towns are located further to the interior, along the Tennessee and Cumberland rivers. But the nearest comparably sized center to the south was the Shiloh site, probably founded after AD 1050 along the Tennessee River to the southeast. Like the Obion site, it too has produced Cahokian artifacts and possible other parallels with greater Cahokia. Unlike Obion, there are possible secondary sites with one or more platform mounds that may indicate the existence of a three-tiered settlement hierarchy at some point in the region's history (Welch 2001).

From excavations at Shiloh, archaeologists recovered sherds from two Ramey Incised jars, several Cahokia triangular points, pieces of at least two Cahokia chunkey stones, and a single flintclay figurine pipe. The latter was excavated from a log-lined tomb at the base of an elongate mound isolated on a ridge spur south of the main mound-and-plaza cluster. North of this possible ridge-top mound are Shiloh's seven primary steep-sided rectangular pyramids and an unnumbered array of barely visible "house mounds" (Welch 2001). As excavations have shown, Mound A was built up through many repeated stage enlargements and blanket mantles using earth potentially engineered and almost certainly selected for its red and white colors (Fig. 6.6; Anderson and Cornelison 2002). Both rectangular and circular wall trench buildings occupied the summits of the large earthen platforms and the small mounds. The circular buildings contained central hearths comparable to their Cahokian counterparts, and perhaps functioned similarly. In any event, the extent of the residential component of Shiloh is unclear. Especially unusual is a possible Mississippian palisade wall 1 km long located far to the west of the mounds that, as a group, cover less than a 6 ha area.

There were a series of prominent Mississippian towns north and east of Shiloh in the vicinity of Nashville, Tennessee, suggestive of a hotbed of early Mississippian political activity. In fact, there was a possible exodus of some population segment from this region southward to the Ocmulgee site at Macon Plateau, Georgia (Hally 1994). People at the Kincaid site, strategically located at the confluence of the Tennessee and Cumberland rivers with the Ohio River, could have controlled the movement of dugouts through the three-rivers region, potentially making this site key in understanding Mississippian history in this area. The site is relatively large, its nineteen or twenty earthen pyramids covering a palisaded area of roughly 30 ha (Muller 1986:200). Its highest pyramid (Mx 8) stood over 9 m above the land surface, and its largest (Mx 10) was 6 m high and covered an area of 8700 m^2. According to Jon Muller (1986, 1997),

6.6 Shiloh Mound A excavations, 2001 (courtesy David G. Anderson)

the resident population who presumably built these pyramids at the
Kincaid site included only several hundred people, a low estimate based
on a modicum of excavated data and matched by a low rural population
estimate of less than 1500 people, in turn inferred from surface survey
data (Butler 1977; Muller 1978, 1986:table 6.7).

Kincaid was probably founded in the middle of the Black Bottom sometime in the late eleventh or early twelfth century (Cole *et al.* 1951; Muller
1986). The chronology at Kincaid remains "hard to pin down" (Muller
1986:180). "The mean of all radiocarbon dates…in the locality is
AD 1180" (Muller 1978:275). At the Angel site, up the Ohio, the earliest
radiocarbon dates fall around AD 1050, and it is likely that Kincaid was
under construction and occupied after AD 1100, as verified in part by
the presence of three Ramey Incised jar rimsherds, two dated by Cole
et al. (1951) to the middle phase of Kincaid's occupation (presumably,
the "Kincaid" phase, see Muller 1986:185).[22] Possibly dating to this same
phase, if not earlier, is a series of log tombs in a small mound at the site's
northeastern end (Cole *et al.* 1951:112). The earliest tombs were in the
mound's lower stratum, where three log-covered tombs contained the
bodies of several people, one with a headdress and another decapitated

(Cole *et al.* 1951:107–9). There is no indication in the small-scale non-mound excavations by the University of Chicago at Kincaid to support a pre-eleventh-century date, given the wall trench structures and their associated Mississippian debris. However, Cole and coworkers (1951:80–2) report a large single-set-post building atop an early stage of one pyramid (Mx 7) reminiscent of the early Obion buildings (and pre-Mississippian styles in the American Bottom).

Notably, the late "Tinsley Hill" phase of Kincaid's occupation correlates with the finding of possible Moorehead phase Cahokian wares (so-called Tippett's Bean Pots [beakers] and Cahokia Cordmarked pottery, see Cole *et al.* 1951:151). Apparently, the Kincaid site was abandoned by about AD 1400. Recent work by Charles Cobb and Brian Butler (2002) has traced the dispersal of people from the collapse of Black Bottom society deep into the southern Illinois interior. Their work also supports the overall abandonment of the Lower Ohio River floodplain and adjacent areas as part of the fourteenth- through fifteenth-century "Vacant Quarter" (Williams 1990; see also Wesler 1991). In the Mississippi Alluvial Plain and adjacent bluff edges around the confluence of the Ohio and Mississippi Rivers, some two dozen fortified administrative centers were abandoned by AD 1400 (Fig. 6.7).

The Mississippi valley remained well populated south of Memphis. However, after AD 1200, there is little hint of Cahokia's existence in the Midsouth, the latest such appearance being the early Moorehead phase Cahokian pottery at both Winterville and Lake George in the lower Yazoo Basin of western Mississippi. The occurrence of this pottery appears coincident with the reconstruction of those former Coles Creek centers into dense, compact, Plaquemine-Mississippian capitals, their twenty-three and twenty-five steep-sided pyramids standing up to 16 m tall and covering site-areas of 20 and 22 ha, respectively (Brain 1989; Williams and Brain 1983). At the same time, the Moundville polity consolidated its apical position over the Black Warrior valley more than 300 km to the east (Steponaitis and Knight 1998). With Cahokia's influence observable, and Moundville's hypothetical, it may be no wonder that a defensive ditch surrounded Lake George (Fig. 6.8). Like so many Mississippian towns of the time up and down the Mississippi River, defense appears an overriding factor in their plans. Where the farmers were during all this time is not yet known (cf. Rogers and Smith 1995; Pauketat 2000a).

Neither Lake George nor Winterville survived as a political force in the Lower Mississippi valley beyond AD 1400 (consider Anderson's [1994a, 1994b] political factionalism and "cycling" model). Moundville too had become a mere ceremonial burial ground by that time, and many other

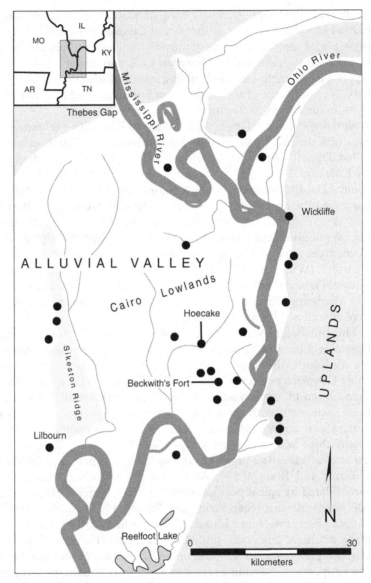

6.7 Mississippian towns in the Ohio–Mississippi river confluence area (adapted from Lewis 1991)

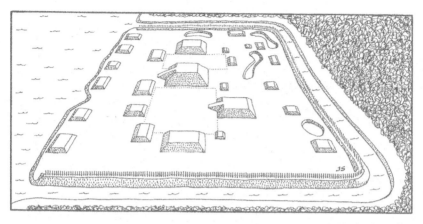

6.8 Oblique view of the Lake George site, southeastern Mississippi (redrawn from Morgan 1999 by Jack Scott)

middle-river Mississippian peoples left their homelands for points to the far west, south, and southeast. The dénouement of this seemingly panregional deterioration of political centers was a singular mortuary event at the Caddoan site of Spiro in eastern Oklahoma (Brown 1996).

Spiro's political history as a regional center probably began a little before AD 1200 and perhaps involved some sort of migrations along the Arkansas River (see Schambach 2002). Although the paramount site of a probable three-tiered settlement hierarchy, Spiro's real claim to fame is owed to the "Great Mortuary," a hoard of wealth objects buried with members of Spiro's elite at about AD 1400 (see Brown 1996). Here was an assortment of hundreds of the finest examples of woven, chipped-stone, groundstone, baked clay, and carved objects known from the Midwest and Midsouth (Brown 1996). There were arrows, clubs, tools, pots, smoking pipes, body ornaments, and garments from the southern Plains, the Mississippi valley, the Deep South, and Cahokia. In the one burial event, the Spiroan elite claimed for themselves the glory of all of the various Mississippian domains of their memory. In the process, they memorialized a single Mississippian culture in a way that it had never previously existed. Twentieth-century archaeologists reified the Spiroan creation as the Southeastern Ceremonial Complex or, simply, the Southern Cult (Muller 1989; Waring 1968; Waring and Holder 1945). Today, V. James Knight, James Brown, and George Langkford (2001) recognize that there were many local variants to the SECC, as it morphed through time and across space.

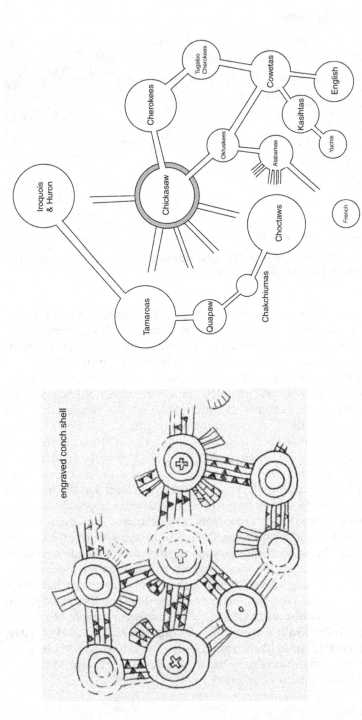

6.9 Cartography on a Mississippian engraved conch shell, Spiro, Oklahoma (left) and on the 1737 Chickasaw map (after Lafferty 1994; Phillips and Brown 1978; Waselkov 1989)

Political history and the Southern Cults

The Southeastern Ceremonial Complex was defined as a set of motifs posited to represent the central cultural themes and cosmological principles of all Mississippian peoples. The four-quartered earth or sun symbol, the war club, the bi-lobed arrow, the thunderbird eye, the raptor's tail feathers, and the serpentine earth-monster signify the central principles and deities of the Mississippian cosmos, the temples that housed the bones of the ancestors, and the relationship of people and supernatural powers (Fig. 1.3). Sets of these motifs emphasizing various themes, sometimes arranged in panels, are found in rock art from Wisconsin south to Tennessee and Missouri.

Mark Wagner and Mary McCorvie's (2002) analysis of the rock art on open-air ledges at an interior mesa-top village in southern Illinois that post-dates Kincaid's collapse shows that peoples inscribed their cosmos into their village space. The petroglyphs on three individual panels seem to be grouped to commemorate an upper world of thunderbird deities, an earthly human realm, and an underworld of serpents and earth. Similar inscriptions across the Mississippianized north and into the Midsouth bespeak interconnectedness to the Mississippian world. But to what degree did each group of people reshape and regroup the motifs, and thus affect a contemporary sense of what the Southeastern Ceremonial Complex was all about?

The peoples of the terminal phases of the Cahokian polity and the thirteenth- and fourteenth-century centers of Spiro, Lake George, Winterville, and Moundville were almost certainly aware of each other. In the seventeenth and early eighteenth centuries, the Chickasaw used buckskin maps to travel from place to place (Waselkov 1989). Their cartographic symbols match the iconography of at least one pre-Columbian pot (Fig. 6.9). At contact, both Plains sign language and, along the Gulf Coast, Mobilean trade jargon permitted communication between travelers and traders (Drechsel 1994). In this way, and presumably compounded by the migrations of people from place to place, cultural practices may have developed far away from their origin points. Such a cultural transmission of ideas may have occurred simply by virtue of the power of esoterica (Helms 1992). Mesoamerican linguistic traits entered the Southeast probably in this manner (Nicklas 1994). Then again, social movements or political-religious cults may have facilitated the cultural transmission of Mississippianism. The possible mid-eleventh-century Cahokian cult(s) is the precursor to the "ancestor-warrior" cults signified in later Mississippian iconography (Emerson et al. 2003; Knight et al. 2001).

As the idea of a series of cults hints, there was not one iconographic complex but any number of "Southern Cults" associated with different Mississippian places and peoples. The full complement of Mississippian iconographic elements is not found anywhere, save perhaps in the Spiroan hoard. Using that hoard, Philip Phillips and James Brown (1978) defined a number of different schools of Mississippian artisans who, in turn, seem associated with specific places. Certain motifs are more or less common to the various schools, regions, or times (Muller 1989). The multiple meanings of the symbols would have been differentially emphasized or valued from region to region according to the social and political exigencies of the times and places. That emphasis or valuation would have contributed to the shape of social and political histories. For instance, Mark Rees (1997) has made the case that fish, not maize, symbolized the surplus owed to the chiefs of certain late Mississippian Arkansas peoples, giving those political cultures qualities that diverged from other Mississippian realms. Likewise, the political concern with controlling the value embodied by portable finished goods – as at Spiro – versus that embodied by public works and human sacrifice – as at Cahokia – implicated labor and gender in very different ways, and thus led to very different social and political histories (Pauketat 1997a, 1997b).

As with political relations, gender relations were neither static nor uniform, but were always under construction and subject to politicization. The gendered referents in falcon-dancer motifs and statuary objects – beginning with the Cahokian flintclay figurines – are telling of such a politicization of gender (see Koehler 1997; Trocolli 1999). As exemplified in the meanings of centrally made ritual pots, noted earlier, the effects of the continued politicized negotiation of gender extended into the realm of the quotidian – into daily domestic routines, agricultural production, and culinary practices – that underwrote the political economies of regions. The quotidian converged with the political in the spaces and practices of public rituals, such as the historically known Green Corn Ceremony (Bell 1990; Howard 1968; Witthoft 1949). Gender mattered, and thus it is either explicitly portrayed or implicit in much of Southeastern Ceremonial Complex art. Thus, gendered history also mattered, although archaeologists have only recently begun to think in such terms. This is patently obvious in the contrasting political tactics used by early sixteenth-century male and female rulers in their encounters with the Hernando de Soto expedition (see Clayton et al. 1993).

7   The struggle for identity

During the tenth century, Plum Bayou peoples had emigrated or were emigrating from central Arkansas. There may have been small-scale movements of other Red-Filmed Horizon people in the vicinity of the Ohio–Mississippi river confluence. Finally, there seem to have been limited movements of Midsouthern families or kin groups into greater Cahokia. With the consolidation of Cahokia midway through the eleventh century, migrations across or into northern Illinois and southern Wisconsin seem evident, coinciding with intrusive villages and possible Cahokian outposts in formerly Late Woodland territories. By the late eleventh century, a pan-regional socio-religious phenomenon – a possible Cahokian cult and a Long-Nosed God Horizon – appeared among disparate peoples as far removed from one another as Louisiana is from southern Minnesota. Disparate people wore the insignia of a Cahokian(ist?) affiliation (Gibbon 1974). *Pax Cahokiana* reigned in the Mississippi valley. It would end, and the lid that Cahokia had kept on the Mississippian(ized) world would be lifted.

The drawn-out collapse of Cahokia

At the end of the eleventh century, the greater Cahokian cultural hegemony pervaded all social life in that region. How one's home was sited referenced the Cahokian master plan. The pots used to cook meals and the tools used to slice meat, cut wood, or till the earth all evoked one's obligations to or relationships with Cahokians. Human bodies as units of value seem inseparable from the construction of the new central political-administrative landscape with its many memorials of earth, wood, and sacrificial victims. The effects were probably felt well outside the region.

Indeed, a Cahokian ethos – a set of ideas, beliefs, and a game – seems to have attracted followers and encouraged emulators with such zeal as to appear religious in character. The fervor to be like Cahokia or Cahokians was played out in the chunkey games of community plazas, painted in the ritual paintings of cave walls, and embodied by would-be rulers and

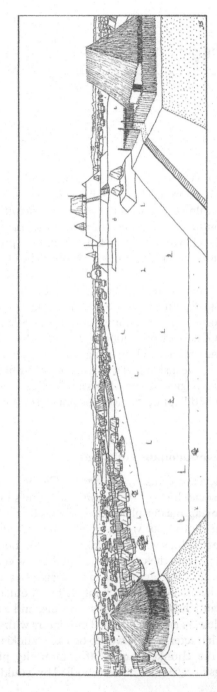

7.1 Artist's reconstruction of Cahokia, c. AD 1175 (rescaled from a Lloyd Townsend mural, drawing by Jack Scott)

religious leaders wearing special earpieces and garments and emulating the powerful ancestor veneration and temple rites of Cahokia. To be sure, if Cahokia did not usher a wave of interactions and migrations along northern and southern frontiers, then it toppled the first domino. There were historical consequences.

Perhaps as early as the tenth century and certainly by the eleventh, upper Midwestern and Midsouthern settlements were fortified. Several of the partially excavated northern settlements even appear to have burned. Yet a critical contrast tells all: throughout this early period, greater Cahokia existed without palisade walls. The capital grounds of Cahokia itself were not walled. None of the outlier towns was walled. Not a single village or farmstead had a defensive palisade. No evidence of internal conflict exists. No evidence that external enemies ever fell upon Cahokia's inner sanctum can be found. Moreover, compared to contemporaneous peoples in the north, few chipped-stone arrowheads are found amid the refuse of everyday life.

Yet, already in the first few decades after AD 1100, there are material and spatial signs of (1) the widening distance between people of upper and lower statuses, and (2) political factions within Cahokia's domain. At that time and over the next century, the Stirling phase residents of Cahokia and East St. Louis built a series of elite-sized pole-and-thatch domiciles and non-domestic buildings, some surrounded by compound walls or located near huge marker posts 1 m wide (Fig. 7.1). The work on the earthen pyramids, if anything, increased so that most of the mounds for which we have some construction data have Stirling phase construction fills. All of these constructions necessarily displaced people, who presumably moved to more marginal areas in the vicinity (e.g., Jackson et al. 1992). For instance, the construction of Cahokia's woodhenge at the end of the Lohmann phase entailed dismantling scores of neighborhood houses. In their place, a series of sixty upright cedar posts, about 30–40 cm in diameter and perhaps 10 m high, were set in large postholes in the ground to form a circle initially 130 m in diameter, too large to have supported a roof (Pauketat 1994, 1998a). The principal investigator, Warren Wittry (1977), found bits of red cedar posts in two of the post pits, and the snapped base of another red cedar post left behind in a third, an aborted extraction attempt 900 years ago (Pauketat 1998a). This was the earliest and largest example of a sacred monument similar to the "world center shrines" or sun-circle constructions of the Plains Indians (Hall 1985). At Cahokia over the next century, this post-circle monument was rebuilt at least four times, and probably more (based on scattered post-pits). Each time it was rebuilt, the number of posts in the circle (always a multiple of twelve) and the diameter of the circle changed.[23]

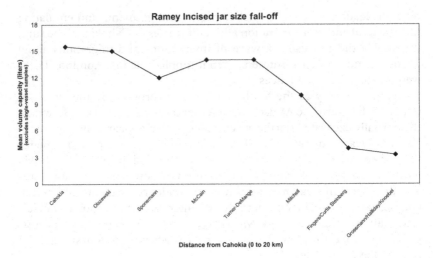

7.2 The distribution of Ramey Incised jars in greater Cahokia during the Stirling phase (adapted from Pauketat and Emerson 1991)

The earliest Ramey Incised pottery known was found among the broken sherds and garbage in a house just north of the first woodhenge construction. The paste characteristics and regional distribution of this pottery, with its redundant iconic messages about the relationship of the user to the cosmos, warrants the view that Ramey Incised jars were made by a few potters and used to redistribute comestibles during communal feasts (Fig. 7.2; Emerson 1989; Pauketat and Emerson 1991).[24] At about this time, and continuing through the twelfth century, domestic groups at Cahokia began routinely storing certain foodstuffs in subterranean pits *indoors*. With time, households increasingly built their houses with less attention to the old Cahokia master grid and with a heightened concern for neighborhood platform mounds or other landmarks in the vicinity (Collins 1997; Mehrer and Collins 1995). Moreover, late Stirling and Moorehead phase houses became increasingly segregated into "household clusters" consisting of at least two or three buildings of different sizes (Pauketat 1998a).

By AD 1150, all of the known Richland complex villages and their associated homesteads or field houses were abandoned, with the only known occupation in that district being one or two hamlets in the adjacent Silver Creek valley to the east (Holley *et al.* 2000; Pauketat 2003b). If there was a local motivation for this upland abandonment it remains a mystery. However, at about this same time, a 20,000-log palisade wall complete with bastions spaced at regular intervals was set into a wall trench 3 km long

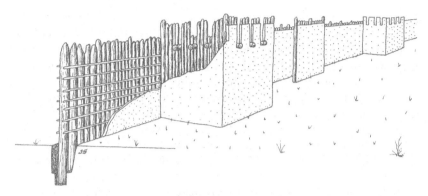

7.3 Artist's reconstruction of a section of Cahokia's palisade wall (redrawn from Iseminger *et al.* 1990 by Jack Scott)

around downtown Cahokia (Fig. 7.3). James Porter (1974) suspected that the Mitchell site palisade wall was constructed at about this time. Palisade walls were definitely built at the East St. Louis site and at the small mesa-top village of Olin 15 km further north of Mitchell (Sidney Denny, personal communication, 2000; J. Kelly 1997). A wall may have surrounded another interior upland village on the northern rim of the American Bottom (Woods and Holley 1991).

Moreover, a fire was ignited at East St. Louis near the end of the late Stirling phase, burning down storage huts and houses and terminating the use of at least one pyramid and its associated elite residential compound (Pauketat 2004). Whether or not two isolated late Stirling phase burned houses at Cahokia were incinerated in the same moment is unknown (Collins 1990; Pauketat 1987, 1995). Yet even if these events were spread out over a period of years, the late twelfth century would seem to have been a turning point in the history of Cahokia.

One might suspect that palisade wall construction held profound social consequences, even if the walls were never put to military use. These consequences may be evident in the subsequent Moorehead phase. Between AD 1200 and 1275, the residents of the American Bottom were importing a restricted array of exotic raw materials and finished goods: marine shell, galena from the Ozarks, fluorite crystal from the Lower Ohio valley, bifacial Ramey knives chipped from Mill Creek and Kaolin cherts, and ceremonial axe heads, one highly polished variety chipped from southern Illinois cherts and another "long-stemmed" variety imported from Tennessee (Koldehoff n.d.; Pauketat 1983, 1992, 1994; Pauketat and Koldehoff 2002; Trubitt 2000). During this time, Cahokians depicted themselves using "Braden" style falcon-warrior motifs (Brown and Kelly

2000). Many of these motifs, display objects, and ritual goods are found around Cahokia's "East Plaza," which John Kelly (1997) has described as the new Moorehead phase space for Cahokia's political-ritual gatherings. Within a few decades, Ramey Incised jars ceased being made, and the social gatherings and related mound-top ceremonies around the East Plaza employed well-made earthenware plates decorated with sunburst motifs (rather than the four-quartered motifs of Ramey Incised jars). The substitution of plates for Ramey Incised jars would seem to indicate an added emphasis on the act of eating in public even while de-emphasizing either the act of public cooking in jars or the take-home potential of the jars.

This evidence for elaborations of ritual media and iconic content belies a significantly diminished and reorganized regional political economy. Cahokia's effects on and interactions with the north had for all intents and purposes ceased as Cahokians turned their attentions southward. In Cahokia's own residential sectors, we see the reasons why. The Moorehead phase population of the Cahokia site numbered 3000–4500 people, down 60 percent from its Lohmann phase levels (Pauketat and Lopinot 1997). The Mitchell site, 10 km north of Cahokia, was the only other town known in the region at this time, with token occupations of platform-mound tops known at East St. Louis and the upland Emerald site. No other pyramid construction or population concentrations are known (the dating of St. Louis remains uncertain, but it bears some overall resemblance to the Mitchell site). Thus, Cahokia and Mitchell (and perhaps St. Louis) after AD 1200 were the apical settlements of a two- to three-tiered settlement hierarchy, depending on the relationship of Cahokia and Mitchell to each other and to their support populations who, by and large, still lived in dispersed single-family farmsteads.

Tallying up the bones and artifacts in the refuse of Moorehead phase households at Cahokia and beyond produces the evidence of a reduced reliance on the meaty elements of deer (L. Kelly 1990, 1997) and the scaled-back production of domestic pottery and textiles. Regarding the latter, the skilled production of finely made angled-shoulder jars seems to have diminished rapidly during the Moorehead phase. The earlier Ramey Incised and Powell Plain jars required skilled potters who used slabbing techniques, simple molds, scraping to thin vessel walls, and at least a two-piece manufacturing procedure. If this procedure can be called specialized owing to the necessary skilled labor, then the later "Cahokia Cordmarked" jars of the Moorehead phase did not entail such a specialized chaîne opératoire. The later jars were shaped using simple coiling techniques aided by the paddle and anvil (Pauketat 1998a). The cords evident in the cordwrapped paddle impressions left on the pot exteriors were increasingly "S" twist, which, along with the virtual disappearance of spindle whorls following AD 1200, may indicate a simplification of the textile production process and an increasingly household-level production of fabric (Susan Alt, personal communication, 2002).

The causes of political collapse

The causes of Cahokia's collapse are less well understood than its emergence owing to the fewer settlement data available to archaeologists. Clearly, there were significant social changes that, minimally, included the abandonment of a whole upland farming district and the increased factionalization of the remaining floodplain community. Some feel that climate change and the localized deterioration of the environment may have led directly to political collapse. Certainly, there were two long dry spells "around AD 1200 ... back-to-back, each lasting 25 years" that brought the warmer and moist Medieval Warm Period to a close (Ollendorf 1993:175). The severity and impacts of these dry spells on native agricultural production in such a temperate Midwestern climate are uncertain. Additionally, there was at least some localized sedimentation of creek channels, possibly adversely affecting drainage and producing flash floods (Lopinot and Woods 1993). There may also have been hydrologic changes in the American Bottom leading to a rising of the water table (Milner 1998). Doubtless there were also cumulative effects of two centuries of significant numbers of farmers chopping and burning wood for housing and fuel.

However, the detrimental effects of these environmental factors remain hypothetical. Some actually contradict others or, worse, archaeological data. For example, did the two dry spells lead to a rising water table? Would a rising water table have forced people out of the well-drained and elevated uplands first, as actually occurred? Would a depleted wood supply have allowed people to construct a 20,000-log palisade wall (and rebuild it repeatedly)? Would not the wood supply have recovered, given the diminished population of the region beginning in the second half of the twelfth century? These environmental factors are insufficient to explain sociopolitical change unless they are integrated in models that account for how people accommodated the natural changes. That is, ditches could have been dug to drain fields. Wood shortages and agricultural production could have been and presumably were administered by Mississippian leaders. Extra stores presumably were held aside for lean years. Cahokians were probably proactive and not merely reactive. Thus, how they lived in this environment is what matters in any explanation, which takes us back to the theories of practice, cultural landscapes, and corporeality necessary to explain the historical processes at work in the pre-Columbian Mississippi valley.

It is certainly true that prolonged drought might have taxed the storage capacity of a community, depending on how that community was governed. Diminished production might have threatened the ability of a particular office-holder to retain the loyalty of her or his followers. And a palisade wall might have exacerbated factionalism in the region, meaning that new problems might emerge under the same social conditions that, in earlier years, would not have been problematic at all.[25] Thus, in the final analysis, the question of the effects of climatic and environmental change is still a question of how social coordination or political management succeeded or failed. Our explanations of Cahokia's demise must situate natural changes in a broader understanding of social and political history. Attempts to do this to date have produced the realization that the collapse of Cahokia was a two-step process.

The dry spells following AD 1200 correlate with the beginning of the Moorehead phase, and thus may reasonably be projected to have further strained an already ailing central-place redistributive economy. The potential strains may have been greater in the twelfth century than they would have been in the eleventh, since the demographic profile of the region and the political stakes had changed. We can imagine two events sufficient to throw the legitimating ideology of the ruling elite or the sacrality of Cahokia's *sanctum sanctorum* into doubt. The first involves enemies breaching the palisade wall and violating the sacred spaces of the central precinct and the ancestral bones of the elite ancestors curated in the temples. This scenario may have played out in the burning and scaled-back occupation of the East St. Louis site. And it may help explain why Monks Mound would fall into disuse even while the East Plaza was developed. The second involves a great earthquake centered in New Madrid, Missouri, of the sort that rocked the mid-continent in 1811–12. According to William Woods (2001), just such an earthquake occurred in the late thirteenth century and may have caused the severe slumpage of Monks Mound's western side – still visible today – that seems to have occurred after the pyramid reached its final proportions in the late twelfth century. The effect might have been similar to the penetration and defilement by enemies.

Whatever combination of factors was involved, the initial step in the process of Cahokian collapse was fundamentally a political one. The increasingly top-heavy economy and monument-laden spaces of Cahokia grew out of proportion to the shrinking farming population. The presumed results, factionalism in the late Stirling and Moorehead phases of greater Cahokia, provided the context for the second step in the process of Cahokian collapse. The second step follows what may be a Moorehead phase reorganization of the Cahokia polity.

The Moorehead phase society of the American Bottom was made up of domestic groups who had assumed administrative responsibilities that they had not possessed earlier. Their larger houses and multiple-building and pit household clusters – all oriented toward local pyramids or landmarks – probably correlate with larger households and greater household-level management of domestic stores. Likewise, the possession by domestic groups of more "prestige goods" (of a sort) accords with their enhanced greater economic responsibilities (cf. Trubbitt 2000). The high-status Cahokians may have become increasingly removed from the mundane realm of economic management as they imagined themselves great warriors through their art and weaponry.

The second step in the process of Cahokian collapse terminates the "reorganized" and "stabilized" Moorehead phase polity and may have been abrupt. The beginning to this second step is indicated by a series of consistent radiocarbon dates from several late Mississippian cemeteries pinpointing them to the period AD 1275–1300 (Emerson and Hargrave 2000; Emerson et al. 2003a). No cemetery is known to post-date them. In fact, there are only several known Sand Prairie phase (AD 1275–1400) houses and even fewer sites at and outside of Cahokia proper. At the Sponemann site immediately north of Cahokia, the Sand Prairie phase occupation appears to overlap with the use of the site by immigrant Oneota hunter-farmers, who lived in the largely vacant American Bottom for another hundred years or so (Jackson et al. 1992). To all intents and purposes, most Mississippians appear to have left the region permanently during the second half of the thirteenth century and the first few decades of the fourteenth.

Why total emigration occurred cannot be explained entirely by the factional politics of earlier years. It is plausible that the same kind of factional disputes and violations of Moorehead phase temples may have led to the departure of certain kin groups, who from all appearances moved far to the south and west. Many of them may have migrated south to join friends and families at the fortified centers of the Ohio–Mississippi confluence, which were still going strong in the thirteenth and fourteenth centuries. Some probably moved north into the rich Illinois River valley. Others may have gone west immediately.

A Cahokian diaspora?

Although we remain uncertain precisely how the demographic fissioning of the Cahokia polity happened, we can be relatively confident that

Cahokians primarily included Siouan-speaking peoples. This is the case given the locations of Siouan peoples at contact and given modern studies of the Siouan languages with their complex terminology describing politics and kin organization (e.g., Bailey 1995; Fowler 1999; Gartner 1996; O'Shea and Ludwickson 1992). Most importantly, archaeologists rely on the oral history of the Siouan-speaking peoples themselves to understand what happened between Cahokia's collapse and the arrival of the French traders and missionaries centuries later (Dorsey 1886; McGee 1897).

According to their oral histories, the Dhegiha-Siouans – who include the Osage, Kansa, Ponca, Omaha, and Quapaw – initially splintered in their homeland somewhere in the vicinity of the Ohio–Mississippi river confluence prior to the sixteenth century. The Quapaw went south, ultimately ending up in central Arkansas (Hoffman 1994; Vehik 1993). The others went west, with the Osage settling just beyond the former greater Cahokia region, south of the Missouri River. The Omaha and Ponca traveled farthest up the Missouri River into Nebraska. Meanwhile, the Chiwere-Siouan-speaking people originated in the north, near Green Bay, Wisconsin. Of these, the Ho-Chunk (or Winnebago) peoples remained, and are today credited with the Gottschall Rock Shelter paintings (Salzer and Rajnovich 2000). Other Chiwere-Siouan peoples – the Missouri, Oto, and Ioway – moved west into the eastern Plains.

Once again, migration appears to have engendered dramatic changes in political arrangements and material culture of these former Mississippians. The Dhegiha-Siouans, for instance, continued to play some variant of the chunkey game and to maintain a heterarchically complex array of political offices and ritual privileges. The cosmos for Osage peoples at contact was divided into upper and lower divisions, and they practiced a form of dual political organization, even down to having two principal leaders (Bailey 1995).[26] The parallels with the dualism of Mound 72 are readily apparent (Fowler 1999).

However, some things it seems are best forgotten. The Dhegihans did not construct earthen pyramids subsequent to their westward movements. In addition, wall trench architecture disappeared among the western Chiwere and Dhegiha peoples. Pottery decorations among some peoples, particularly the Chiwere-speaking peoples, are reminiscent of Ramey antecedents, but they are even more commonly associated with various Oneota peoples to the north, some of whom are thought to be lineal descendants of Cahokianized northerners, but not Cahokians themselves.

In our attempts to connect the dots between likely descendants of Mississippians and the First Nations, we can begin at Cahokia. Several researchers recognize that the processes whereby the uniquely sprawling agglomeration of pyramid-and-plaza neighborhoods coalesced at Cahokia may have predetermined the character of its dissolution. Just as the courtyard groups seem to be the basis for earlier, pre-Mississippian re-settlement and site abandonment, so the pyramid-and-plaza groups may have engendered corporate or sub-community identities that were the basis for the fissioning of the American Bottom population. If Cahokia had formed through an aggregation of distinctive groups, so it may have dissolved as such once the factionalized groups began to slough off at the end of the twelfth century. Pyramid-and-plaza-based identities, in other words, may have served as cleavage planes for the fissioning and dispersal of the population. Conceivably, such factional divisions could have been perpetuated in places such as Southeast Missouri where a dozen or so fortified centers vied with one another for the rights and privileges due to their kin groups.

It is potentially significant to note that Midsouthern centers – even the early ones such as Obion, Shiloh, Beckwith's Fort, etc. – are little larger than one of Cahokia's various "mound-and-plaza" groups. Just a handful – Lake George, Winterville, perhaps Kincaid – may be the scalar equivalents of two or three of Cahokia's mound groups. Many of the later towns in the Lower Mississippi Valley are "small ceremonial centers" – some appearing to be little more than individual elite com-pounds (Phillips *et al.* 1951:315ff). Greater Cahokia had been made up of many compounds and groups of compounds (so perhaps we should call it a "compound center"). As a result, it was a qualitatively different political animal by virtue of the sheer scale of the central political-administrative complex and the distinctive heterarchical, kin-based, and possibly ethnic-based pluralism of the place (*à la* Alt 2001; Emerson 2002; Emerson and Hargrave 2000; Pauketat 2002, 2003b). Its mode of consolidation and collapse may have been just as different.

By the end of the thirteenth century, when the fortified centers and their support settlements around the Ohio–Mississippi river confluence were also abandoned, the balkanization of the Mississippian world was complete. The transformed cultural identities that emerged from the in-teracting small-scale polities – including for example the "Cairo Lowlands phase" – seem to have entailed complete abandonment of the Ohio–Mississippi river confluence. At AD 1400 major migrations took place, probably including the Siouan movements further south and west. Those peoples vacating parts of western and central Kentucky and Tennessee may have moved further to the east and southeast (Williams 1990), per-haps following in the footsteps of earlier Mississippian emigrants who had headed for Macon Plateau.

Warfare

Wherever they moved, the liminal experience of resettlement once again up-ended the traditions of peoples. The large early Mississippian polities were gone, and the agricultural peoples so liberated were simultaneously subjected to a level of violence hitherto unknown in the history of the continent. Endemic warfare appeared across eastern North America, seen variously as an upsurge in the construction of palisades, as a disappearance of dispersed farmsteads, and as the increased rate of traumatic injury and death (Milner 1999).

Along the central Illinois River valley, violence seems to have become progressively worse through time. Consider this brief historical outline. First, the initial Mississippian people appear as intruders during the Lohmann and early Stirling phases. At places such as the Eveland village outpost we see trappings of Cahokia and the new northern Mississippianized world, including the ceremonious beheading of four men perhaps in a commemorative sacrifice to a Cahokianist cult (Conrad 1989; Harn 1991). Like other northern settlements, burned houses hint at possible violent conflict of a sort. By AD 1200, the creolized local Mississippian population of that region lived in a series of large towns, each with one large public building to one side, sometimes situated atop an earthen platform mound. These towns were interspersed on the bluff crests overlooking the wide floodplain of the Illinois River. Periodically, an entire town appears to have been burned to the ground. At the fourteenth-century site of Orendorf, Lawrence Conrad (1989, 1991) and Tom Emerson and their coworkers excavated a series of four superimposed villages. Each was suspected to have been home to several hundred people. Each in its turn had been burned to the ground.

This sort of village-based warfare spilled out into the Plains, exacerbated by the migrations of peoples from the east whose lifestyles, languages, or claims to the land apparently could not be peacefully reconciled with those of the peoples already there. During the mid-1300s, eastern Siouan-speakers and even some Algonkian-speakers migrated into an area of the middle Missouri river in present-day South Dakota occupied by Caddoan-speaking proto-Arikara, all as part of the so-called "Initial Coalescent Tradition." The results include the infamous Crow Creek massacre (Willey 1990; Willey and Emerson 1993). At the 7 ha Crow Creek site, scores of lodges had occupied the steep loess bluffs overlooking the Missouri River. An earlier fortification at this site had been allowed to deteriorate, leaving the village unprotected. At some point, the residents sensed a new threat and began work on a fortification ditch and a new bastioned palisade wall. However, before the work could be completed,

7.4 Skeletal remains at the Crow Creek site, South Dakota (courtesy
Thomas E. Emerson)

the enemy attacked. Most of the men, women, and children of the village were massacred. At least 486 bodies were heaped into one portion
of the incomplete 300 m long, 3 m deep fortification ditch. The lower
incidence of young women indicated to the analysts that they either were
captured and carried off, or managed to run away as the male defenders stood their ground. The high incidence of post-mortem scavenging
of the bodies indicates that they lay dead on the ground for a period of
time before someone returned to bury the bodies in the still-open ditch
(Fig. 7.4).

Warfare was becoming a no-holds-barred proposition on the eastern
Plains and back in the Mississippian heartland. Whereas early Mississippians infrequently touted their arrows and falcon imagery, and perhaps
occasionally raided the settlement of a political rival, their warfare was
actually a low-frequency and high-status activity. Young men from prominent families would have gained status during surgical strikes against
an enemy. In contrast, late Mississippian and proto-historic warfare was
much less of an aristocratic pursuit. The enemy killed all people indis-
criminately. The intent was not merely prestige, but an early form of ethnic cleansing. In one fifteenth-century cemetery in central Illinois, "one
third of all adults were killed by their enemies" from blows to the head,

arrow wounds, or scalpings (Milner 1999:126; see Santure et al. 1990). Many of these people showed evidence of parry fractures on the arms, produced by the force of a blunt instrument across a long bone, caused when they had attempted to fend off attackers, ultimately unsuccessfully.

Warfare along the Mississippi near Memphis retained vestiges of its original aristocratic character. But the Mississippi valley was not spared from the no-holds-barred warfare of the period, as evident first in the archaeological remains of the Powers phase. Powers Fort was a modest 5 ha town with four earthen pyramids at AD 1300, one of the series of probably competing towns spread across this part of the Mississippi alluvial valley. It was the center of a series of smaller settlements, at least ten of which are known and two of which James Price and James B. Griffin (1979) dug in their entirety (see also Morse and Morse 1983:258). At the small settlement of Snodgrass, Price and Griffin found ninety houses in the neat rows and columns of a 1 ha palisaded rectangular village burned to the ground. The burning seems to have been part of a general assault that led to the abandonment of Powers Fort and all other Powers phase sites by AD 1375 or so.

This sort of warfare continued, perhaps contributing to the general abandonment of the Ohio–Mississippi confluence area at AD 1400 and the opening of the Vacant Quarter. South of present-day Memphis, Tennessee, the Hernando de Soto expedition became embroiled in the long-standing feuds of native elites in 1541. Having crossed to the west side of the Mississippi, the chroniclers tell of one polity where the central town, the province, and the people all had the same name – "Casquin."

The cacique, accompanied by many nobles, came out to receive the governor [Hernando de Soto] and offered him . . . his own house in which to lodge, this being on a high hill erected artificially, on one side of the pueblo, where there were twelve or thirteen large houses in which the curaca had all his family, consisting of wives and servants, who were numerous (Clayton et al. 1993:391).

[T]his cacique Casquin and his parents, grandparents, and ancestors for many centuries previously had war with the lord or lords of another province, called Capaha, which bordered upon his own . . . Casquin now saw the good opportunity that was offered him to take revenge for all his past injuries with the aid of foreign strength and power . . . Casquin set out from his pueblo . . . He led his men out formed in squadrons . . . They marched three days . . . [and after crossing a swamp] marched two days more, and early on the third they reached some high hills from which the principal pueblo of Capaha could be seen . . . five hundred large and good houses . . . with a ditch or moat . . . fifty paces wide . . . [T]he cacique Capaha . . . got into one of the canoes that were in the moat and went through the canal to the Rio Grande [i.e., the Mississippi] to take refuge on a fortified island he had there. The Indians of the pueblo who could get canoes followed their lord . . . [or] fled to the woods . . . After the Casquines ascertained that there was no one in the pueblo to oppose them, they showed well the hatred and rancor that

7.5 Timucuans raid enemy village, Florida, AD 1564 (engraving by Theodore de Bry)

they felt against its inhabitants, for they killed the men on whom they could lay hands, numbering more than 150, and took off their scalps to carry to their own country... They sacked the whole pueblo, particularly robbing the lord's house with more satisfaction and enjoyment than any of the others because they were his. They captured many boys, children, and women... [T]he Casquins went to the temple... threw out on the ground the bones and dead bodies that were in the chests... [and] stamped and kicked them in an excess of contempt and disdain. (Clayton *et al.* 1993:394, 397–98)

Today, archaeologists think that the site of Parkin was the capital of Casquin, and the Bradley site was probably the capital of Capaha (or "Pacaha," see D. Morse and P. Morse 1990). Archaeologists have excavated cemetery plots and isolated burial places associated with both phases, and have found high rates of traumatic death. Given the absence of mass graves, it seems that killings occurred on an opportunistic basis, with little discrimination based on age or sex. Most of these killings probably occurred outside the fortifications of sites such as Parkin, where Phyllis Morse (1981) has noted that survey has located no rural settlements – neither hamlets nor farmsteads. Presumably, any farmer so unwise as to live alone in an isolated location, *c.* AD 1500 ± 100, did not live long (Fig. 7.5).

7.6 The largest platform mound at the proto-Historic Fatherland site,
Louisiana (earthen ramp in foreground)

For this reason, most of the entire population of one chiefdom lived
inside the fortifications of the principal town. The result was an accumulation of refuse inside the walls of the settlement. Over the years, the sites
themselves became mounds of midden not unlike a Near Eastern tell.
The Parkin, Rose Mound, Castile Landing, and other "St. Francis type"
sites dating to this late pre-contact and proto-historic period in northeastern Arkansas are elevated up to 2.5 m above the natural landforms
of the area (see Phillips *et al.* 1951:329–34).

Pre-Columbian conclusions

As perhaps exemplified in the Great Mortuary at Spiro at the start of the
fifteenth century, the formerly exclusive and high-status symbols of the
early Mississippian world had become devalued or communalized three
to four centuries later (Knight 1997). At Spiro, it took an incredible hoard
likened to King Tut's tomb to achieve what eleventh-century Cahokians
could have done with a few dozen shell beads and some chunkey stones.
Late Mississippian peoples south of the Vacant Quarter yet practiced
collective rituals associated with sacred temples and platform mounds,
but even these were pale reflections of what they had been (Fig. 7.6).

7.7 Elite Timucuan woman carried on a litter, AD 1564 (engraving by Theodore de Bry)

Increasingly, political power, value, and meaning were reckoned through warfare.

This is not to say that the so-called late Mississippian and proto-historic "complex chiefdoms" of the American Southeast were not politically complex. Several had well-documented tributary relations that defined three-tiered settlement hierarchies (Steponaitis 1978). Southern lords, borne by porters on litters, greeted de Soto as if he and his military attachés were fellow aristocrats (Fig. 7.7; Hally and Smith 1992). Some Indian rulers embodied their lordliness as lardliness – one captured cacique being so heavy as to necessitate quadripedal locomotion during his escape attempt (Clayton *et al.* 1993). The Timucuan caciques and the Natchez "Great Sun" possessed the power to execute men for violating military rules (see Conrad 1989; Swanton 1946). Their own deaths, in both places, commanded special public rituals – the burning of the home and possessions in the Timucuan case and the sacrifice of children and women in the Natchez case.

The Natchez case, finally, brings us full circle. It is the only known case of anything similar to the Cahokian interments in Mound 72. Interestingly, the archaeologists who have studied the most elaborate of the historic Southeastern polities described in the accounts of early

Europeans – the Natchez, Apalachee, Coosa, and Powhatan confederacies or principalities – have had a difficult time finding definitive evidence of hierarchy and tribute. This has led some to doubt the sorts of complexity described by Europeans, particularly those Spanish and French authors biased by their own monarchist ideologies (Muller 1997). It leads others to doubt the ability of archaeologists to reconstruct the past without historical documentation.

I lay the blame not on a lack of documentary information, but on overly simplistic or monolithic models of society. The utility of thinking in terms of static settlement hierarchies clearly has limitations. That is, the ranking of sites into two- or three-tiered settlement hierarchies probably masks what were complex and dynamic relations among the people between and within supposed settlement tiers. It also ignores other historical factors that shaped society, economy, and polity. For example, there would have been a greater administrative burden associated with large-scale labor projects in early Mississippian times at places such as Cahokia, probably making them more complex (heterarchically) than the low-intensity public events of later hierarchical regimes. In fact, public works projects seem relatively unimportant in the creation of value and the legitimation of authority among the Natchez, Apalachee, Coosa, and Powhatan. Perhaps the difficulty in reconciling European accounts of tribute-taking and hierarchy with the archaeology of the historic-period polities points out that political complexity is not simply a matter of hierarchy, giving us more reason to seek a detailed understanding of ancient Cahokia and the Mississippians.

8   Conclusion

Cahokia still makes my jaw drop!

> Elizabeth Garland (La Crosse, Wisconsin, 2001)

What really happened in the Mississippi valley a thousand years ago? Henry Brackenridge pondered that question, as have many who have since stood atop Monks Mound, walked over Aztalan, or viewed the silhouette of Toltec's pyramids at sundown. He and others saw in the Mississippian tumuli shades of Mesoamerica, Egypt, or some other civilization of Moundbuilders.

While archaeologists debunked the extreme versions of the Moundbuilder Myth years ago, certain interpretations of archaeologists are still subject to biases that have their roots in that myth. These are apparent whenever researchers play down American Indian history or minimize social complexity without weighing all of the evidence. The trick of course is to guard against these biases in one's own thinking. Thankfully, newer theories of practice, human agency, corporeality, landscape, and historical-processualism, joined with a heightened appreciation of oral history, can lead us to rethink Cahokia and the Mississippian peoples of eastern North America.

Rethinking Cahokia

In the environment-heavy explanations of Cahokia up through the 1990s, the floodplain of the American Bottom was thought isomorphic with a natural region that, in turn, enabled Mississippian adaptation. The Cahokia, East St. Louis, and St. Louis sites, along with outlying towns, were considered a loose aggregation of semi-autonomous chiefdoms comparable to the other Mississippian polities across the Southeast. Greater Cahokia's many large mounds were thought unremarkable, built by the resident population but not requiring a significant outlay of labor (see Milner 1998). The single-family homesteads dispersed in the floodplain were thought to be trophically autonomous and, therefore, politically

independent (Mehrer 1995, 2000). Once it coalesced, the Cahokia chiefdom like its other Mississippian counterparts suffered from an inherently
unstable political system exacerbated by a deteriorating environment,
causing it to come crashing down. End of story.

However, the empirical realities of the extensive datasets from the
greater Cahokia region are bursting the seams of the environment-based,
downsized-Cahokia scenario. The big three sites of the central political-
administrative complex are unique in North America in terms of both size
and proximity, and cannot be easily fitted within a standard spatial model
of Mississippian settlement. Likewise, there seems little theoretical or empirical basis for the assertion that the ability to feed one's family translates
into political autonomy for farmers living within one or two days' walk
of Monks Mound (see Hally 1993; contra Mehrer 1995). If everyone
was politically autonomous, what conceivable reason could there have
been for the formation of social relationships of obligation or debt that
would bind people into a larger community or commonwealth? Indeed,
are there any pre-industrial food producers anywhere in the world under
similar conditions who were genuinely autonomous?[27]

The danger of such a minimalist position – uninformed by any social
theory – is its susceptibility to interpretive biases ultimately linked to the
myths of the Moundbuilders and the unchanging Indian. Recent theories
enable the transcendence of the old biases by encouraging archaeological observations of how the lived experiences of people continuously
constructed traditions, cultural regions, political economies, and pan-
regional horizons. By tracking the variability of cultural practices and representations within and between settlements over time, the abrupt and
rapid historic events of Cahokia's consolidation may be first recognized
and second correlated with the general trends across the mid-continent.
Such correlations afford opportunities to understand the motivations behind the consolidation of Cahokia, the reasons for Cahokian(ized) incur-
sions, and the diffusion of Mississippian culture into distant lands.

To do this, we must first *make observations at the appropriate scales of
analysis* (Emerson 2002). With respect to issues of farmer autonomy,
archaeologists now know that the recent *floodplain-based* syntheses, written at the end of the FAI-270 highway project, unintentionally omitted a
significant component of the regional population (Pauketat 2002). The
new evidence from the Richland villages indicates relatively unambigu-
ously that the floodplain farmsteads are not the archetypal rural settlement but occupied a niche somewhere between Cahokia and the upland
village (cf. Smith 1995). This is easily demonstrated by the regional distribution of Cahokia's finery, exotic raw materials, and restricted-access
woods and plants (see Fig. 5.3). The higher concentrations of peoples in

the Richland villages have comparatively few such items that presumably were redistributed from the central floodplain administrators, probably via upland towns or outposts, such as the Grossmann site (Alt 2003). Thus, a centralized-redistributive economy is apparent in the greater Cahokia region once we enlarge our field of vision to include the outer tier of rural upland sites.

Still, identifying an economic pattern is a long way from an explanation of what happened in the Mississippi valley. An economy, after all, is a composite description of the materiality, spatiality, and corporeality of the lived experiences and cultural practices of people (Pauketat 2003a). Understanding the greater Cahokia economy necessarily means seeing such things as the sub-Mound 51 feasting refuse, the death rituals of Mound 72, or the resettlement of the countryside as the active, ongoing creations of Cahokians living a centralized agricultural lifestyle. To wit, the feasts at Cahokia brought together people in spaces that redefined cultural identities (Pauketat *et al.* 2002). The Lohmann phase sacrifices of women do not simply reflect an established Cahokian order; they helped create that order (Emerson and Pauketat 2002). The large-scale resettlement of people *c.* AD 1050 constituted a new pluralism and quite possibly a new hierarchical solidarity to the regional culture of greater Cahokia (Pauketat 2003b).

In all of these ways, Cahokians politicized or co-opted the pre-Mississippian sense of community. That sense of community was probably inseparable from cosmological principles of agricultural fertility and became a metaphor for polity, possibly making the abrupt political consolidation both more palatable and unavoidable (Emerson 1989, 1997a, 1997c; Emerson and Pauketat 2002; Pauketat 2000a, 2000b). Thus, one could call Cahokia a "communal" and "heterarchical" society at the same time that one calls it "hegemonic" and "hierarchical" (Pauketat and Emerson 1999).

At the opposite end of the settlement hierarchy from the upland rural settlements is the sprawling central political-administrative complex, so large as to necessitate a Lohmann and early Stirling phase regional economy with the funds and labor sufficient to level huge plazas, fill in extensive low areas, and build or rebuild the many earthen pyramids, numerous large pole-and-thatch buildings, huge marker posts, woodhenge, compound walls, etc., dating to that period. Like the Richland villages, the central political-administrative sprawl seems internally differentiated and suggestive of substantial heterarchical complexity. Various social units represented by pyramid-and-plaza groups at the Cahokia, East St. Louis, and St. Louis sites may have been ranked or unranked one to another. The "group-oriented" Cahokian mortuaries of the ridge-top mounds are the probable remains of these high-ranking "corporate" groups; their mortuaries are profoundly different from the ordinary cemeteries of farmers and possibly unique to greater Cahokia (Emerson et al. 2003).

Perhaps each of the pyramid-and-plaza groups within the big three sites of the central political-administrative complex was home to families or the scene of ritual performances or social functions not found or conducted at the others. Possibly, the ridge-top mounds at Cahokia, East St. Louis, St. Louis, and Mitchell were exclusive family or lineage facilities. However, given that Cahokia was contemporaneous with East St. Louis, and probably St. Louis, these sites and their ridge-top mounds can hardly be viewed as evidence of politically autonomous centers. Instead, they strongly suggest heterarchical segmentation at the top that, ultimately, may have laid the foundations for the factionalism of the twelfth century. Melvin Fowler (1999:188–9) captures this sense of heterarchical complexity in his summary of the Mound 72 burials:

Who were these people? They were leaders of a segment of Cahokian society. Because of their power and status they were buried in splendor ... [and] commemorated for a few generations by the addition of more interments.
Many interpret the buildup of early Mississippian Cahokia as having been rapid. I have heard it suggested that there was probably one great leader who brought this about. Since Mound 72 is the only burial mound that has been carefully excavated at Cahokia, speculation has suggested that the individual buried on the raptor-shaped platform of beads (Burial 13) *was* that great leader. I think not. He, and his associated burials, were powerful early Mississippian chiefs, but, they were probably leaders of only one of the many communities that made up early Cahokia ... Early Cahokia was probably made up of groups of chiefdoms whose headquarters were at Cahokia but whose power and wealth lay, perhaps, in the hinterlands in the American Bottom and beyond. It was the binding of these chiefdoms into a single political entity dominated by Monks Mound, and the leader headquartered there, that made Cahokia the center of the four quarters of the universe in its time.

The heterarchical complexity of the central political-administrative complex is most atypical of other, later Mississippian domains. It is also unusual compared to other world civilizations. Few ceremonial centers, early cities, or political capitals covered as large an area as the American Bottom's central political-administrative complex. Consider that the Cahokia site alone – at 8 km^2 – is as large or larger than any number of Old World city-states and New World centers from formative periods. Moreover, depending on how one draws the boundaries, the central political-administrative complex is considerably larger than 8 km^2.

Consider also that the initial phases of central Mexican cities had populations ranging from 5000 people (at Monte Albán) to upwards of 20,000 (at Cuilcuilco and Teotihuacan, see Blanton et al. 1993:73, 115;

1999:89–92). Many Uruk period city-states in Mesopotamia, early Harappan polities, Shang period cities in China, or Andean capitals in Peru had central populations ranging from several thousand to 30,000 or so people (see Pollock 1999; papers in Nichols and Charlton 1997). Also like Cahokia, some of the largest and most impressive monuments were built during the coalescent or founding phases of such civilizations, marking the rise of new orders (Blanton *et al.* 1996; Trigger 1990). More than expressions of domination, these constructions were themselves "negotiations" that generated an *esprit de corps* among the builders (Pauketat 2000b). At some of these, there are burials of founding figures, rulers, and sacrificial victims not unlike Mound 72 and the ridge-top tombs of greater Cahokia.

Do these similarities mean that Cahokia was a state? Some people have always thought so. Others have spent their careers vehemently denying it. Some have imagined the northern intrusions to be the consequences of Cahokian economic control in the upper Midwest; others refuse even to consider the proposition. It seems that both sides believe that statehood automatically means a strongly centralized political power, class stratification, opulent royal burials, craft specialization, a standing army, long-distance trade, and the extraction of tribute from a vast hinterland. Some like that idea, others do not (contrast O'Brien 1991 and Muller 1987). But drawing lines between chiefdoms, states, or any other kind of society unnecessarily reifies governments as uniform institutions the world over. In addition, it overstates the historical importance of institutions and ruling elites as if they – and no one else – had the power to make history. But we must keep in mind that the cross-cultural generalizations about governments – that chiefdoms are politically unstable and "cycle" or that state-level bureaucracies involve stable four- and five-tiered settlement hierarchies, etc. – are in the end only generalizations. They are not explanations of the historical diversity that actually exists in the real world (see Anderson 1994a, 1994b; Feinman and Marcus 1998; Wright 1984).

Rethinking state-making and pan-regional culture

Creative reconsiderations of complexity from contemporary historically oriented perspectives recognize that the diversity of early cities, the divergent histories of places, the migrations of peoples, and the complexities of identity, plurality, and heterarchy are not merely epiphenomenal. More recent theories of complex societies pay more attention to the histories of cultural constructions, which go a long way toward elucidating civilizations as political cultures or as great traditions (see chapter 1).

They share a growing recognition that people make their own history and continuously construct and imagine the institutions and governments thought by others, wrongly, to determine history.

Marshall Sahlins (1985) has said that the *chief makes the state*. In actuality, of course, it was the particular syncretic mix of cooperating, collaborating, accommodating, and resisting people, practices, and representations that made states. This is all the more reason to understand "the state" as a cultural hegemony – not as an absolute exploitative structure – that co-opts to some extent the experiences and lived traditions of people and articulates the ancient and invented traditions under a single umbrella (e.g., Kus and Raharijaona 2001; Pauketat 1994). Considering political formation in such terms allows for considerably more variability in the kinds and degrees of governance and statecraft than some older models of chiefdoms and states permit (see Yoffee 1993). It is consistent with the growing recognition of cross-cultural variability and historically unique pathways of various polities (Blanton *et al.* 1996; Brumfiel 1994, 1995). It is also consistent with a sense that culture contact, migration, diaspora, and identity formation are more fundamental processes in the development of complex societies than is the evolution of political institutions (Pauketat 2001a, 2001b). There may be many kinds of polities and forms of government, contingent on historical specificities (rather than the specificities being contingent on a uniform type of political institution). There may be any number of developmental trajectories and historical consequences of the rise and demise of polities that should not be expected to follow a progressive outline.

In the end, a pre-Columbian city if not a novel kind of American Indian polity is not outside the realm of the possible. Given the scale and genesis of early Cahokia's central political-adminstrative complex, and given that the regional population appears at once stratified, corporate, and heterarchical, it seems useful to rethink the coming together of the many pyramid-and-plaza subcommunities, if not the resettled farmers, in terms of a singular episode of pre-Columbian *state-making*. This is not to say that Cahokia was a state in the typical sense of that word (e.g., Feinman and Marcus 1998). Perhaps Cahokians would have built a territorial state if they had invented writing or extended their territory through conquest warfare (see Box 12). But Cahokia coalesced when social classes were either non-existent or underdeveloped. As a result, Cahokians and their collaborators appear to have overstated the new order through dramatic public-works projects, giant feasts, and impressive death rites. Cahokians were, quite clearly, actively stratifying the regional or pan-regional population from the beginning. The Mound 72 sacrifices of women with their distinctive corn-rich diets contrast with the modest rural cemeteries

---

Box 12. Why was writing not invented? In other parts of the world, the invention of writing appears to accompany the rise of complex administrative bureaucracies or the conquest state (e.g., Pollock 1999:149–72). In Formative Mesoamerica, some of the first written inscriptions involve commemorations of particular conquests (see Hassig 1992; Spencer 1982). The "proto-writing" of the Moche in Peru seems based in an iconography that was "functioning at different levels of the social hierarchy in different ways. Different individuals or classes of individuals in Moche society had differing levels of pictorial literacy. For the general populace, the images seem to have been locked firmly into oral traditions directly tying the overall production of cultural memory to mnemonic visualization, pictorial cueing, and patterns of rhetoric occasioned by important events and accompanied by the circulation of ideologically invested artwork. For religious specialists, the images were polyvalent... comprising an iconic, semasiographic system," which is to say the "notational forms that use marks to convey meaning in a non-verbally tied manner" (Jackson 2002:107).

Cahokian iconography had perhaps taken the first step toward a proto-writing, having settled on a "partitive" iconography – a series of discrete motifs extricable from other design contexts (DeBoer 1991) – such as the forked eye, Braden style head, the ogee, etc. that become part of the Southeastern Ceremonial Complexes. It is noteworthy that the Natchez were recorded to carve the "hieroglyphic sign of the nation that declares war" on a bark marker "near one of their villages," reminiscent of Mesoamerican place glyphs on conquest memorials (Wesler 2001:131, citing Du Pratz 1975:373–4). However, the sociopolitical landscape before AD 1600 or so was probably not nearly urban enough to engender the increased reliance on a hieroglyphic notational system for record-keeping purposes. Had the Mississippians continued on their own for a few more centuries, the pre-contact pattern of endemic warfare, migration, and increased social stratification, and the militarization of Southern Cult symbolism, might have seen the rise of a Mesoamerican-style writing system.

---

and point to a stratification of social groups and genders (Emerson *et al.* 2003a; Hargrave and Hedman 2001). The Tract 15A residential neighborhood may point to an intra-subcommunity stratification of ordinary domestic houses as well. The floodplain farmsteads and the upland Richland complex seem to point to similar emergent stratification at a regional scale.

One might think of early Cahokian state-making in the sense that I intend as a "confederation" of different cultural groups, village identities, or ethnic entities. Certainly, some confederacies are difficult to distinguish from states, as evident in a recent discussion of the pre-Incan Tiwanaku "state" in Peru (Goldstein 2000). A similar state-like confederation emerged during the early twentieth century among the Swat Pathans in northeastern Pakistan, albeit brought about by the British. The Swat formed a state from a confederation of formerly acephalous tribal segments through strategic alliances and chance events that saw a number of politicized kin-based factions come together to elect one man as ruler (Barth 1968:127–8).

Such rulers are seldom mere despots. Among the Moche of Peru, for instance, rulers co-opted the religious powers of shamans, presumably giving them added legitimacy (Bawden 1996). Likewise, the first king of the early eighteenth-century Merina state in Madagascar could not merely impose his will. State formation there was characterized by a pervasive co-optation of traditional domestic, communal, mortuary, and linguistic practices, making the performance of traditional practices unthinkable outside the state (see Kus 1983; Kus and Raharigaona 2001).

For Cahokia, more refined measures of the rate and scale of regional resettlement at AD 1050, especially as this may relate to the identity of the executed women in Mound 72, ultimately will provide the definitive measure of governance and economic centrality. Rapid and large-scale resettlement of both central neighborhoods and rural districts would bespeak top-down Cahokian state-making. A more gradual drawn-out resettlement would argue for a more decentered confederation process. At the moment, the evidence suggests something in between (Pauketat 2003b).

Additional clarity relative to the problem of Cahokia's governance and centrality is available in the evidence of Cahokia's "civilizing" effects in the northern and southern portions of the Mississippi valley. There is ample evidence of many intermittent encounters of Cahokians or their intermediaries with others across the mid-continent. Cahokia probably was the site of pilgrimage as well. Yet it seems that the numbers of possible Cahokian pots and lithic artifacts in certain northern contexts (e.g., the Trempealeau region) surpass what a few northern pilgrims could have carried home. Instead, there seems substantial evidence of a network of politicos tied to each other and to Cahokia via the insignia of the Long-Nosed God. Given the additional accouterments found along with the ear ornaments – Cahokian arrowheads, shell beads, flintclay figurines, chunkey stones, and Ramey Incised, Powell Plain, and Monks Mound Red pots – I suggest that the network was established via a possible cult of Red Horn and the associated adoption ceremony (following Hall 1991, 2000; see also Emerson 2002). Such a suite of objects does argue for an integrated cultural phenomenon rather than undirected diffusion. Might it also argue that founding members of northern villages and southern centers were Cahokians or their fictive kin, and that these men and women were laid to rest in the log-lined tombs of Kincaid, Hoecake, and Shiloh, as in the ridge-top mortuary chambers of greater Cahokia?

That is, *Cahokians may be said directly or indirectly to have caused Mississippianism.* At a minimum, data from a range of sites suggest some important and direct contacts between Cahokians, Cahokian intermediaries, and northern Woodland peoples (Stoltman 1991, 2000). There was probably a Cahokian presence at a number of late eleventh- and early twelfth-century settlements in Wisconsin, eastern Iowa, and central and northern Illinois. Some of the Cahokians may have been emissaries, traders, or factional refugees. Some of them may also have become the marriage partners of northerners, giving northern families direct access to Cahokian culinary practices, pottery technologies, agricultural knowledge, and bloodlines.

There were also other Mississippianized peoples, if not other Mississippian movements, that had profound historical effects to the far north and distant south. Whether direct or indirect and Cahokian or other Mississippian, these phenomena demand an explanation of the question of why local people would involve themselves in some larger pan-regional movement(s) or organizing force(s). The answer may lie in the novelty and perceived supernatural power behind Mississippian places, particularly Cahokia and its people. It may also lie in the very real threat of Cahokia and any number of northern organized war parties, perhaps realized in the social disruptions, migrations, and conflagrations to the north. Some may have resisted or avoided the expanding terminal Late Woodland–Cahokian–Mississippian alliance network in the late eleventh century. Yet the evidence of migrations and the anecdotal evidence of violence suggest that all northern terminal Late Woodland people were affected in some way.

Summary

Archaeological evidence and the oral history of Siouan-speaking peoples seem to converge in ways "too close ... to dismiss" (Salzer and Rajnovich 2000:65–6), and the evidence for historical processes at the scale of the village, the cultural region, and the Mississippian ethnoscape is strong, and growing stronger. That evidence suggests that the formation of

Cahokia was unique, different from everything that preceded or followed it. Its peculiar combination of communal, heterarchical, and temple-fertility themes hint that the Cahokian phenomenon – if not the entire Mississippian experience – was contingent on pan-regional migrations, the attendant plurality and hybridity of populations, and the invention of new traditions by a host of people (Pauketat 2003b).

The greater Cahokian phenomenon may have been but the first of a series of political-religious movements that produced the well-known Mississippian places, but it *was* the first, the founding center perhaps commemorated in ways we are only beginning to understand. It is arguable that Cahokians in the late eleventh and early twelfth centuries were engaged in state-making even if they did not realize a full-fledged territorial state. State-making can happen in various contexts ranging from so-called confederacies to complex chiefdoms. Such a process probably would have been centered on a historical figure or figures. Quite possibly at the center of the Cahokian political-religious happening, if not also at those of later Southern Cults, was the legend of Red Horn and sons, embodied by the dual interments in Mound 72's Lohmann phase beaded burial, along with the other men and women sacrificed and buried with the other accouterments of the legend: arrows, gaming stones and copper rods, shell beads, and falcon imagery. But such a movement, whoever the personage or personages at the heart of it, was created by many collaborators and at many sites of cultural production, engendering a diverse and dynamic cultural landscape.

The order of Cahokia and its cult-like effects made it a pan-regional cultural force. Cahokia may have been an incipient urban place, the only such city in the eastern Woodlands, with spiritual power and cultural draw that was difficult to resist. Those who did might have found themselves on the losing side of a new set of alliances articulated by Cahokians. Cahokian war parties, or those of intermediaries, probably flexed their muscles from time to time, if only to keep the peace and ensure the order of *pax Cahokiana*. Common to chiefdoms and states around the world, however, was the hiving off of various claimants to offices, rival families, or dissatisfied kin groups who might easily set themselves up as the equivalents of "stranger-kings" in distant lands. They were autonomous, yes, but allied to the Cahokians or to the idea of Cahokia. The kin-based alliances, fictive or real, were sealed by the ritual adoption of people through the Long-Nosed God ceremonies.

Later phases – perhaps even more critical to the dissemination of Mississippianism – were characterized as much by political disintegration. With the factionalizing, emigrations, and eventual break-up of Cahokia, other competing polities carved up the Ohio–Mississippi confluence region into smaller territories. They recast the themes of the earlier Mississippians, emphasizing warrior imagery, and generating an elite stratum of warrior chiefs across the Midsouth. Competitive emulation and attempts to reclaim the Mississippian heritage of earlier years led to memorials that recalled what had never really existed at places such as Spiro. Thus, it seems that Mississippian civilization was in this way both real and imagined.

Real or imagined, the true measure of a civilization may be the extent to which it shaped subsequent historical developments. To wit, at contact, Mississippian populations occupied the entire eastern seaboard, the southern Coastal Plain, the Midsouth below Memphis, and the upper Midwest north of greater Cahokia. The facts of European contact help explain why the Mississippians did not develop anything else that compared to early Cahokia.

But there were environmental constraints as well that played into the hand that history dealt American Indians. To some extent, the ample precipitation did not force Mississippian agriculturalists to invest in the construction and management of irrigation systems in ways that might have further developed political administrations into bureaucracies. Likewise, only single crops could be produced during any one year, unlike the warmer year-round climates in portions of Mexico where two crops may be produced annually.

That is, surplus production had limits in the American mid-continent, requiring extensification more than intensification. Perhaps extensification of production is precisely what we see in greater Cahokia: the inner floodplain farmsteads seem counterbalanced by an outer tier of upland villages. If correct, we should consider that with extensification comes a high administrative cost. Cahokians may have been unable effectively to manage distant fields and farmers, perhaps leading to the growth of autonomous communities or political factions and emigrations that brought about the downfall of a central political regime. The end of the Medieval Warm Period could only have added fuel to the internal decentralizing forces of the larger Mississippian economies.

Clearly, after waves of infectious disease decimated particular polities and regions on the heels of the Hernando de Soto *entrada* and the other exploratory parties that followed, what remained of the Mississippians were peoples who regrouped into confederacies of towns, ultimately giving birth to the "civilized" southeastern tribes. Viable populations remained in pockets across the eastern United States, unintentionally configured either to inhibit or to enable European colonization. The Caddo controlled much of the commerce between interior Indian groups and the Spanish presidios and missions. The Powhatan held the Chesapeake and intervened at a critical juncture in the lives of Jamestown residents, adding their own sense of republican governance to the ideas of the founding fathers. The Creek confederacy held key portions of the Deep South and, along with other resistant Indian nations, shaped the policies and possibilities of the European powers and the young United States. The powerful Osage, for a time, blocked the expansion of Jefferson's America.

The future of the Mississippian past

The rest, as they say, is history. Unfortunately, that history was biased. Worse, those historical biases – the minimization of the significance of American Indian accomplishments – continue to influence the thinking of new generations of citizens, sometimes simply by omissions of fact. For instance, only since the 1980s have the Mississippians been included among the world civilizations and recognized in high school and college level textbooks. Previously, they received no mention. So today many laypersons and policy-makers alike remain ignorant of the names and significance of places such as Cahokia, Aztalan, Toltec, Kincaid, Obion, or Trempealeau. The Shiloh site is known as a National Military Park, but few realize the site was sacred long before North and South spilled blood there.

This ignorance of the North American past is a legacy of the European conquest of North America, aided by the enduring effects of the Moundbuilder Myth. The effects are not simply negligible, but have led to a tradition of obliterating both archaeological and historical sites that is still alive today in the eastern United States. Henry Brackenridge (1818) was at a loss to explain to Thomas Jefferson why his St. Louis newspaper account of the nearby great mounds attracted no attention! The members of the Stephen Long expedition delayed in St. Louis, mapping the St. Louis mounds and also attempting to dispel a misguided newspaper account of a race of pygmy Moundbuilders (Pool 1989:8).

But the enlightened few were not able to save the Big Mound, Cemetery Mound, and Powell Mound from destruction in the nineteenth and early twentieth centuries. Instead, Warren Moorehead encountered deeply in-grained local and state resistance, and even had to argue against the opinions of professional geologists, to get the State of Illinois to purchase the central precinct of Cahokia. The Euroamerican citizens of the ex-panding mercantile, then industrial, and now service-oriented economies have viewed and still view pre-Columbian settlements, cemeteries, and mounds as a curious nuisance.

There have been problems with looting, graves dug into, rock art sawed apart, and even refuse pits mined for their artifacts. However, the real

8.1 The modern threat: belly-scraper moving earth near the Grossmann site, St. Clair County, Illinois (2002)

destruction continues in the name of progress and development. In recent years, whole Mississippian village sites have been bladed away in an afternoon by the armies of trucks that lay the groundwork for shopping malls, condominiums, subdivisions, department stores, and parking lots (Fig. 8.1). The sandy ridge beneath one residential portion of outer Cahokia was mined for sand and the site was simply sucked away, even as the owner in 1995 denied archaeologists a chance to investigate it properly at no cost to himself. A realty company subdividing an upland farm field and building single-family homes illegally bulldozed away a large reported Mississippian site in 2003.

"They're f_ing dead!" yelled one subdivision contractor as I prevented him from digging away a Mississippian cemetery with a backhoe. "Who cares?!"

His question should prompt us to consider carefully what can be done about the accelerating destruction of archaeological sites. Quite apparently, the archaeology of American Indians does not matter to many transplanted and alienated wage-earners and petty capitalists who did not bury *their* dead in the unmarked cemeteries and settlements of the past. Unfortunately, the lived traditions of many people in the mid-continent today are not only ethnocentric; they are actively anti-historical and anti-preservationist. Pre-Columbian history is at best natural science to them and, at worst, something to be "cleansed" from the landscape. More than one archaeologist has been asked to "clean" a site to make way for development. Unscrupulous archaeological contractors have built businesses by being efficient site cleaners.

In the mid-continent and Midsouth, history cleansing occurs through the total modification of the landscape. The new ethnocentric version of history is inscribed directly into the landscape with bulldozers, belly-scrapers, and dump trucks. The past is merely an obstacle to the future. It is a history of expanding markets and capital developments created by grading away the natural contours, Indian mounds, and ancient habitation sites of ages past.

The worst cases of such a cleansing of history by the powers of capital originate in the Mississippi Alluvial Valley in southeast Missouri and northeast Arkansas. There, "land-levelers" are used to reduce the subtle topography of ridges and swales to perfectly flat rice fields that can be flooded by tapping into the ancient waters of deep aquifers (see Morse and Morse 1983). There, hundreds of square kilometers – entire rural counties – have been flattened, completely erasing the remains of houses and pits on the high ridges and dragging the scrapings and scattered artifacts and bones into shallow depressions, all to feed a global rice market. Entire Mississippian towns and outlying farmsteads have been expunged off the face of the earth by land-levelers and heavy machinery (Fig. 8.1).

From certain minimalist or environment-heavy perspectives, one Mississippian polity is pretty much like the next. The loss of a few sites – even a few polities – may seem no big deal to them; there were always more Mississippian houses, potsherds, and mounds somewhere else, and these archaeologists are usually content with a few small samples of supposedly representative artifact assemblages. This is most unfortunate. From cultural-historical vantagepoints, and especially from the newer historical-processual perspectives of cultural construction, each settlement holds critical historical information about the variability, intra-polity plurality, and social history of the real people of the past. Losing one of them is an insult to history. It has been compared repeatedly and justifiably to ripping chapters out of history books. To extend the analogy, the destruction of the monuments, cemeteries, and settlements of entire polities is nothing less than book burning.

There is hope, if archaeologists keep pace with destruction and address the education of a dubious public and the voices of an ignored people. To do this requires an archaeological ethic of the sort advocated by William Nickerson and embodied in the salvage archaeology of Charles Bareis, Lawrence Conrad, Warren Wittry, and others. It requires the kind of enthusiasm of the Civil War veterans who began the intensified surveys of the Mississippi valley, the emphasis on systematic digging seen in the

8.2 Cahokia's Braden-style falcon dancer design on an Interstate 255 overpass, St. Clair County, Illinois

Chicago Method and the New Deal archaeology, and the logistical organization and publication track-record of the FAI-270 Highway Mitigation Project admired by James B. Griffin, and today carried on through the "Transportation Archaeology" of Thomas Emerson and John Walthall in Illinois (Walthall *et al.* 1997). It requires an expansion of the cooperative networks of researchers and First Nations peoples who will together preserve the landscapes of the past and pay homage to the peoples whose distant histories remain active constituents of the contemporary world.

The "greatest puzzle of this continent" remains to be pieced together. We must piece it together, and inscribe the landscape with a new history of the past (Fig. 8.2).

Notes

1. Upon first setting eyes on Cahokia with a group of archaeologists in 1984 or 1985, Robert Carneiro is said to have made such an exclamation. However, his recollection is not clear, and today he remains uncertain whether he thinks Cahokia was or was not the center of an actual kingdom. "But there's no doubt it was big and elaborate. It could easily have been a state. And if it was a state, and the state had a ruler, as in all likelihood it did, then he could have legitimately been called a king, and his domain, therefore, a kingdom." Yet he adds, Cahokia may turn out "not to have been a kingdom after all" (R. Carneiro, personal communication, June 2003).

2. The idea of a "Middle Mississippi" cultural tradition, where "Middle" refers to the geographic center of the valley, sprang from the early pottery analysis of William Henry Holmes (1903), and has usually been used in a geographical sense to isolate those peoples with a set of "classic" traits – shell-tempered pottery, platform mounds, wall trench houses, and warrior/ancestor symbol sets (Griffin 1967; Knight 1986; cf. Morse and Morse 1983; Muller 1997). Sometimes Middle Mississippian is also used as a temporal construct to refer to the middle of the Mississippian period (AD 1200–1400).

3. The regional chronology presented here is based on Hall's (1991) radiocarbon calibrations (see also Pauketat 1994 and Pauketat and Emerson 1997). Obviously, the phases are rough approximations of real time, but the fifty-to seventy-five-year durations are consistent with the number of times houses were rebuilt or repaired at continuously occupied sites (Pauketat 2003b).

4. A subsequent "Sand Prairie" phase at Cahokia is barely recognizable on the ground, owing to the low population density and the abandonment of Cahokia as a seat of government, and has no significance as a pan-regional chronological construct.

5. An earlier map exists of the northern American Bottom showing the mounds of St. Louis, Pulcher, and a combined East St. Louis–Cahokia group, apparently dating to 1816. It has been attributed to the Stephen Long expedition by Milner (1998:fig. 1.1), although Long arrived in St. Louis three years later.

6. I am indebted here to Phillip Millhouse and Tom Emerson, ardent admirers of Nickerson. It is unclear to what extent Nickerson learned techniques from his time at the Peabody Museum or innovated techniques later borrowed and incorporated into the "Chicago method" (elsewhere also credited to Samuel Barrett at the Aztalan site in Wisconsin by Muller [1986:15]).

7. To jump into the controversies, compare Pauketat 1998b with Milner 1998, Emerson 1997a with Mehrer 2000, or Pauketat 1997b and Yerkes 1991 with Muller 1997. See also the differential emphasis placed on trade by Emerson and Hughes 2000 versus Kelly 1991a, 1991b, or the historical importance of Cahokia advocated by Anderson 1997 or Stoltman 2000 versus Milner 1998. Not all of the respective positions of these archaeologists remain controversial. To the extent that some do, the debate often boils down to semantic differences or a failure to take into account all of the archaeological evidence.

8. Under modern conditions, with chemical fertilizers, pesticides, and herbicides, the upland prairie loams (Tama, Virden, Muscatine) in the greater Cahokia region produce 3–12 percent more corn per unit farmland than the best floodplain loams (Beaucoup), 26–33 percent more than the most friable floodplain fine sandy loams (Landes) and about 5–16 percent more than upland forest soils (Alford, Iva, Fayette), using average corn yields provided by Olsen et al. (2000). On a modern corn-yield map of Illinois, there are two high-productivity (>75 bushels/acre) zones in the uplands of St. Clair County that correspond with the large villages of the Richland complex (see Ollendorf 1993:fig. 3.2; and see chapter 5).

9. A possible note may be helpful here concerning an earlier short-lived social experiment known from the "Weeden Island" culture area of northwestern Florida at around AD 400. No unambiguous evidence of ascribed social ranking exists. However, Milanich et al. (1984) document the planned construction of a modest mound center, arranged to reference the rising summer solstice sun, and the elaborate mortuary rites seemingly managed by a shaman-like person at the McKeithen site. This person's death heralded the ritual closure of a mound-top building and the abandonment of the site.

10. See also the "corporate" polities reviewed by Blanton et al. (1996) and the heterarchical or factionalized governments referenced by Brumfiel (1994, 1995).

11. Wagner's summary did not include the sub-Mound 51 data and the wealth of tobacco evidence from a ritual feasting pit in the middle of Cahokia (Pauketat et al. 2002).

12. The regional distributional pattern is a bit more complex: upland Richland communities of farmers did keep chunkey stones, some of which look to be the classic Cahokia varieties. These were not buried with people but left in the village. Of course, Adair noted that at contact in the lower Mississippi valley chunkey stones were "exempt from being buried with the dead." In eleventh- and twelfth-century greater Cahokia, chunkeys are known from burials only with the groups of Cahokian elite in their ridge-top mounds (Mound 72, Rattlesnake Mound, Wilson Mound).

13. Cahokia had been thought by James Porter (1974) to be a northern link in a "chain" of pre-Mississippian mound centers spaced every 20 to 30 km up the Jackson, Bois Brule, and American Bottoms from Thebes Gap (see also Milner 1990, 1998). The chain-settlement idea remains unverified by excavations, although the Cahokia, the Pulcher, and possibly the tiny two-mound Morrison sites may have been pre-Mississippian centers at AD 1000 surrounded by smaller sedentary settlements. Other sites in the hypothetical

pre-Mississippian settlement chain may actually post-date AD 1050. These were probably subordinate to Cahokia to varying degrees and in different ways.

14. An interesting bias has emerged against Mississippian tributary-economic models, most commonly proffered to explain the Moundville polity in Alabama (e.g., Steponaitis 1978; Welch 1991). For some, tribute implies "political complexity" and is presumably eschewed for that reason (L. Kelly 2000; Milner 1998; Muller 1997). Lucretia Kelly (2000:247–8) has summarized one argument as follows: "Milner (1998) estimated the human population density for the American Bottom and calculated the contribution that deer may have made to the diet. He concludes that the deer population would have been almost decimated or much reduced" as a result and, "evoking the schlep effect, he concludes that only the meatiest portions would be brought back" by Cahokian hunters. She continues: "Milner may not be fully aware of the faunal data from the Emergent Mississippian, which may be the reason he does not account for the dramatic increase in the proportion of deer remains at Cahokia in the early Mississippian." However, not wishing to support what she calls the "domination model," Kelly states that "other provisioning mechanisms such as ritual feasting" are preferred over "any kind of formalized tribute/taxation system." Of course, the difference is in part a semantic one, and Kelly overly dichotomizes the contrasts. After all, the provisions brought to "ritual feasts" would clearly qualify as tribute for some analysts. The difference is also one of perception – when does a gift become tribute? – much like it probably was for Cahokians themselves. Since a writing system had not been developed, we are unable to read the accounts of scribes and record-keepers, as possible among early states in other parts of the world.

15. For instance, bird-man, feather, serpentine, and barred eye or "ogee" motifs appear for the first time incised on potsherds thought to have been used in religious rites or by (male?) shamans during the Lohmann phase (Emerson 1989; Wilson 1996). Spider webs and sun symbols appear on spindle whorls at Cahokia, perhaps more frequently used by women.

16. The contexts of hoe blade finds give us additional reason to suspect centralized redistribution of hoe blades. The large cache of hoe blades at East St. Louis points in this direction, but so may smaller caches that may not be evenly distributed across the rural landscape. More importantly, Alt (2003) has documented the association of hoe blade offerings with ritual temple refuse at the Grossmann site. These whole hoe blades were burned along with bags of maize kernels, roof thatch, quartz crystals, Burlington chert cores, pots, and a Cahokian flintclay figurine. This refuse is similar to several other special refuse deposits that Emerson (1997a, 1997c) has called "Green Corn Ceremonial" pits.

17. Brad Koldehoff (personal communication, 2002) suggests that the raw material for many of the Cahokia chunkey stones is Yankeetown Orthoquartzite, which outcrops in southwestern Illinois.

18. Of course, northern galena was not as common at Cahokia as was galena from the Ozarks (Walthall 1981), and copper was scarce. Thus, doubt about the *economic* importance of the north to Cahokians is justified (see Emerson 2002;

Milner 1990, 1998; Pauketat and Emerson 1997; Pauketat 1998b). Indeed, Emerson (1999) and Henning (2001) wonder if the scarcity of northern goods at Cahokia may mean that various northern peoples were *not* on good terms with Cahokians.

19. Aztalan may be an ideal case study in the power of controlling "the gaze" (*sensu* Said 1978). Not only can one see the entirety of the settlement only from the platform mounds, the site itself is not visible from the west until one walks to within a few hundred meters of the palisade wall.

20. Neither did Rome directly cause the pervasive warfare along its northern imperial frontier.

21. Prominent Cahokian researchers from the 1960s through the 1990s were trained at Beloit College and at the University of Wisconsin campuses of Madison and Milwaukee, imparting a northern Midwestern outlook on excavation inherited from William Nickerson, the University of Chicago, and the Smithsonian Institution's River Basin survey in the Great Plains, and based on the experiences of archaeologists at the Cahokia, Mitchell, Knoebel, and Orendorf sites, among others. In and around the American Bottom, an ideology of complete site excavation took hold with the FAI-270 project (Bareis and Porter 1984; Walthall *et al.* 1997). That ideology unfortunately does not characterize many Midsouthern and southeastern Mississippianists, with few exceptions.

22. The Duffy and Yankeetown pottery, local to the lower Ohio drainage, at Kincaid also appears as "exotic" wares in greater Cahokia, and may signal additional contacts between the two peoples.

23. Wittry (1977) considered at least one of the woodhenge constructions to have been an astronomical observatory. Unfortunately, the alignments of this one example are not possible with any of the other subsequent constructions, casting some doubt on this interpretation (Pauketat 1996). Recently, Melvin Fowler (1999) has postulated that a similar woodhenge may have been located in the Mound 72 area.

24. Milner's (1998:91) aspersions to the contrary notwithstanding, the argument by myself and Thomas Emerson that Ramey Incised was probably centrally made for redistribution is supported by a growing body of Stirling phase pottery assemblages (i.e., including recent early Stirling phase Richland complex data and excluding Moorehead phase containers for which insufficient regional data are available).

25. Ross Hassig, on the basis of his familiarity with Old and New World warfare, has repeatedly pointed out to me that palisade walls are not passive structures for defense only. Instead, they represent a potential offensive threat that may necessitate the construction of walls around each respective enemy's home. The theory is that a wall permits one's military force to strike at an enemy with maximum manpower, leaving only a minimum of defenders to guard their town. This is particularly true of a palisade with bastions, from which a small force of archers could prevent an enemy from breaching the wall.

26. This proved confusing to Thomas Jefferson, William Clark, and a host of Anglo-American agents who assumed that there was one chief, not two (see Rollings 1992).

27. The "rituality" explanation also implies that all producers were autonomous, and suffers from chronic theoretical underdevelopment. Calling Cahokia a "ritual center that served to pull people into its orbit" is non-explanatory (cf. Kelly 2002:145). The same can be said for all political capitals in all epochs, from Uruk to Cuzco to Washington, DC! Was Cahokia more of a ritual place than these others?

References

Adair, Mary J. 2000 Tobacco on the Plains: Historical Use, Ethnographic Accounts, and Archaeological Evidence. In *Tobacco Use by Native North Americans: Sacred Smoke and Silent Killer*, edited by J. C. Winter, pp. 171–201. University of Oklahoma Press, Norman.

Adams, Robert McCormick 1941 *Archaeological Investigations in Jefferson County, Missouri 1939–1940*. Transactions of the Academy of Science of St. Louis 30 (5), St. Louis.

1949 Archaeological Investigations in Jefferson County, Missouri. *The Missouri Archaeologist* 11 (3–4) (whole volume).

Ahler, Steve A. and P. J. DePuydt 1987 *A Report on the 1931 Powell Mound Excavations, Madison County, Illinois*. Reports of Investigations, 43, Illinois State Museum, Springfield.

Alt, Susan M. 1999 Spindle Whorls and Fiber Production at Early Cahokian Settlements. *Southeastern Archaeology* 18:124–33.

2001 Cahokian Change and the Authority of Tradition. In *The Archaeology of Traditions: Agency and History before and after Columbus*, edited by T. R. Pauketat, pp. 141–56. University Press of Florida, Gainesville.

2002 The Knoebel Site: Tradition and Change in the Cahokian Suburbs. Unpublished Masters thesis, Department of Anthropology, University of Illinois, Urbana.

2003 More than Mounds: Mississippian Ritual in the Cahokian Uplands. Paper presented at the 68th Annual Meeting of the Society for American Archaeology, April 9–13, Milwaukee, Wisconsin.

Alvord, Clarence W. 1965 [1922] *The Illinois Country 1673–1818*. Loyola University Press, Chicago.

Ambrose, Stanley H., Jane Buikstra, and Harold W. Kruger 2001 Gender and Status Differences in Diet at Mound 72, Cahokia, Revealed by Isotopic Analysis of Bone. Paper presented at the 66th Annual Meeting of the Society for American Archaeology, New Orleans.

Anderson, Benedict 1983 *Imagined Communities*. Verso, London.

Anderson, David G. 1994a *The Savannah River Chiefdoms: Political Change in the Late Prehistoric Southeast*. University of Alabama Press, Tuscaloosa.

1994b Factional Competition and the Political Evolution of Mississippian Chiefdoms in the Southeastern United States. In *Factional Competition in the New World*, edited by Elizabeth M. Brumfiel and John W. Fox, pp. 61–76. Cambridge University Press, Cambridge.

1997 The Role of Cahokia in the Evolution of Southeastern Mississippian Society. In *Cahokia: Domination and Ideology in the Mississippian World*, edited by T. R. Pauketat and T. E. Emerson, pp. 248–68. University of Nebraska Press, Lincoln.

2001 Climate and Culture Change in Prehistoric and Early Historic Eastern North America. *Archaeology of Eastern North America* 29:143–89.

Anderson, David G. and John E. Cornelison 2002 Excavations at Mound A, Shiloh: The 2002 Season. Paper presented at the 59th Southeastern Archaeological Conference, November 6–9, Biloxi, Mississippi.

Anderson, David G. and Robert C. Mainfort, eds. 2001 *The Woodland Southeast.* University of Alabama Press, Tuscaloosa.

Anderson, David G., David W. Tahle, and Malcolm R. Cleaveland 1995 Paleoclimate and the Potential Food Reserves of Mississippian Societies: A Case Study from the Savannah River Valley. *American Antiquity* 60:258–86.

Appadurai, Arjun 1996 *Modernity at Large: Cultural Dimensions of Globalization.* University of Minnesota Press, Minneapolis.

Bailey, Garrick A. 1995 *The Osage and the Invisible World from the Works of Francis La Flesche.* University of Oklahoma Press, Norman.

Bareis, Charles J. and James W. Porter, eds. 1984 *American Bottom Archaeology: A Summary of the FAI-270 Project Contribution to the Culture History of the Mississippi River Valley.* University of Illinois Press, Urbana.

Barker, Alex W. 2002 Myths and Monsters: Decoding Ritual Images of a Mysterious Ancient American Religion. *Archaeology* 55 (4):40–5.

Barker, Alex W., Craig E. Skinner, M. Steven Shackley, Michael D. Glascock, and J. Daniel Rogers 2002 Mesoamerican Origin for an Obsidian Scraper from the Precolumbian Southeastern United States. *American Antiquity* 67: 103–8.

Barrett, S. A. 1933 *Ancient Aztalan* (1970 reprint). Greenwood Press, Westport, Connecticut.

Barth, Fredrik 1968 [1959] *Political Leadership among Swat Pathans.* The Athlone Press, London.

Bawden, Garth 1996 *The Moche.* Blackwell, Oxford.

Bell, Amelia R. 1990 Separate People: Speaking of Creek Men and Women. *American Anthropologist* 92:332–45.

Bell, Robert E. 1958 *Guide to the Identification of Certain American Indian Projectile Points.* Special Bulletin 1 of the Oklahoma Anthropological Society, Oklahoma City.

1984a Arkansas Valley Caddoan: The Harlan Phase. In *Prehistory of Oklahoma*, edited by R. E. Bell, pp. 221–40. Academic Press, Orlando.

Bell, Robert E., ed. 1984b *Prehistory of Oklahoma.* Academic Press, Orlando.

Benn, David W. and William Green 2000 Late Woodland Cultures in Iowa. In *Late Woodland Societies: Tradition and Transformation across the Midcontinent*, edited by T. E. Emerson, D. L. McElrath, and A. C. Fortier, pp. 429–96. University of Nebraska Press, Lincoln.

Benn, David W. and Gina Powell 2002 *Data Recovery Excavations at the Terminal Late Woodland Period Union Bench Site (13DB497), Dubuque County, Iowa.* Report prepared for the Iowa Department of Transportation, Bear Creek Archaeology Inc., Cresco, Iowa.

Bennett, John 1942 W. B. Nickerson – Pioneer in Scientific Archaeology. *American Antiquity* 8:122–4.

Birmingham, Robert A. and Leslie E. Eisenberg 2000 *Indian Mounds of Wisconsin*. University of Wisconsin Press, Madison.

Blake, Leonard W. 1955 The Lambert-St. Louis Airport Site. *The Missouri Archaeologist* 17:27–39.

Blanton, Richard E., Gary M. Feinman, Stephen A. Kowalewski, and Linda M. Nicholas 1999 *Ancient Oaxaca*. Cambridge University Press, Cambridge.

Blanton, Richard E., Gary M. Feinman, Stephan A. Kowalewski, and Peter N. Peregrine 1996 A Dual-Processual Theory for the Evolution of Mesoamerican Civilization. *Current Anthropology* 37:1–31.

Blanton, Richard E., Stephen A. Kowalewski, Gary M. Feinman, and Laura M. Finstein 1993 *Ancient Mesoamerica: A Comparison of Change in Three Regions* (second edition). Cambridge University Press, Cambridge.

Boewe, Charles, ed. 2000 *John D. Clifford's Indian Antiquities*. University of Tennessee Press, Knoxville.

Booth, Don, Timothy R. Pauketat, and Andrew Fortier 2001 Competitors or Colleagues: The Archaeology of the East St. Louis Mound Group. Paper presented at the 47th Annual Midwest Archaeological Conference, October 12–14, La Crosse, Wisconsin.

Brackenridge, Henry Marie 1814 *Views of Louisiana Together with a Journal of a Voyage up the Missouri River, in 1811* (1962 edition). Quadrangle Books Inc., Chicago.

1818 On the Population and Tumuli of the Aborigines of North American. In a Letter from H. M. Brackenridge, Esq. to Thomas Jefferson – Read Oct. 1, 1813. *Transactions of the American Philosophical Society* 1 (new series):151–9. Philadelphia.

Brain, Jeffrey P. 1989 *Winterville: Late Prehistoric Culture Contact in the Lower Mississippi Valley*. Mississippi Department of Archives and History, Archaeological Report 23, Jackson.

Braun, David P. and Stephen Plog 1982 Evolution of "Tribal" Social Networks: Theory and Prehistoric North American Evidence. *American Antiquity* 47:504–626.

Brewer, W. H. 1883 Report on the Cereal Production of the United States. In *Report on the Productions of Agriculture as Returned at the Tenth Census (June 1, 1880)*. Department of the Interior, Census Office, Government Printing Office, Washington, DC.

Browman, David L. 2002 Origins of Stratigraphic Excavation in North America. In *New Perspectives on the Origins of Americanist Archaeology*, edited by D. L. Browman and S. Williams, pp. 242–64. University of Alabama Press, Tuscaloosa.

Brown, James A. 1996 *The Spiro Ceremonial Center: The Archaeology of Arkansas Valley Caddoan Culture in Eastern Oklahoma*. University of Michigan, Museum of Anthropology, Memoir 29, Ann Arbor.

Brown, James A. and John E. Kelly 2000 Cahokia and the Southeastern Ceremonial Complex. In *Mounds, Modoc, and Mesoamerica: Papers in Honor of Melvin L. Fowler*, pp. 469–510. Illinois State Museum Scientific Papers 28, Springfield.

Brown, James A., Richard A. Kerber, and Howard D. Winters 1990 Trade and the Evolution of Exchange Relations at the Beginning of the Mississippian Period. In *The Mississippian Emergence*, edited by B. D. Smith, pp. 251–80. Smithsonian Institution Press, Washington, DC.

Brumfiel, Elizabeth 1994 Factional Competition in the New World: An Introduction. In *Factional Competition in the New World*, edited by Elizabeth M. Brumfiel and John W. Fox, pp. 3–13. Cambridge University Press, Cambridge.

—— 1995 Heterarchy and the Analysis of Complex Societies: Comments. In *Heterarchy and the Analysis of Complex Societies*, edited by R. M. Ehrenreich, C. L. Crumley, and J. E. Levy, pp. 125–31. Archeological Papers of the American Anthropological Association 6. Washington, DC.

—— 1996 The Quality of Tribute Cloth: The Place of Evidence in Archaeological Argument. *American Antiquity* 61:453–62.

Bryson, R. A., D. A. Baerreis, and W. M. Wendland 1970 The Character of Late-Glacial and Post-Glacial Climatic Changes. In *Pleistocene and Recent Environments of the Central Great Plains*, edited by W. Dort, Jr. and J. K. Jones, pp. 53–74. University of Kansas Press, Lawrence.

Buchner, C. Andrew 1998 A Forked Eye Ramey Incised Jar from Mississippi County, Arkansas. *Field Notes: Newsletter of the Arkansas Archeological Society* 283:8–9.

Bunzell, Ruth 1929 *The Pueblo Potter: A Study of Creative Imagination in Primitive Art*. Columbia University Press, New York.

Butler, Brian M. 1977 Mississippian Settlement in the Black Bottom, Pope and Massac Counties, Illinois. Unpublished PhD dissertation, Southern Illinois University, Carbondale.

Chapman, Carl H. 1980 *The Archaeology of Missouri, II*. University of Missouri Press, Columbia.

Claflin, John 1991 The Shire Site: Mississippian Outpost in the Central Illinois Prairie. In *New Perspectives on Cahokia: Views from the Periphery*, edited by J. B. Stoltman, pp. 155–76. Prehistory Press, Madison, Wisconsin.

Clayton, Lawrence A., Vernon James Knight, Jr., and Edward C. Moore, eds. 1993 *The De Soto Chronicles: The Expedition of Hernando de Soto to North America in 1539–1543*. University of Alabama Press, Tuscaloosa.

Cobb, Charles R. 2000 *From Quarry to Cornfield: The Political Economy of Mississippian Hoe Production*. University of Alabama Press, Tuscaloosa.

Cobb, Charles R., and Brian M. Butler 2002 The Vacant Quarter Revisited: Late Mississippian Abandonment of the Lower Ohio Valley. *American Antiquity* 67:625–41.

Cole, Fay-Cooper, Robert Bell, John Bennett, Joseph Caldwell, Norman Emerson, Richard MacNeish, Kenneth Orr, and Roger Willis 1951 *Kincaid: A Prehistoric Illinois Metropolis*. University of Chicago Press, Chicago.

Cole, Fay-Cooper and Thorne Deuel 1937 *Rediscovering Illinois: Archaeological Explorations in and around Fulton County*. University of Chicago Press, Chicago.

Collins, James M. 1990 *The Archaeology of the Cahokia Mounds ICT-II: Site Structure*. Illinois Cultural Resources Study 10. Illinois Historic Preservation Agency, Springfield.

1997 Cahokia Settlement and Social Structures as Viewed from the ICT-II. In *Cahokia: Domination and Ideology in the Mississippian World*, edited by T. R. Pauketat and T. E. Emerson, pp. 124–40. University of Nebraska Press, Lincoln.

Collins, James M. and Dale R. Henning 1996 The Big River Phase: Emergent Mississippian Cultural Expression on Cahokia's Near Frontier, the Northeast Ozark Rim, Missouri. *Midcontinental Journal of Archaeology* 21:79–104.

Connerton, Paul 1989 *How Societies Remember*. Cambridge University Press, Cambridge.

Conrad, Lawrence A. 1989 The Southeastern Ceremonial Complex on the Northern Middle Mississippian Frontier: Late Prehistoric Politico-Religious Systems in the Central Illinois River Valley. In *The Southeastern Ceremonial Complex: Artifacts and Analysis*, edited by P. Galloway, pp. 93–113. University of Nebraska Press, Lincoln.

1991 The Middle Mississippian Cultures of the Central Illinois River Valley. In *Cahokia and the Hinterlands: Middle Mississippian Cultures of the Midwest*, edited by T. E. Emerson and R. B. Lewis, pp. 119–56. University of Illinois Press, Urbana.

Cottier, John W. 1977 An Area Archaeological Construction. *The Missouri Archaeologist* 38:49–69.

Crumley, Carole L. 1995 Heterarchy and the Analysis of Complex Societies. In *Heterarchy and the Analysis of Complex Societies*, edited by R. M. Ehrenreich, C. L. Crumley, and J. E. Levy, pp. 1–5. Archeological Papers of the American Anthropological Association 6. Washington, DC.

Culin, Stewart 1992 [1907] *Games of the North American Indians*. University of Nebraska Press, Lincoln.

Dalan, Rinita 1997 The Construction of Mississippian Cahokia. In *Cahokia: Domination and Ideology in the Mississippian World*, edited by T. R. Pauketat and T. E. Emerson, pp. 89–102. University of Nebraska Press, Lincoln.

DeBoer, Warren R. 1988 Subterranean Storage and the Organization of Surplus: The View from Eastern North America. *Southeastern Archaeology* 7:1–20.

1991 The Decorative Burden: Design, Medium, and Change. In *Ceramic Ethnoarchaeology*, edited by W. A. Longacre, pp. 144–61. University of Arizona Press, Tuscon.

1993 Like a Rolling Stone: The Chunkey Game and Political Organization in Eastern North America. *Southeastern Archaeology* 12:83–92.

DeHaas, Wills 1869 Archaeology of the Mississippi Valley. *Proceedings of the American Association for the Advancement of Science* 17:288–302.

DeMott, Rodney C., Derrick J. Marcucci, and Joyce A. Williams 1993 *The Archaeology of the Cahokia Mounds ICT-II: Testing and Lithics. Part II: Chipped Lithic Materials*. Illinois Cultural Resource Study 9, Illinois Historic Preservation Agency, Springfield.

DePratter, Chester B. 1983 Late Prehistoric and Early Historic Chiefdoms in the Southeastern United States. Unpublished PhD dissertation, University of Georgia, Athens. University Microfilms, Ann Arbor.

Diaz-Granados, Carol M. and James R. Duncan 2000 *The Petroglyphs and Pictographs of Missouri*. University of Alabama Press, Tuscaloosa.

Diaz-Granados, Carol M., Marvin W. Rowe, Marian Hyman, James R. Duncan, and John R. Southon 2001 AMS Radiocarbon Dates for Charcoal from Three Missouri Pictographs and Their Associated Iconography. *American Antiquity* 66:481–92.

Dincauze, Dena F. and Robert J. Hasenstab 1989 Explaining the Iroquois: Tribalization on a Prehistoric Periphery. In *Centre and Periphery: Comparative Studies in Archaeology*, edited by T. C. Champion, pp. 67–87. Unwin Hyman, London.

Dobres, Marcia-Anne 2000 *Technology and Social Agency*. Blackwell, Oxford.

Dorsey, J. O. 1886 Migrations of Siouan Tribes. *The American Naturalist* 20:211–22.

Douglas, John G. 1976 Collins: A Late Woodland Ceremonial Complex in the Woodfordian Northeast. Unpublished PhD dissertation, University of Illinois, Urbana-Champaign.

Drechsel, Emanuel J. 1994 Mobilean Jargon in the "Prehistory" of Southeastern North America. In *Perspectives on the Southeast: Linguistics, Archaeology, and Ethnohistory*, edited by P. B. Kwachka, pp. 25–43. University of Georgia Press, Athens.

Du Pratz, Antoine Simon Le Page 1975 [1763] *The History of Louisiana*, edited by J. G. Tregle. Louisiana State University Press, Baton Rouge.

Duncan, James R. and Carol Diaz-Granados 2000 Of Masks and Myths. *Midcontinental Journal of Archaeology* 25:1–26.

Emerson, Thomas E. 1982 *Mississippian Stone Images in Illinois*. Illinois Archaeological Survey Circular 6, Urbana.

1989 Water, Serpents, and the Underworld: An Exploration into Cahokia Symbolism. In *The Southeastern Ceremonial Complex: Artifacts and Analysis*, edited by P. Galloway, pp. 45–92. University of Nebraska Press, Lincoln.

1991a The Apple River Mississippian Culture of Northwestern Illinois. In *Cahokia and the Hinterlands: Middle Mississippian Cultures of the Midwest*, edited by T. E. Emerson and R. B. Lewis, pp. 164–82. University of Illinois Press, Urbana.

1991b Some Perspectives on Cahokia and the Northern Mississippian Expansion. In *Cahokia and the Hinterlands: Middle Mississippian Cultures of the Midwest*, edited by T. E. Emerson and R. B. Lewis, pp. 221–36. University of Illinois Press, Urbana.

1997a *Cahokia and the Archaeology of Power*. The University of Alabama Press, Tuscaloosa.

1997b Reflections from the Countryside on Cahokian Hegemony. In *Cahokia: Domination and Ideology in the Mississippian World*, edited by T. R. Pauketat and T. Emerson, pp. 190–228. University of Nebraska Press, Lincoln.

1997c Cahokian Elite Ideology and the Mississippian Cosmos. In *Cahokia: Domination and Ideology in the Mississippian World*, edited by T. R. Pauketat and T. E. Emerson, pp. 190–228. University of Nebraska Press, Lincoln.

1999 The Langford Tradition and the Process of Tribalization on the Middle Mississippian Borders. *Midcontinental Journal of Archaeology* 24:3–56.

2002 An Introduction to Cahokia 2002: Diversity, Complexity, and History. *Midcontinental Journal of Archaeology* 27:127–48.

Emerson, Thomas E. and Eve Hargrave 2000 Strangers in Paradise? Recognizing Ethnic Mortuary Diversity on the Fringes of Cahokia. *Southeastern Archaeology* 19:1–23.

Emerson, Thomas E., Eve Hargrave, and Kristin Hedman 2003a Death and Ritual in Early Rural Cahokia. In *Theory, Method, and Technique in Modern Archaeology*, edited by R. J. Jeske, and D. K. Charles. Bergin and Garvey, Westport, Connecticut (in press).

Emerson, Thomas E. and Randall E. Hughes 2000 Figurines, Flint Clay Sourcing, the Ozark Highlands, and Cahokian Acquisition. *American Antiquity* 65:79–101.

Emerson, Thomas E., Randall E. Hughes, Mary R. Hynes, and Sarah U. Wisseman 2002 Implications of Sourcing Cahokia-Style Flint Clay Figures in the American Bottom and the Upper Mississippi River Valley. *Midcontinental Journal of Archaeology* 27:309–38.

2003b The Sourcing and Interpretation of Cahokia-Style Figurines in the Trans-Mississippi South and Southeast. *American Antiquity* 68:287–313.

Emerson, Thomas E. and Douglas K. Jackson 1984 *The BBB Motor Site (11-Ms-595)*. American Bottom Archaeology, FAI-270 Site Reports 6, University of Illinois Press, Urbana.

Emerson, Thomas E. and Timothy R. Pauketat 2002 Embodying Power and Resistance at Cahokia. In *The Dynamics of Power*, edited by M. O'Donovan, pp. 105–25. Center for Archaeological Investigations, Occasional Paper 30, Southern Illinois University, Carbondale.

Emerson, Thomas E. and William I. Woods 1993 Saving the Great Nobb: A Case Study in the Preservation of Cahokia's Monks Mound through Passive Management. *Illinois Archaeology* 5:100–7.

Engelke, Georgia M. 1983 *The Great American Bottom*. C. Sarne Corporation, St. Louis.

Esarey, Duane and Timothy R. Pauketat 1992 *The Lohmann Site: An Early Mississippian Center in the American Bottom*. American Bottom Archaeology, FAI-270 Site Reports 25, University of Illinois Press, Urbana.

Feinman, Gary M. and Joyce Marcus, eds. 1998 *Archaic States*. School of American Research Press, Santa Fe.

Fenneman, N. M. 1914 Physiographic Boundaries within the United States. *Annals of the Association of American Geographers* 4:84–137.

Finiels, Nicolas de 1989 *An Account of Upper Louisiana*, edited by C. J. Ekberg and W. E. Foley. University of Missouri Press, Columbia.

Finney, Fred A. and James B. Stoltman 1991 The Fred Edwards Site: A Case of Stirling Phase Culture Contact in Southwestern Wisconsin. In *New Perspectives on Cahokia: Views from the Periphery*, edited by J. B. Stoltman, pp. 229–52. Prehistory Press, Madison, Wisconsin.

Fortier, Andrew C. 1998 Pre-Mississippian Economies in the American Bottom of Southwestern Illinois, 3000 BC–AD 1050. *Research in Economic Anthropology* 19:341–92.

Fortier, Andrew C. and Douglas K. Jackson 2000 The Formation of a Late Woodland Heartland in the American Bottom, Illinois cal AD 650–900. In *Late Woodland Societies: Tradition and Transformation across the Midcontinent*,

190   References

edited by T. E. Emerson, D. L. McElrath, and A. C. Fortier, pp. 123–47. University of Nebraska Press, Lincoln.

Fortier, Andrew C., Richard B. Lacampagne, and Fred A. Finney 1984 *The Fish Lake Site*. American Bottom Archaeology, FAI-270 Site Reports 8, University of Illinois, Urbana.

Fortier, Andrew C. and Dale L. McElrath 2002 Deconstructing the Emergent Mississippian Concept: The Case for the Terminal Late Woodland in the American Bottom. *Midcontinental Journal of Archaeology* 27:171–215.

Fowler, Melvin L. 1969 The Cahokia Site. In *Explorations into Cahokia Archaeology*, edited by M. L. Fowler, pp. 1–30. Illinois Archaeological Survey, Bulletin 7, Urbana.

1997 *The Cahokia Atlas: A Historical Atlas of Cahokia Archaeology* (revised edition). Studies in Archaeology 2, Illinois Transportation Archaeological Research Program, University of Illinois, Urbana.

1999 Who Were These People? In *The Mound 72 Area: Dedicated and Sacred Space in Early Cahokia*, by Melvin L. Fowler, Jerome Rose, Barbara Vander Leest, and Steven A. Ahler, pp. 183–9. Illinois State Museum, Reports of Investigations 54, Springfield.

Fowler, Melvin L., Jerome Rose, Barbara Vander Leest, and Steven A. Ahler 1999 *The Mound 72 Area: Dedicated and Sacred Space in Early Cahokia*. Illinois State Museum, Reports of Investigations 54, Springfield.

Frazer, Sir James G. 1947 *The Golden Bough: A Study in Magic and Religion* (abridged edition). Macmillan, New York.

Fritz, Gayle J. 1990 Multiple Pathways to Farming in Precontact Eastern North America. *Journal of World Prehistory* 4:387–435.

1992 "Newer," "Better" Maize and the Mississippian Emergence: A Critique of Prime Mover Explanations. In *Late Prehistoric Agriculture: Observations from the Midwest*, edited by W. I. Woods, pp. 19–43. Studies in Illinois Archaeology 8, Illinois Historic Preservation Agency, Springfield.

Garland, Elizabeth B. 1992 *The Obion Site: An Early Mississippian Center in Western Tennessee*. Cobb Institute of Archaeology, Report of Investigation 7, Mississippi State University, Mississippi.

Gartner, William G. 1996 Archaeoastronomy as Sacred Geography. *The Wisconsin Archeologist* 77:128–50.

Gibbon, Guy E. 1974 A Model of Mississippian Development and Its Implications for the Red Wing Area. In *Aspects of Upper Great Lakes Anthropology*, edited by E. Johnson, pp. 129–37. Minnesota Prehistoric Archaeology Series 11. Minnesota Historical Society, St. Paul.

Gibbon, Guy E. and Clark A. Dobbs 1991 The Mississippian Presence in the Red Wing Area, Minnesota. In *New Perspectives on Cahokia: Views from the Periphery*, edited by James B. Stoltman, pp. 281–305. Prehistory Press, Madison, Wisconsin.

Goldstein, Lynne G. 1991 The Implications of Aztalan's Location. In *New Perspectives on Cahokia: Views from the Periphery*, edited by James B. Stoltman, pp. 209–28. Prehistory Press, Madison, Wisconsin.

2000 Mississippian Ritual as Viewed through the Practice of Secondary Disposal of the Dead. In *Mounds, Modoc, and Mesoamerica: Papers in Honor of*

Melvin L. Fowler, edited by S. Ahler, pp. 193–206. Illinois State Museum Scientific Papers 28, Springfield.

Goldstein, Lynne G. and John D. Richards 1991 Ancient Aztalan: The Cultural and Ecological Context of a Late Prehistoric Site in the Midwest. In *Cahokia and the Hinterlands: Middle Mississippian Cultures of the Midwest*, edited by T. E. Emerson and R. B. Lewis, pp. 193–206. University of Illinois Press, Urbana.

Goldstein, Paul S. 2000 Communities without Borders: The Vertical Archipelago and Diaspora Communities in the Southern Andes. In *The Archaeology of Communities: A New World Perspective*, edited by M. A. Canuto and J. Yaeger, pp. 182–209. Routledge, London.

Gose, Peter 1991 House Rethatching in an Andean Annual Cycle: Practice, Meaning, and Contradiction. *American Ethnologist* 18:39–66.

Green, William 1997 Middle Mississippian Peoples. *The Wisconsin Archeologist* 78:202–23.

Green, William and Roland L. Rodell 1994 The Mississippian Presence and Cahokia Interaction at Trempealeau, Wisconsin. *American Antiquity* 59:334–59.

1952a Culture Periods in Eastern United States Archeology. In *Archeology of Eastern United States*, edited by J. B. Griffin, pp. 352–64. University of Chicago Press, Chicago.

1952b An Interpretation of the Place of Spiro in Southeastern Archaeology. *The Missouri Archaeologist* 14:89–106.

1960 A Hypothesis for the Prehistory of the Winnebago. In *Culture in History: Essays in Honor of Paul Radin*, edited by S. A. Diamond, pp. 809–65. Columbia University Press, New York.

1961 Some Correlations of Climatic and Cultural Change in Eastern North American Prehistory. *Annals of the New York Academy of Sciences* 95:710–17.

1967 Eastern North American Archaeology: A Summary. *Science* 156 (3772):175–91.

1985 An Individual's Participation in American Archaeology 1928–1985. *Annual Review of Anthropology* 14:1–23.

Gums, Bonnie 1993 Groundstone Tools, Modified Rock, and Exotic Materials. In *The Archaeology of the Cahokia Mounds ICT-II: Testing and Lithics, Part III*. Illinois Cultural Resources Study 9, Illinois Historic Preservation Agency, Springfield.

1985 Medicine Wheels, Sun Circles, and the Magic of World Center Shrines. *Plains Anthropologist* 30:181–93.

1986 Upper Mississippi and Middle Mississippi Relationships. *The Wisconsin Archeologist* 67:365–9.

1989 The Cultural Background of Mississippian Symbolism. In *The Southeastern Ceremonial Complex*, edited by P. Galloway, pp. 239–78. University of Nebraska Press, Lincoln.

1991 Cahokia Identity and Interaction Models of Cahokia Mississippian. In *Cahokia and the Hinterlands: Middle Mississippian Cultures of the Midwest*, edited by T. E. Emerson and R. B. Lewis, pp. 3–34. University of Illinois Press, Urbana.

1993 Red Banks, Oneota, and the Winnebago: Views from a Distant Rock. *The Wisconsin Archeologist* 74:10–79.

1997 *An Archaeology of the Soul: North American Indian Belief and Ritual.* University of Illinois Press, Urbana.

2000 Sacrificed Foursomes and Green Corn Ceremonialism. In *Mounds, Modoc, and Mesoamerica: Papers in Honor of Melvin L. Fowler,* edited by S. R. Ahler, pp. 245–53. Illinois State Museum Scientific Papers 28, Springfield.

Hally, David J. 1993 The Territorial Size of Mississippian Chiefdoms. In *Archaeology of Eastern North America: Papers in Honor of Stephen Williams,* edited by J. B. Stoltman, pp. 143–68. Archaeological Report 25, Mississippi Department of Archives and History, Jackson, Mississippi.

Hally, David J., ed. 1994 *Ocmulgee Archaeology: 1936–1986.* University of Georgia Press, Athens.

Hargrave, Eve A. and Kristin Hedman 2001 *The Halliday Site (11-S-27): Investigations into Early Mississippian Mortuary Behavior.* Illinois Transportation Archaeological Research Program, Research Reports 50, University of Illinois, Urbana-Champaign.

Hargrave, M. L., G. A. Oetelaar, N. H. Lopinot, B. M. Butler, and D. Billings 1983 *The Bridges Site 11-Mr-11: A Late Prehistoric Settlement in the Central Kaskaskia Valley,* Center for Archaeological Investigations, Research Paper 38, Southern Illinois University, Carbondale.

Harl, Joseph L. 1991 An Alternative Explanation for the Shift from a Late Woodland to a Mississippian Lifestyle Based on Evidence from the Bridgeton Site (23SL442) and Other Sites along the Lower Missouri River Valley. Unpublished Masters thesis, Department of Anthropology, Washington University, St. Louis.

Harn, Alan D. 1991 The Eveland Site: Inroad to Spoon River Mississippian Society. In *New Perspectives on Cahokia: Views from the Periphery,* edited by J. B. Stoltman, pp. 129–53. Prehistory Press, Madison, Wisconsin.

Hart, John P. 1999 Maize Agriculture Evolution in the Eastern Woodlands of North America: A Darwinian Perspective. *Journal of Archaeological Method and Theory* 6:137–80.

Hassig, Ross 1992 *War and Society in Ancient Mesoamerica.* University of California Press, Berkeley.

Helms, Mary W. 1992 Long-Distance Contacts, Elite Aspirations, and the Age of Discovery in Cosmological Context. In *Resources, Power, and Interregional Interaction,* edited by E. M. Schortman and P. A. Urban, pp. 157–74. Plenum Press, New York.

Henning, Dale 2001 Plains Village Tradition: Eastern Periphery and Oneota Tradition. In *Handbook of North American Indians: Plains,* edited by R. J. DeMalle, pp. 222–33. Smithsonian Institution Press, Washington, DC.

Hobsbawm, Eric 1983 Introduction: Inventing Traditions. In *The Invention of Tradition,* edited by E. Hobsbawm and T. Ranger, pp. 1–14. Cambridge University Press, Cambridge.

Hoffman, Michael P. 1990 The Terminal Mississippian Period in the Arkansas River Valley and Quapaw Ethnogenesis. In *Towns and Temples along the Mississippi,* edited by D. H. Dye and C. A. Cox, pp. 208–26. University of Alabama Press, Tuscaloosa.

1994 Ethnic Identities and Cultural Change in the Protohistoric Period of Eastern Arkansas. In *Perspectives on the Southeast: Linguistics, Archaeology, and Ethnohistory*, edited by P. B. Kwachta, pp. 61–70. University of Georgia Press, Athens.

Holley, George R. 1989 *The Archaeology of the Cahokia Mounds ICT-II: Ceramics*. Illinois Cultural Resources Study 11, Illinois Historic Preservation Agency, Springfield.

1995 Microliths and the Kunnemann Tract: An Assessment of Craft Production at the Cahokia Site. *Illinois Archaeology* 7:1–68.

2000 Late Woodland on the Edge of Looking Glass Prairie: A Scott Joint-Use Archaeological Project Perspective. In *Late Woodland Societies: Tradition and Transformation across the Midcontinent*, edited by T. E. Emerson, D. L. McElrath, and A. C. Forter, pp. 149–62. University of Nebraska Press, Lincoln.

Holley, George R., Rinitia A. Dalan, and Phillip A. Smith 1993 Investigations in the Cahokia Site Grand Plaza. *American Antiquity* 58:306–19.

Holley, George R., Neal H. Lopinot, William I. Woods, and John E. Kelly 1989 Dynamics of community organization at prehistoric Cahokia. In *Proceedings of the 21st Annual Chacmool Conference*, edited by S. MacEachern, D. J. W. Archer, and R. Garvin, pp. 339–49. University of Calgary Archaeological Association, Calgary.

Holley, George R., Kathyrn E. Parker, Harold W. Watters, Jr., J. N. Harper, Michels Skele, Jennifer E. Ringberg 2001 *The Prehistoric Archaeology of the Lembke Locality, Scott Joint-Use Archaeological Project*. Report submitted to the Illinois Department of Transportation, Southern Illinois University, Edwardsville.

Holmes, William H. 1903 Aboriginal Pottery of the Eastern United States. In *Twentieth Annual Report of the Bureau of American Ethnology*, pp. 1–201. Smithsonian Institution, Washington, DC.

House, John H. 1996 East-Central Arkansas. In *Prehistory of the Central Mississippi Valley*, edited C. H. McNutt, pp. 137–54. University of Alabama Press, Tuscaloosa.

Howard, James H. 1968 *The Southeastern Ceremonial Complex and Its Interpretation*. Missouri Archeological Society, Memoir 6, Columbia.

Howland, Henry R. 1877 Recent Archaeological Discoveries in the American Bottom. *Buffalo Society of Natural Sciences, Bulletin* 3 (5):204–11.

Hunt, William J., Jr. 1974 Late Woodland–Mississippian Relationshiops at the River Bend East Site (23SL70), St. Louis County, Missouri. Unpublished Masters thesis, University of Nebraska, Lincoln.

Iseminger, William R., Timothy R. Pauketat, Brad Koldehoff, Lucretia S. Kelly, and Leonard Blake 1990 *Archaeology of the Cahokia Palisade: The East Palisade Investigations*. Illinois Cultural Resources Study 14, Illinois Historic Preservation Agency, Springfield.

Ives, David J. 1975 *The Crescent Hills Prehistoric Quarrying Area*. Museum Brief 22, University of Missouri, Columbia.

1984 The Crescent Hills Prehistoric Quarrying Area: More than Just Rocks. In *Prehistoric Chert Exploitation: Studies from the Midcontinent*, edited by B. M.

194   References

Butler and E. E. May, pp. 187–95. Occasional Paper 2, Center for Archaeological Investigations, Southern Illinois University, Carbondale.

Jackson, Douglas K., Andrew C. Fortier, and Joyce A. Williams 1992 *The Sponemann Site 2 (11-Ms-517): The Mississippian and Oneota Occupations.* American Bottom Archaeology, FAI-270 Site Reports 24, University of Illinois Press, Urbana.

Jackson, Margaret A. 2002 Proto-Writing in Moche Pottery at Cerro Mayal, Peru. In *Andean Archaeology II: Art, Landscape, and Society,* edited by H. Silverman and W. H. Isbell, pp. 107–35. Kluwer Academic/Plenum Publishers, New York.

James, J. Alton 1928 *The Life of George Rogers Clark.* University of Chicago Press, Chicago.

Johannessen, Sissel 1984 Paleoethnobotany. In *American Bottom Archaeology,* edited by C. J. Bareis and J. W. Porter, pp. 197–214. University of Illinois Press, Urbana.

1993 Food, Dishes, and Society in the Mississippi Valley. In *Foraging and Farming in the Eastern Woodlands,* edited by C. M. Scarry, pp. 182–205. University Press of Florida, Gainsville.

Johnson, Eldon 1991 Cambria and Cahokia's Northwestern Periphery. In *New Perspectives on Cahokia: Views from the Periphery,* edited by J. B. Stoltman, pp. 307–17. Monographs in World Archaeology 2, Prehistory Press, Madison, Wisconsin.

Johnson, Jay K. 1987 Cahokia Core Technology in Mississippi: The View from the South. In *The Organization of Core Technology,* edited by J. K. Johnson and C. A. Morrow, pp. 187–205. Boulder, Colorado, Westview Press.

Jones, Charles C. 1999 [1873] *Antiquities of the Southern Indians, Particularly of the Georgia Tribes* (edited by F. T. Schnell). University of Alabama Press, Tuscaloosa.

Jones, Joseph 1876 *Explorations of the Aboriginal Remains of Tennessee.* Smithsonian Contributions to Knowledge 259, Washington, DC.

Justice, Noel D. 1987 *Stone Age Spear and Arrow Points of the Midcontinental and Eastern United States.* University of Indiana Press, Bloomington.

Kehoe, Alice B. 1997 The History of Wisconsin Archaeology. *The Wisconsin Archaeologist* 78:11–20.

1998 *The Land of Prehistory: A Critical History of American Archaeology.* Routledge, London.

Kelly, John E. 1990a The Emergence of Mississippian Culture in the American Bottom Region. In *The Mississippian Emergence,* edited by B. D. Smith, pp. 113–52. Smithsonian Institution Press, Washington, DC.

1990b Range Site Community Patterns and the Mississippian Emergence. In *The Mississippian Emergence,* edited by B. D. Smith, pp. 67–112. Smithsonian Institution Press, Washington, DC.

1991a Cahokia and Its Role as a Gateway Center in Interregional Exchange. In *Cahokia and the Hinterlands: Middle Mississippian Cultures of the Midwest,* edited by T. E. Emerson and R. B. Lewis, pp. 61–80. University of Illinois Press, Urbana.

1991b The Evidence for Prehistoric Exchange and Its Implications for the Development of Cahokia. In *New Perspectives on Cahokia: Views from the*

Periphery, edited by J. B. Stoltman, pp. 65–92. Monographs in World Archaeology 2, Prehistory Press, Madison, Wisconsin.

1993 The Pulcher Site: An Archaeological and Historical Overview. In *Highways to the Past: Essays on Illinois Archaeology in Honor of Charles J. Bareis*, edited by Thomas E. Emerson, Andrew C. Fortier, and Dale L. McElrath. *Illinois Archaeology* 5:434–51.

1997 Stirling-Phase Sociopolitical Activity at East St. Louis and Cahokia. In *Cahokia: Domination and Ideology in the Mississippian World*, edited by T. R. Pauketat and T. E. Emerson, pp. 141–66. University of Nebraska Press, Lincoln.

2000 Introduction. In *The Cahokia Mounds*, by W. K. Moorehead, pp. 1–35. University of Alabama Press, Tuscaloosa.

2002 The Pulcher Tradition and the Ritualization of Cahokia: A Perspective from Cahokia's Southern Neighbor. *Southeastern Archaeology* 21:136–48.

Kelly, John E., Andrew C. Fortier, Steven J. Ozuk, and Joyce A. Williams 1987 *The Range Site: Archaic through Late Woodland Occupations (11-S-47)*. American Bottom Archaeology, FAI-270 Site Reports 16, University of Illinois Press, Urbana.

Kelly, John E. and Brad Koldehoff 1996 The Nature and Context of the Mississippian Occupation on Cahokia's Western Periphery: The Fingerhut and Powell Tracts. Paper presented at the 17th Annual Mid-South Archaeological Conference, Memphis, Tennessee.

Kelly, John E., Steven J. Ozuk, and Joyce A. Williams 1990 *The Range Site 2: The Emergent Mississippian Dohack and Range Phase Occupations*. American Bottom Archaeology, FAI-270 Site Reports 20, University of Illinois Press, Urbana.

Kelly, Lucretia S. 1979 *Animal Resource Exploitation by Early Cahokia Populations on the Merrell Tract*. Illinois Archaeological Survey Circular 4, Urbana.

1997 Patterns of Faunal Exploitation at Cahokia. In *Cahokia: Domination and Ideology in the Mississippian World*, edited by T. R. Pauketat and T. E. Emerson, pp. 69–88. University of Nebraska Press, Lincoln.

2000 Social Implications of Faunal Provisioning for the Cahokia Site: Initial Mississippian, Lohmann Phase. Unpublished PhD dissertation, Department of Anthropology, Washington University, St. Louis.

Kidder, Tristram R. 1992 Coles Creek Period Social Organization and Evolution in Northeast Louisiana. In *Lords of the Southeast: Social Inequality and the Native Elites of Southeastern North America*, edited by A. W. Barker and T. R. Pauketat, pp. 145–62. Archaeological Papers of the American Anthropological Association 3, Washington, DC.

2002 Woodland Period Archaeology of the Lower Mississippi Valley. In *The Woodland Southeast*, edited by D. G. Anderson and R. C. Mainfort, pp. 66–90. University of Alabama Press, Tuscaloosa.

2003 Investigating the Plaza at the Raffman Site (16MS20), Northeast Louisiana. Manuscript in the possession of the author.

Kidder, Tristram R. and Gayle J. Fritz 1993 Subsistence and Social Change in the Lower Mississippi Valley: Excavations at the Reno Brake and Osceola Sites, Louisiana. *Journal of Field Archaeology* 20:281–97.

2002 Other Worlds, Heroes, and Power: After the Decline of Cahokia. Paper presented before the Pre-Columbian Society of Washington, DC, in the "Ancient Cities of Power and Splendor: New Light on Cahokia and the Southeast" conference, September 21. Washington, DC.

Knight, Vernon James, Jr. 1986 The Institutional Organization of Mississippian Religion. *American Antiquity* 51:675–87.

1989 Symbolism of Mississippian Mounds. In *Powhatan's Mantle: Indians in the Colonial Southeast*, edited by P. H. Wood, G. A. Waselkov, and M. T. Hatley, pp. 279–91. University of Nebraska Press, Lincoln.

1997 Some Developmental Parallels between Cahokia and Moundville. In *Cahokia: Domination and Ideology in the Mississippian World*, edited by T. R. Pauketat and T. E. Emerson, pp. 227–49. University of Nebraska Press, Lincoln.

2001 Feasting and the Emergence of Platform Mound Ceremonialism in Eastern North America. In *Feasts: Archaeological and Ethnographic Perspectives on Food, Politics, and Power*, edited by M. Dietler and B. Hayden, pp. 311–33. Smithsonian Institution Press, Washington, DC.

Knight, Vernon James, Jr., James A. Brown, and George E. Langkford 2001 On the Subject Matter of Southeastern Ceremonial Complex Art. *Southeastern Archaeology* 20:129–53.

Knight, Vernon James, Jr. and Vincas P. Steponaitis 1998 *Archaeology of the Moundville Chiefdom*. Smithsonian Institution Press, Washington, DC.

Koehler, Lyle 1997 Earth Mothers, Warriors, Horticulturalists, Artists, and Chiefs: Women among the Mississippian and Mississippian-Oneota Peoples, AD 1000–1750. In *Women in Prehistory: North America and Mesoamerica*, edited by C. Claassen and R. A. Joyce, pp. 211–26. University of Pennsylvania Press, Philadelphia.

Koldehoff, Brad 1982 A Coles Creek Vessel from Cahokia's Hinterland. *Illinois Antiquity* 14 (2–3):20–3.

1987 The Cahokia Flake Tool Industry: Socioeconomic Implications for Late Prehistory in the Central Mississippi Valley. In *The Organization of Core Technology*, edited by J. Johnson and C. Morrow, pp. 151–86. Boulder, Colorado, Westview Press.

1989 Cahokia's Immediate Hinterland: The Mississippian Occupation of Douglas Creek. *Illinois Archaeology* 1:39–68.

1990a Household Specialization: The Organization of Mississippian Chipped-Stone-Tool Production. Unpublished Masters thesis, Southern Illinois University, Carbondale.

1990b Lithics. In *The Archaeology of the Cahokia Palisade: The East Palisade Investigations*, by W. R. Iseminger, T. R. Pauketat, B. Koldehoff, L. S. Kelly, and L. Blake, pp. 77–108. Illinois Cultural Resources Study 14, Illinois Historic Preservation Agency, Springfield.

1995 Lithics. In *The Fingers and Curtiss Steinberg Road Sites*, by J. E. Kelly, B. Koldehoff, and K. E. Parker, pp. 41–53, 80–9. Transportation Archaeological Research Reports 1, Illinois Transportation Archaeological Research Program, University of Illinois, Urbana.

2002 *The Woodland Ridge Site and Late Woodland Land Use in the Southern American Bottom*. Transportation Archaeological Research Reports 15,

Illinois Transportation Archaeological Research Program, University of Illinois, Urbana.

Koldehoff, Brad and Phillip J. Carr 2001 Chipped stone technology: patterns of procurement, production, and consumption. In *Excavations at Wickliffe Mounds*, by K. Wesler, chapter 10 (CD-ROM). University of Alabama Press, Tuscaloosa.

Koldehoff, Brad, Charles O. Witty, and Mike Kolb 2000 Recent Investigations in the Vicinity of Mounds 27 and 28 at Cahokia: The Yale Avenue Borrow Pit. *Illinois Archaeology* 12:199–217.

Kozuch, Laura 2002 *Olivella* Beads from Spiro and the Plains. *American Antiquity* 67:697–709.

Kreisa, Paul P. 1987 Late Prehistoric Settlement Patterns in the Big Bottoms, Fulton County, Kentucky. In *Current Archaeological Research in Kentucky*, vol. 1, edited by D. Pollack, pp. 78–99. Kentucky Heritage Council, Frankfort.

Kroeber, A. L. 1953 *Cultural and Natural Areas of Native North America*. University of California Press, Berkeley.

Kruchten, Jeffery D. 2000 Early Cahokian Fluidity on the Fringe: Pfeffer Mounds and the Richland Complex. Paper presented at the 57th Southeastern Archaeological Conference, November 8–11, Macon, Georgia.

Kus, Susan M. 1983 The Social Representation of Space: Dimensioning the Cosmological and the Quotidian. In *Archaeological Hammers and Theories*, edited by J. A. Moore and A. S. Keene, pp. 277–98. Academic Press, New York.

Kus, Susan M. and Victor Raharigaona 2001 To Dare to Wear the Cloak of Another before Their Very Eyes: State Co-optation and Local Re-appropriation in Mortuary Rituals of Central Madagascar. In *Social Memory, Identity, and Death: Anthropological Perspectives on Mortuary Rituals*, edited by M. Chesson, pp. 114–31. Archeological Papers of the American Anthropological Association 10, Washington, DC.

Kuttruff, L. Carl 1972 *The Marty Coolidge Site, Monroe County, Illinois*. Southern Illinois Studies 10, Southern Illinois University, Carbondale.

Lafferty, Robert H., III 1994 Prehistoric Exchange in the Lower Mississippi Valley. In *Prehistoric Exchange Systems in North America*, edited by T. G. Baugh and J. E. Ericson, pp. 177–213. Plenum Press, New York.

Lafferty, Robert H., III and James E. Price 1996 Southeast Missouri. In *Prehistory of the Central Mississippi Valley*, edited by C. H. McNutt, pp. 1–45. University of Alabama Press, Tuscaloosa.

Lekson, Stephen H. 1999 *The Chaco Meridian: Centers of Political Power in the Ancient Southwest*. Altamira Press, Walnut Creek, California.

Lewis, R. Barry 1991 The Early Mississippi Period in the Confluence Region and Its Northern Relationships. In *Cahokia and the Hinterlands: Middle Mississippian Cultures of the Midwest*, edited by T. E. Emerson and R. B. Lewis, pp. 274–94. University of Illinois Press, Urbana.

Little, Elizabeth A. 1987 Inland Waterways in the Northeast. *Midcontinental Journal of Archaeology* 12:55–76.

1994 A New Crop of Data on the Cahokian Polity. In *Agricultural Origins and Development in the Midcontinent*, edited by W. Green, pp. 127–53. Office of the State Archaeologist, Report 19, University of Iowa, Iowa City.

Lopinot, Neal H., Michael D. Conner, J. H. Ray, and J. K. Yelton 1998 *Prehistoric and Historic Properties on Mitigation Lands, Horseshoe Lake Peninsula, Madison County, Illinois*. St. Louis District Historic Properties Management Report 55, US Army Corps of Engineers, St. Louis.

Lopinot, Neal H. and William I. Woods 1993 Wood Overexploitation and the Collapse of Cahokia. In *Foraging and Farming in the Eastern Woodlands*, edited by C. M. Scarry, pp. 206–31. University Press of Florida, Gainesville.

Ludwickson, John, J. N. Gunderson, and C. Johnson 1993 Select Exotic Artifacts from Cattle Oiler 39ST224, a Middle Missouri Tradition Site in Central South Dakota. *Plains Anthropologist* 38:151–68.

Lynott, Mark J. 1987 Thermoluminescence Dating of Prehistoric Ceramics in Southeast Missouri: A Progress Report. *Society for Archaeological Sciences Newsletter* 10 (2):2–5.

Lynott, Mark J., Thomas W. Boutton, James E. Price, and Dwight E. Nelson 1986 Stable Carbon Isotopic Evidence for Maize Agriculture in Southeast Missouri and Northeast Arkansas. *American Antiquity* 51:51–65.

McAdams, William 1887 *Records of Ancient Races in the Mississippi Valley*. C. R. Barns, St. Louis.

McConaughy, Mark A. 1991 The Rench Site Late Late Woodland/Mississippian Farming Hamlet from the Central Illinois River Valley: Food for Thought. In *New Perspectives on Cahokia: Views from the Periphery*, edited by J. B. Stoltman, pp. 101–28. Monographs in World Archaeology 2, Prehistory Press, Madison, Wisconsin.

McConaughy, Mark A., ed. 1993 *Rench: A Stratified Site in the Central Illinois River Valley*. Illinois State Museum, Reports of Investigations 49, Springfield.

McElrath, Dale L., Thomas E. Emerson, and Andrew C. Fortier 2000 Social Evolution or Social Response? A Fresh Look at the "Good Gray Cultures" after Four Decades of Midwest Research. In *Late Woodland Societies: Tradition and Transformation across the Midcontinent*, edited by T. E. Emerson, D. L. McElrath, and A. C. Forter, pp. 3–36. University of Nebraska Press, Lincoln.

McElrath, Dale L. and Andrew C. Fortier 2000 The Early Late Woodland Occupation of the American Bottom. In *Late Woodland Societies: Tradition and Transformation across the Midcontinent*, edited by T. E. Emerson, D. L. McElrath, and A. C. Forter, pp. 97–121. University of Nebraska Press, Lincoln.

McGee, W. J. 1897 The Siouan Indians: A Preliminary Sketch. In *Bureau of American Ethnology, Annual Report* 15, pp. 153–204. Washington, DC.

Mainfort, Robert C., Jr. 1996 The Reelfoot Lake Basin, Kentucky and Tennessee. In *Prehistory of the Central Mississippi Valley*, edited by C. H. McNutt, pp. 77–96. University of Alabama Press, Tuscaloosa.

Mallam, R. Clark 1976 *The Iowa Effigy Mound Manifestation: An Interpretive Model*. Office of the State Archaeologist, Report 9, University of Iowa, Iowa City.

Marshall, John B. 1992 The St. Louis Mound Group: Historical Accounts and Pictorial Depictions. *The Missouri Archaeologist* 53:43–79.

Marshall, Richard A. 1987 A Brief Comparison of Two Emergent Mississippi Substage Settlement Patterns in Southeast Missouri and Northwest

Mississippi. In *The Emergent Mississippian: Proceedings of the Sixth Mid-South Archaeological Conference, June 6–9, 1985*, edited by R. A. Marshall, pp. 160–6. Cobb Institute of Archaeology, Occasional Papers 87-01. Mississippi State University, Mississippi.

Marshall, Richard A. and James F. Hopgood 1964 A Test Excavation at Hoecake, 23MI8, Mississippi County, Missouri. *Missouri Archaeological Society Newsletter* 177:3–5.

Mason, Ronald J. and Gregory Perino 1961 Microblades at Cahokia, Illinois. *American Antiquity* 26:553–7.

Mehrer, Mark W. 1995 *Cahokia's Countryside: Household Archaeology, Settlement Patterns, and Social Power*. Northern Illinois University Press, DeKalb.

2000 Heterarchy and Hierarchy: The Community Plan as Institution in Cahokia's Polity. In *The Archaeology of Communities: A New World Perspective*, edited by M. A. Canuto and Y. Yaeger, pp. 44–57. Routledge, London.

Mehrer, Mark W. and James M. Collins 1995 Household Archaeology at Cahokia and in Its Hinterlands. In *Mississippian Communities and Households*, edited by J. D. Rogers and B. D. Smith, pp. 32–57. University of Alabama Press, Tuscaloosa.

Milanich, Jerald T., Ann S. Cordell, Vernon J. Knight, Jr., Timothy A. Kohler, and Brenda J. Sigler-Lavelle 1984 *McKeithen Weeden Island: The Culture of Northern Florida AD 200–900*. Academic Press, Orlando, Florida.

Miller, Daniel 2001 Alienable Gifts and Inalienable Commodities. In *The Empire of Things: Regimes of Value and Material Culture*, edited by F. R. Myers, pp. 91–115. School of American Research Press, Santa Fe.

Mills, Barbara 2000 Gender, Craft Production, and Inequality. In *Women and Men in the Prehispanic Southwest: Labor, Power, and Prestige*, edited by P. L. Crown, pp. 301–43. School of American Research Press, Santa Fe.

Milner, George R. 1984a *The Robinson's Lake Site*. American Bottom Archaeology FAI-270 Site Reports 10, University of Illinois Press, Urbana.

1984b Social and Temporal Implications of Variation among American Bottom Mississippian Cemeteries. *American Antiquity* 49:468–88.

1986 Mississippian Period Population Density in a Segment of the Central Mississippi Valley. *American Antiquity* 51:227–38.

1990 The Late Prehistoric Cahokia Cultural System of the Mississippi River Valley: Foundations, Florescence, and Fragmentation. *Journal of World Prehistory* 4:1–43.

1992 Health and Cultural Change in the Late Prehistoric American Bottom, Illinois. In *What Mean These Bones? Studies in Southeastern Bioarchaeology*, edited by M. L. Powell, pp. 52–69. University of Alabama Press, Tuscaloosa.

1993 Settlements amidst Swamps. *Illinois Archaeology* 5:374–80.

1998 *The Cahokia Chiefdom: The Archaeology of a Mississippian Society*. Smithsonian Institution Press, Washington, DC.

1999 Warfare in Prehistoric and Early Historic Eastern North America. *Journal of Archaeological Research* 7:105–51.

Miracle, Preston 1998 Faunal Remains. In *The Archaeology of Downtown Cahokia: The Tract 15A and Dunham Tract Excavations*, by T. R. Pauketat, pp. 309–31. Illinois Transportation Archaeological Research Program, Studies in Archaeology 1, University of Illinois, Urbana.

Moore, Clarence B. 1998 *The Lower Mississippi Valley Excavations of Clarence Bloomfield Moore*, edited by D. F. Morse and P. A. Morse. University of Alabama Press, Tuscaloosa.

Morgan, William N. 1999 [1980] *Precolumbian Architecture in Eastern North America*. University Press of Florida, Gainesville.

Morse, Dan F. and Phyllis A. Morse 1983 *The Archaeology of the Central Mississippi Valley*. Academic Press, New York.

1990a Emergent Mississippian in the Central Mississippi Valley. In *The Mississippian Emergence*, edited by B. D. Smith, pp. 153–74. Smithsonian Institution Press, Washington, DC.

1990b The Spanish Exploration of Arkansas. In *Columbian Consequences*, Vol. 2: *Archaeological and Historical Perspectives in the Spanish Borderlands East*, edited by D. H. Thomas, pp. 197–210. Smithsonian Institution Press, Washington, DC.

2000 Social Interaction between the American Bottom of Cahokia and the Crowley's Ridge Lowlands Division of the Lower Mississippi River AD 800–1200. In *Mounds, Modoc, and Mesoamerica: Papers in Honor of Melvin L. Fowler*, edited S. R. Ahler, pp. 347–60. Illinois State Museum, Scientific Papers 28, Springfield.

Morse, Phyllis A. and Dan F. Morse 1990 The Zebree Site: An Emergent Early Mississippian Expression in Northeast Arkansas. In *The Mississippian Emergence*, edited by B. D. Smith, pp. 51–66. Smithsonian Institution Press, Washington, DC.

Moulton, Gary E., ed. 1985 *The Papers of Chief John Ross*, vol. 2: 1840–1866. University of Oklahoma Press, Norman.

1986 *The Definitive Journals of Lewis & Clark: From the Ohio to the Vermilion*, vol. 2: University of Nebraska Press, Lincoln.

1986 *Archaeology of the Lower Ohio River Valley*. Academic Press, Orlando, Florida.

1987 Salt, Chert, and Shell: Mississippian Exchange and Economy. In *Specialization, Exchange, and Complex Societies*, edited by E. Brumfiel and T. Earle. Cambridge University Press, Cambridge, pp. 10–21.

1989 The Southern Cult. In *The Southeastern Ceremonial Complex: Artifacts and Analysis*, edited by P. Galloway, pp. 11–26. University of Nebraska Press, Lincoln.

1995 Regional Interaction in the Later Southeast. In *Native American Interactions: Multiscalar Analyses and Interpretations in the Eastern Woodlands*, edited by M. S. Nassaney and K. E. Sassaman, pp. 317–40. University of Tennessee Press, Knoxville.

1997 *Mississippian Political Economy*. Plenum Press, New York.

Nassaney, Michael S. 1991 Spatial-Temporal Dimensions of Social Integration during the Coles Creek Period in Central Arkansas. In *Stability, Transformation, and Variation: The Late Woodland Southeast*, edited M. S. Nassaney and C. R. Cobb, pp. 177–220. Plenum Press, New York.

1992 Communal Societies and the Emergence of Elites in the Prehistoric American Southeast. In *Lords of the Southeast: Social Inequality and the Native Elites of Southeastern North America*, edited by A. W. Barker and

T. R. Pauketat, pp. 111–43. Archeological Papers of the American Anthropological Association 3, Washington, DC.

1994 The Historical and Archaeological Context of Plum Bayou Culture in Central Arkansas. *Southeastern Archaeology* 13:36–55.

2001 The Historical-Processual Development of Late Woodland Societies. In *The Archaeology of Traditions: History and Agency before and after Columbus*, edited by T. R. Pauketat, pp. 157–73. University Press of Florida, Gainesville.

Nelson, Margaret C. and Michelle Hegmon 2001 Abandonment Is Not as It Seems: An Approach to the Relationship between Site and Regional Abandonment. *American Antiquity* 66:213–36.

Nichols, Deborah L. and Thomas H. Charlton, eds. 1997 *The Archaeology of City-States: Cross-Cultural Approaches*. Smithsonian Institution Press, Washington, DC.

Nickerson, William B. 1913 Archaeology of Jo Daviess County Illinois 1895–1901. Explorations of W. B. Nickerson – Reporting to the Peabody Musium [*sic*] of American Archaeology, Harvard University. Unpublished report in the possession of the author.

Nicklas, T. Dale 1994 Linguistic Provinces of the Southeast at the Time of Columbus. In *Perspectives on the Southeast: Linguistics, Archaeology, and Ethnohistory*, edited by P. B. Kwachka, pp. 1–13. University of Georgia Press, Athens.

O'Brien, Michael J., Thomas D. Holland, Robert J. Hoard, and Gregory L. Fox 1994 Evolutionary Implications of Design and Performance Characteristics of Prehistoric Pottery. *Journal of Archaeological Method and Theory* 1:259–304.

O'Brien, Michael J. and W. Raymond Wood 1998 *The Prehistory of Missouri*. University of Missouri Press, Columbia.

O'Brien, Patricia J. 1972 *A Formal Analysis of Cahokia Ceramics from the Powell Tract*. Illinois Archaeological Survey Monograph 3, Urbana.

1978 Steed-Kisker: A Western Mississippian Settlement System. In *Mississippian Settlement Patterns*, edited by B. D. Smith, pp. 1–20. Academic Press, New York.

1991 Early State Economics: Cahokia, Capital of the Ramey State. In *Early State Economics*, edited by H. J. M. Claessen and P. van de Velde, pp. 143–75. Transaction Publishers, London.

1994 Prehistoric Politics: Petroglyphs and the Political Boundaries of Cahokia. *Gateway Heritage* (Summer):30–47.

O'Shea, John M. and John Ludwickson 1992 Omaha Chieftainship in the Nineteenth Century. *Ethnohistory* 39:316–52.

Ollendorf, Amy L. 1993 Changing Landscapes in the American Bottom (USA): An Interdisciplinary Investigation with an Emphasis on the Late-Prehistoric and Early-Historic Periods. Unpublished PhD dissertation, University of Minnesota, Minneapolis.

Olsen, K. R., J. M. Lang, J. D. Garcia-Paredes, R. N. Majchrzak, C. I. Hadley, M. E. Woolery, and R. M. Rejesus 2000 *Average Crop, Pasture, and Forestry Productivity Ratings for Illinois Soils*. College of Agricultural, Consumer and Environmental Sciences, Office of Research, Bulletin 810, Urbana, Illinois.

Overstreet, David F. 2000 Cultural Dynamics of the Late Prehistoric Period in Southern Wisconsin. In *Mounds, Modoc, and Mesoamerica: Papers in Honor of Melvin L. Fowler*, edited by S. R. Ahler, pp. 405–38. Illinois State Museum Scientific Papers Series 28. Springfield.

Parmalee, Paul 1958 Marine Shells of Illinois Indian Sites. *Nautilis* 71:132–9.

Patterson, Thomas C. 1995 *Toward a Social History of Archaeology in the United States*. Harcourt Brace and Company, Orlando, Florida.

Pauketat, Timothy R. 1983 A Long-Stemmed Spud from the American Bottom. *Midcontinental Journal of Archaeology* 8:1–12.

1984 Notes on Some Non-local Ceramics from an American Bottom Collection. *Illinois Antiquity* 16:4–6.

1987a A Burned Domestic Dwelling at Cahokia. *The Wisconsin Archeologist* 68(3):212–327.

1987c Mississippian Domestic Economy and Formation Processes: A Response to Prentice. *Midcontinental Journal of Archaeology* 12:77–88.

1992 The Reign and Ruin of the Lords of Cahokia: A Dialectic of Dominance. In *Lords of the Southeast: Social Inequality and the Native Elites of Southeastern North America*, edited by Alex W. Barker and Timothy R. Pauketat, pp. 31–51. Archeological Papers of the American Anthropological Association 3, Washington, DC.

1993a Preliminary Observations of Building Density at Cahokia's Tract 15A and Dunham Tract. In *Highways to the Past: Essays on Illinois Archaeology in Honor or Charles J. Bareis*, edited by T. Emerson, A. Fortier, and D. McElrath. *Illinois Archaeology* 5:402–6.

1993b *Temples for Cahokia Lords: Preston Holder's 1955–1956 Excavations of Kunnemann Mound*. Museum of Anthropology, University of Michigan, Memoir 26, Ann Arbor.

1994 *The Ascent of Chiefs: Cahokia and Mississippian Politics in Native North America*. University of Alabama Press, Tuscaloosa.

1995 Additional Notes on the Burned Building beneath Cahokia's Kunnemann Mound. *Illinois Archaeology* 7:102–8.

1996a AG Church Ceramics: Clues to Community Change. *Illinois Archaeology* 8:85–116.

1996b The Place of Post-Circle Monuments in Cahokia Political History. *The Wisconsin Archeologist* 77(3/4):73–83.

1997a Cahokian Political Economy. In *Cahokia: Domination and Ideology in the Mississippian World*, edited by T. R. Pauketat and T. E. Emerson, pp. 30–51. University of Nebraska Press, Lincoln.

1997b Specialization, Political Symbols, and the Crafty Elite of Cahokia. *Southeastern Archaeology* 16:1–15.

1998a *The Archaeology of Downtown Cahokia: The Tract 15A and Dunham Tract Excavations*. Illinois Transportation Archaeological Research Program, Studies in Archaeology 1, University of Illinois, Urbana.

1998b Refiguring the Archaeology of Greater Cahokia. *Journal of Archaeological Research* 6:45–89.

2000a Politicization and Community in the Pre-Columbian Mississippi Valley. In *The Archaeology of Communities: A New World Perspective*, edited by M. A. Canuto and J. Yaeger, pp. 16–43. Routledge, London.

2000b The Tragedy of the Commoners. In *Agency in Archaeology*, edited by M.-A. Dobres and J. Robb, pp. 113–29. Routledge, London.

2001a A New Tradition in Archaeology. In *The Archaeology of Traditions: Agency and History before and after Columbus*, edited by T. R. Pauketat, pp. 1–16. University Press of Florida, Gainesville.

2001b Practice and History in Archaeology: An Emerging Paradigm. *Anthropological Theory* 1:73–98.

2002 A Fourth-Generation Synthesis of Cahokia and Mississippianization. *Midcontinental Journal of Archaeology* 27:149–70.

2003a The Economy of the Moment: Cultural Practices and Mississippian Chiefdoms. In *The Economy of Chiefdoms and States*, edited by G. M. Feinman and L. M. Nicholas. University of Utah Press, Salt Lake City (in press).

2003b Resettled Farmers and the Making of a Mississippian Polity. *American Antiquity* 68:39–66.

Pauketat, Timothy R., ed. 2004 *The Archaeology of the East St. Louis Mound Center: Southside Excavations*. Illinois Transportation Archaeological Research Program, Report of Investigations (in press).

Pauketat, Timothy R. and Susan M. Alt 2003 Mounds, Memory, and Contested Mississippian History. In *Archaeologies of Memory*, edited by R. Van Dyke and S. Alcock, pp. 151–79. Blackwell Press, Oxford.

2004 The Makers and Meaning of a Mississippian Axe Head Cache. Manuscript in possession of the authors.

Pauketat, Timothy R. and Thomas E. Emerson 1991 The Ideology of Authority and the Power of the Pot. *American Anthropologist* 93:919–41.

1997 Introduction: Domination and Ideology in the Mississippian World. In *Cahokia: Domination and Ideology in the Mississippian World*, edited by T. R. Pauketat and T. E. Emerson, pp. 30–51. University of Nebraska Press, Lincoln.

1999 The Representation of Hegemony as Community at Cahokia. In *Material Symbols: Culture and Economy in Prehistory*, edited by J. Robb, pp. 302–17. Occasional Paper 26, Southern Illinois University, Carbondale.

Pauketat, Timothy R., Lucretia S. Kelly, Gayle J. Fritz, Neal H. Lopinot, Scott Elias, and Eve Hargrave 2002 The Residues of Feasting and Public Ritual at Early Cahokia. *American Antiquity* 67:257–79.

Pauketat, Timothy R. and Brad Koldehoff 2002 Cahokian Ritual and the Ramey Field: New Insights from Old Collections. *Southeastern Archaeology* 21:79–91.

Pauketat, Timothy R. and Neal H. Lopinot 1997 Cahokian Population Dynamics. In *Cahokia: Domination and Ideology in the Mississippian World*, edited by T. R. Pauketat and T. E. Emerson, pp. 103–23. University of Nebraska Press, Lincoln.

Pauketat, Timothy R. and Mark A. Rees 1996 Early Cahokia Project 1994 Excavations at Mound 49, Cahokia (11-S-34-2). Unpublished report submitted to the Illinois Historic Preservation Agency, Springfield.

Pauketat, Timothy R., Mark A. Rees, and Stephanie L. Pauketat 1998 *An Archaeological Survey of the Horseshoe Lake State Park, Madison County, Illinois*. Illinois State Museum, Reports of Investigations 55, Springfield.

Peale, Titian Ramsey 1862 Ancient Mounds at St. Louis, Missouri, in 1819. In *Annual Report of the Board of Regents of the Smithsonian Institution for 1861*, pp. 386–91. Government Printing Office, Washington, DC.

Peregrine, Peter N. 1992 *Mississippian Evolution: A World-System Perspective*, Monographs in World Archaeology 1, Prehistory Press, Madison, Wisconsin.

Perino, Gregory 1967 *The Cherry Valley Mounds and Banks Mound 3*. Central States Archaeological Societies, Memoir 1. St. Louis, Missouri.

1968 *Guide to the Identification of Certain American Indian Projectile Points*. Special Bulletin 3 of the Oklahoma Anthropological Society, Oklahoma City.

1971 The Mississippian Component at the Schild Site (No. 4), Greene County, Illinois. In *Mississippian Site Archaeology in Illinois 1*. Illinois Archaeological Survey, Bulletin 8, Urbana.

Phillips, Phillip 1970 *Archaeological Survey in the Lower Yazoo Basin, Mississippi, 1949–1955*. Papers of the Peabody Museum of Archaeology and Ethnology 60. Harvard University, Cambridge, Massachusetts.

Phillips, Phillips and James A. Brown 1978 *Pre-Columbian Shell Engravings from the Craig Mound at Spiro, Oklahoma, Part I*. Peabody Museum Press, Cambridge, Massachusetts.

Phillips, Phillip, James A. Ford, and James B. Griffin 1951 *Archaeological Survey in the Lower Mississippi Alluvial Valley, 1940–1947*. Papers of the Peabody Museum of Archaeology and Ethnology 25, Harvard University, Cambridge, Massachusetts.

Pollock, Susan 1999 *Ancient Mesopotamia: The Eden That Never Was*. Cambridge University Press, Cambridge.

Pool, Kelly J. 1989 A History of Amateur Archaeology in the St. Louis Area. *The Missouri Archaeologist* 50 (whole volume).

Porter, James W. 1974 Cahokia Archaeology as Viewed from the Mitchell Site: A Satellite Community at A.D. 1150–1200. PhD dissertation, Department of Anthropology, University of Wisconsin at Milwaukee. University Microfilms, Ann Arbor.

1977 The Mitchell Site and Prehistoric Exchange Systems at Cahokia: A.D. 1000 ± 300. In *Explorations into Cahokia Archaeology* (second revised edition), edited by M. L. Fowler, pp. 137–64. Illinois Archaeological Survey Bulletin 7, Urbana.

Porubcan, Paula J. 2000 Human and Nonhuman Surplus Display at Mound 72, Cahokia. In *Mounds, Modoc, and Mesoamerica: Papers in Honor of Melvin L. Fowler*, edited by S. Ahler, pp. 207–25. Illinois State Museum Scientific Papers 28, Springfield.

Powell, Mary Lucas 1992 *Status and Health in Prehistory*. Smithsonian Institution Press, Washington, DC.

Price, James E. and James B. Griffin 1979 *The Snodgrass Site of the Powers Phase of Southeast Missouri*. Museum of Anthropology, University of Michigan, Anthropological Papers 66, Ann Arbor.

Putnam, Frederic Ward 1878 Archaeological Explorations in Tennessee. In *Eleventh Annual Report of the Peabody Museum*, vol. 2, pp. 191–206. Harvard University, Cambridge, Massachusetts.

Radin, Paul 1990 [1911] *The Winnebago Tribe*. University of Nebraska Press, Lincoln.

Ramenofsky, Ann F. 1987 *Vectors of Death: The Archaeology of European Contact*. University of New Mexico Press, Albuquerque.

Reed, Nelson A., John W. Bennett, and James W. Porter 1968 Solid Core Drilling of Monks Mound: Technique and Findings. *American Antiquity* 33:137–48.

Rees, Mark A. 1997 Coercion, Tribute, and Chiefly Authority: The Regional Development of Mississippian Political Culture. *Southeastern Archaeology* 16:113–33.

Renfrew, Colin 1975 Trade as Action at a Distance: Questions of Integration and Communication. In *Ancient Civilization and Trade*, edited by J. A. Sabloff and C. C. Lamborg-Karlovsky, pp. 1–60. University of New Mexico Press, Albuquerque.

Rice, Prudence 1987 *The Pottery Sourcebook*. University of Chicago Press, Chicago.

Richards, John D. 1992 Ceramics and Culture at Aztalan: A Late Prehistoric Village in Southeast Wisconsin. Unpublished PhD dissertation, University of Wisconsin, Milwaukee.

Riley, Thomas J., Richard Edging, and Jack Rossen 1990 Cultigens in Prehistoric Eastern North America. *Current Anthropology* 31:425–41.

Ritzenthaler, Robert E. 1985 *Prehistoric Indians of Wisconsin* (3rd edition, revised by L. Goldstein). Milwaukee Public Museum, Milwaukee, Wisconsin.

Rodell, Roland L. 1991 The Diamond Bluff Site Complex and Cahokia Influence in the Red Wing Locality. In *New Perspectives on Cahokia: Views from the Periphery*, edited by J. B. Stoltman, pp. 253–80. Prehistory Press, Madison, Wisconsin.

Rogers, J. Daniel and Bruce D. Smith 1995 *Mississippian Communities and Households*. University of Alabama Press, Tuscaloosa.

Rolingson, Martha A. 1998 *Toltec Mounds and Plum Bayou Culture: Mound D Excavations*. Arkansas Archeological Survey, Research Series 54, Fayetteville.
    2002 Plum Bayou Culture of the Arkansas-White River Basin. In *The Woodland Southeast*, edited by D. G. Anderson and R. C. Mainfort, pp. 44–65. University of Alabama Press, Tuscaloosa.

Rollings, Willard H. 1992 *The Osage: An Ethnohistorical Study of Hegemony on the Prairie-Plains*. University of Missouri Press, Columbia.

Rose, Jerome C. 2000 Mortuary Data and Analysis. In *The Mound 72 Area: Dedicated and Sacred Space in Early Cahokia*, by M. L. Fowler, J. Rose, B. Vander Leest, and S. A. Ahler, pp. 63–82. Illinois State Museum, Reports of Investigations 54, Springfield.

Sahlins, Marshall 1972 *Stone Age Economics*. Aldine, Chicago.
    1985 *Islands of History*. University of Chicago Press, Chicago.

Said, Edward W. 1978 *Orientalism*. Pantheon Books, New York.

Saitta, Dean J. 1994 Agency, Class, and Archaeological Interpretation. *Journal of Anthropological Archaeology* 13:201–27.

Salkin, Philip H. 2000 The Horicon and Kekoskee Phases: Cultural Complexity in the Late Woodland Stage in Southeastern Wisconsin. In *Late Woodland Societies: Tradition and Transformation across the Midcontinent*, edited by T. E. Emerson, D. L. McElrath, and A. C. Fortier, pp. 525–42. University of Nebraska Press, Lincoln.

Salzer, Robert J. and Grace Rajnovich 2000 *The Gottschall Rockshelter: An Archaeological Mystery*. Prairie Smoke Press, St. Paul, Minnesota.

Santure, Sharron K., Alan D. Harn, and Duane Esarey 1990 *Archaeological Investigations at the Morton Village and Norris Farms 36 Cemetery*. Illinois State Museum Reports of Investigations 45, Springfield.

Sassaman, Kenneth E. 1995 The Social Contradictions of Traditional and Innovative Cooking Technologies in the Prehistoric American Southeast. In *The Emergence of Pottery: Technology and Innovation in Ancient Societies*, pp. 223–40. Smithsonian Institution Press, Washington, DC.

Sassaman, Kenneth E. and Michael J. Heckenberger 2001 Roots of the Theocratic Formative of the Archaic Southeast. Paper presented at the Southern Illinois University Visiting Scholar Conference "Hunters and Gatherers in Theory and Archaeological Research," March 23–24, 2001, organized by G. Crothers, Carbondale, Illinois.

Saucier, Roger T. 1994 *Geomorphology and Quaternary Geologic History of the Lower Mississippi Valley*, vol. 1. United States Army Corps of Engineers, Vicksburg.

Saunders, J. W., R. D. Mandel, R. T. Saucier, E. Thurman Allen, C. T. Hallmark, J. K. Johnson, E. H. Jackson, C. M. Allen, G. L. Stringer, D. S. Frink, J. K. Feathers, S. Williams, K. J. Gremillion, M. F. Vidrine, and R. Jones 1997 A Mound Complex in Louisiana at 5400–5000 Years before the Present. *Science* 277:1796–9.

Schambach, Frank 2002 Fourche Maline: A Woodland Period Culture of the Trans-Mississippi South. In *The Woodland Southeast*, edited by D. G. Anderson and R. C. Mainfort, Jr., pp. 91–112. University of Alabama Press, Tuscaloosa.

Schoolcraft, Henry Rowe 1860 *Archives of Aboriginal Knowledge*, 6 vols. J. P. Lippincott, Philadelphia.

Schroeder, Sissel 1999 Maize Productivity in the Eastern Woodlands and Great Plains of North America. *American Antiquity* 64:499–516.

Shelford, Victor E. 1963 *The Ecology of North America*. University of Illinois Press, Urbana.

Simon, Mary L. 2000 Regional Variations in Plant Use Strategies in the Midwest during the Late Woodland. In *Late Woodland Societies: Tradition and Transformation across the Midcontinent*, edited by T. E. Emerson, D. L. McElrath, and A. C. Forter, pp. 37–75. University of Nebraska Press, Lincoln.

Smith, Bruce D. 1975 *Middle Mississippi Exploitation of Animal Populations*. Museum of Anthropology, University of Michigan, Anthropological Papers Number 57, Ann Arbor.

1978 Variation in Mississippian Settlement Patterns. In *Mississippian Settlement Patterns*, edited by B. D. Smith, pp. 479–503. Academic Press, New York.

1984 Mississippian Expansion: Tracing the Historical Development of an Explanatory Model. *Southeastern Archaeology* 3:13–32.

1995 The Analysis of Single-Household Mississippian Settlements. In *Mississippian Communities and Households*, edited by J. D. Rogers and B. D. Smith, pp. 224–49. University of Alabama Press, Tuscaloosa.

Smith, Bruce D., ed. 1990 *The Mississippian Emergence*. Smithsonian Institution Press, Washington, DC.

Smith, Marvin T. and David J. Hally 1992 Chiefly Behavior: Evidence from Sixteenth-Century Spanish Accounts. In *Lords of the Southeast: Social Inequality and the Native Elites of Southeastern North America*, edited by A. W. Barker and T. R. Pauketat, pp. 99–109. Archeological Papers of the American Anthropological Association 3, Washington, DC.

Soja, Edward W. 1989 *Postmodern Geographies: The Reassertion of Space in Critical Social Theory*. Verso, London.

Spencer, Charles S. 1982 *Cuicatlán Cañada and Monte Albán: A Study in Primary State Formation*. Academic Press, New York.

Squier, Ephraim G. and Edwin H. Davis 1998 [184] *Ancient Monuments of the Mississippi Valley*, edited by D. J. Meltzer. Smithsonian Institution Press, Washington, DC.

Stahle, David W. and Daniel Wolfman 1985 The Potential for Archaeological Tree-Ring Dating in Eastern North America. In *Advances in Archaeological Method and Theory 8*, edited by M. B. Schiffer, pp. 279–302. Academic Press, New York.

Steponaitis, Vincas P. 1978 Location Theory and Complex Chiefdoms: A Mississippian Example. In *Mississippian Settlement Patterns*, edited by B. D. Smith, pp. 417–53. Academic Press, New York.

1991 Contrasting Patterns of Mississippian Development. In *Chiefdoms: Power, Economy, and Ideology*, edited by T. Earle, pp. 193–228. Cambridge University Press, Cambridge.

Stoltman, James B. 1991 Cahokia as Seen from the Peripheries. In *New Perspectives on Cahokia: Views from the Periphery*, edited by J. B. Stoltman, pp. 349–54. Prehistory Press, Madison, Wisconsin.

1992 Petrographic Observations on Six Ceramic Vessels Bearing on the Issue of External Cultural Influences at Obion. In *The Obion Site: An Early Mississippian Center in Western Tennessee*, by E. B. Garland, pp. 209–13. Cobb Institute of Archaeology, Report of Investigations 7, Mississippi State University, Mississippi.

2000a A Reconsideration of the Cultural Processes Linking Cahokia to Its Northern Hinterlands during the Period A.D. 1000–1200. In *Mounds, Modoc, and Mesoamerica: Papers in Honor of Melvin L. Fowler*, edited by S. R. Ahler, pp. 439–67. Illinois State Museum Scientific Papers 28, Springfield.

2000b The Role of Petrography in the Study of Archaeological Ceramics. In *Earth Sciences and Archaeology*, edited by P. Goldberg, V. T. Holliday, and C. R. Ferring, pp. 297–326. Kluwer Academic/Plenum Press, New York.

Stoltman, James B. and George W. Christiansen 2000 The Late Woodland Stage in the Driftless Area of the Upper Mississippi Valley. In *Late Woodland Societies: Tradition and Transformation across the Midcontinent*, edited by T. E. Emerson, D. L. McElrath, and A. C. Fortier, pp. 497–524. University of Nebraska Press, Lincoln.

Stuiver, Minze and Gordon W. Pearson 1986 High-Precision Calibration of the Radiocarbon Time Scale, AD 1950–500 BC. *Radiocarbon* 28:805–38.

Swanton, John R. 1946 *The Indians of the Southeastern United States*. Smithsonian Institution Bureau of American Ethnology, Bulletin 137, Washington, DC.

Tanner, Helen H. 1989 The Land and Water Communication Systems of the Southeastern Indians. In *Powhatan's Mantle: Indians in the Colonial Southeast*, edited by P. H. Wood, G. A. Waselkov, and M. T. Hatley, pp. 6–20. University of Nebraska Press, Lincoln.

Theler, James L. and Robert F. Boszhardt 2000 The End of the Effigy Mound Culture: The Late Woodland to Oneota Transition in Southwestern Wisconsin. *Midcontinental Journal of Archaeology* 25:289–312.

Thomas, Cyrus 1985 [1894] *Report on the Mound Explorations of the Bureau of Ethnology*. Smithsonian Institution Press, Washington, DC.

Thornbury, William D. 1965 *Regional Geomorphology of the United States*. John Wiley and Sons, New York.

Thruston, Gates P. 1897 *Antiquities of Tennessee, and the Adjacent States* (2nd edition). Robert Clarke and Company, Cincinatti.

Tiffany, Joseph A. 1982 Hartley Fort Ceramics. *Proceedings of the Iowa Academy of Science* 89:133–50.

1991a Modeling Mill Creek–Mississippian Interaction. In *New Perspectives on Cahokia: Views from the Periphery*, edited by J. B. Stoltman, pp. 319–47. Prehistory Press, Madison, Wisconsin.

1991b Models of Mississippian Culture History in the Western Prairie Peninsula: A Perspective from Iowa. In *Cahokia and the Hinterlands: Middle Mississippian Cultures of the Midwest*, edited by T. E. Emerson and R. B. Lewis, pp. 183–92. University of Illinois Press, Urbana.

Trigger, Bruce G. 1990 Monumental Architecture: A Thermodynamic Explanation of Symbolic Behaviour. *World Archaeology* 22 (2):119–32.

1991 Distinguished Lecture in Archaeology: Constraint and Freedom – A New Synthesis for Archaeological Explanation. *American Anthropologist* 93:551–69.

Trocolli, Ruth 1999 Women Leaders in Native North American Societies: Invisible Women of Power. In *Manifesting Power: Gender and the Interpretation of Power in Archaeology*, edited by T. L. Sweely, pp. 49–61. Routledge, London.

Trubitt, Mary Beth D. 2000 Mound Building and Prestige Goods Exchange: Changing Strategies in the Cahokia Chiefdom. *American Antiquity* 675:669–90.

Van Dyke, Ruth and Susan Alcock, eds. 2003 *Archaeologies of Memory*. Blackwell, Oxford.

Vehik, Susan C. 1993 Dhegiha Origins and Plains Archaeology. *Plains Anthropologist* 38:231–52.

Wagner, Gail E. 2000 Tobacco in Prehistoric Eastern North America. In *Tobacco Use by Native North Americans: Sacred Smoke and Silent Killer*, edited by J. C. Winter, pp. 185–201. University of Oklahoma Press, Norman.

Wagner, Mark J. and Mary R. McCorvie 2002 Mississippian Cosmology and Rock Art at the Millstone Bluff Site, Pope County, Illinois. Paper presented at the 35th Conference on Historical and Underwater Archaeology, January 8–12, Mobile, Alabama.

Wallace, Anthony F. C. 1999 *Jefferson and the Indians: The Tragic Fate of the First Americans.* Belknap Press, Cambridge, Massachusetts.

Walthall, John A. 1980 *Prehistoric Indians of the Southeast: Archaeology of Alabama and the Middle South.* University of Alabama Press, Tuscaloosa.

1981 *Galena and Aboriginal Trade in Eastern North America.* Illinois State Museum, Scientific Papers 17, Springfield.

Walthall, John A. and Thomas E. Emerson 1992 Indians and French in the Midcontinent. In *Calumet and Fleur-de-Lys: Archaeology of Indian and French Contact in the Midcontinent,* edited by J. A. Walthall and T. E. Emerson, pp. 1–13. Smithsonian Institution Press, Washington, DC.

Walthall, John, Kenneth Farnsworth, and Thomas E. Emerson 1997 Constructing (on) the Past. *Common Ground* 2:26–33.

Waring, Antonio J. 1968 The Southern Cult and Muskogean Ceremonial. In *The Waring Papers,* edited by S. Williams, pp. 30–69. Papers of the Peabody Museum of Archaeology and Ethnology 58, Harvard University, Cambridge, Massachusetts.

Waring, Antonio J. and Preston Holder 1945 A Prehistoric Ceremonial Complex in the Southeastern United States. *American Anthropologist* 47:1–34.

Waselkov, Gregory A. 1989 Indian Maps of the Colonial Southeast. In *Powhatan's Mantle: Indians in the Colonial Southeast,* edited by P. H. Wood, G. A. Waselkov, and M. T. Hatley, pp. 21–34. University of Nebraska Press, Lincoln.

Waselkov, Gregory A. and Kathryn E. H. Braund 1995 *William Bartram on the Southeastern Indians.* University of Nebraska Press, Lincoln.

Watkins, Joe 2000 *Indigenous Archaeology: American Indian Values and Scientific Practice.* Altamira Press, Walnut Creek, California.

Webb, Clarence H. and Monroe Dodd, Jr. 1939 Further Excavations of the Gahagan Mound: Connections with a Florida Culture. *Bulletin of the Texas Archeological and Paleontological Society* 11:90–128.

Weiner, Annette 1994 *Inalienable Possessions: The Paradox of Keeping While Giving Away.* University of California Press, Berkeley.

Welch, Paul D. 2001 Archaeology at Shiloh Indian Mounds, 1899–1999. Manuscript in the possession of the author.

Wesler, Kit W. 1991 Ceramics, Chronology, and Horizon Markers at Wickliffe Mounds. *American Antiquity* 56:278–90.

2001 *Excavations at Wickliffe Mounds.* University of Alabama Press, Tuscaloosa.

Whalley, Lucy 1990 Range Phase Floral Remains. In *The Range Site 2: The Emergent Mississippian Dohack and Range Phase Occupations,* by J. E. Kelly, S. J. Ozuk, and J. A. Williams, pp. 515–30. American Bottom Archaeology, FAI-270 Site Reports 20, University of Illinois, Urbana.

Willey, Gordon R. 1966 *An Introduction to American Archaeology,* vol. 1: *North and Middle America.* Prentice-Hall, Englewood Cliffs, New Jersey.

Willey, P. 1990 *Prehistoric Warfare on the Great Plains.* Garland Publishing, New York.

Willey, P. and Thomas E. Emerson 1993 The Osteology and Archaeology of the Crow Creek Massacre. *Plains Anthropologist* 38:227–69.

Williams, J. Raymond 1974 The Baytown Phases in the Cairo Lowlands of Southeast Missouri. *The Missouri Archaeologist* 36 (whole volume).

Williams, Samuel Cole, ed. 1930 *Adair's History of the American Indians*. Promontory Press, New York.

Williams, Stephen 1954 An Archaeological Study of the Mississippian Culture in Southeast Missouri. Unpublished PhD dissertation, Department of Anthropology, Yale University, New Haven, Connecticut. University Microfilms, Ann Arbor.

1963 The Eastern United States. In *Early Indian Farmers and Villages and Communities*, edited by W. G. Haag, pp. 267–325. US Department of the Interior, National Park Service, Washington, DC.

1990 The Vacant Quarter and Other Late Events in the Lower Valley. In *Towns and Temples along the Mississippi*, edited by D. H. Dye, pp. 170–80. University of Alabama Press, Tuscaloosa.

1991 *Fantastic Archaeology: The Wild Side of North American Prehistory*. University of Pennsylvania Press, Philadelphia.

Williams, Stephen and Jeffrey P. Brain 1983 *Excavations at the Lake George Site, Yazoo County, Mississippi, 1958–1960*. Papers of the Peabody Museum of Archaeology and Ethnology 74, Harvard University, Cambridge, Massachusetts.

Williams, Stephen and John M. Goggin 1956 The Long Nosed God Mask in Eastern United States. *The Missouri Archaeologist* 18 (whole volume).

Willoughby, Charles C. 1897 An Analysis of Decorations upon Pottery from the Mississippi Valley. *Journal of American Folklore* 10:9–20.

Wilson, Gilbert L. 1917 *Agriculture of the Hidatsa Indians: An Indian Interpretation*. University of Minnesota, Studies in the Social Sciences 9, Minneapolis.

Wilson, Gregory 1996 Insight through Icons. *Illinois Archaeology* 8:23–37.

Wissler, Clark 1926 *The Relation of Nature to Man in Aboriginal America*. Oxford University Press, New York.

Witthoft, John 1949 *Green Corn Ceremonialism in the Eastern Woodlands*. University of Michigan, Museum of Anthropology, Occasional Contributions 13, Ann Arbor.

Wittry, Warren 1977 The American Woodhenge. In *Explorations into Cahokia Archaeology* (2nd revised edition), edited by M. L. Fowler, pp. 43–8. Illinois Archaeological Survey Bulletin 7, Urbana.

Woods, William I. 2001 Monks Mound: A View from the Top. Paper presented at the 66th Annual Meeting of the Society for American Archaeology, 19 April, New Orleans, Louisiana.

Woods, William I. and George R. Holly 1991 Upland Mississippian Settlement in the American Bottom Region. In *Cahokia and the Hinterlands: Middle Mississippian Cultures of the Midwest*, edited by T. E. Emerson and R. B. Lewis, pp. 46–60. University of Illinois Press, Urbana.

Wright, Henry T. 1984 Prestate Political Formations. In *On the Evolution of Complex Societies: Essays in Honor of Harry Hoijer 1982*, edited by T. K. Earle, pp. 41–77. Undena Publications, Malibu.

Yerkes, Richard W. 1983 Microwear, Microdrills, and Mississippian Craft Specialization. *American Antiquity* 48:499–518.

1991. Specialization in Shell Artifact Production at Cahokia. In *New Perspectives on Cahokia: Views from the Periphery*, edited by J. B. Stoltman, pp. 49–64. Prehistory Press, Madison, Wisconsin.

Yerkes, Richard W. and Linda M. Gaertner 1997 Microwear Analysis of Dalton Artifacts. In *Sloan: A Paleoindian Dalton Cemetery in Arkansas*, by D. F. Morse, pp. 58–71. Smithsonian Institution Press, Washington, DC.

Yoffee, Norman 1993 Too Many Chiefs? (Or, Safe Texts for the '90s). In *Archaeological Theory: Who Sets the Agenda?*, edited by N. Yoffee and A. Sherratt, pp. 60–78. Cambridge University Press, Cambridge.

Yoffee, Norman, Suzanne K. Fish, and George R. Milner 1999 Comunidades, Ritualities, Chiefdoms: Social Evolution in the American Southwest and Southeast. In *Great Towns and Regional Polities in the Prehistoric American Southwest and Southeast*, edited by J. E. Neitzel, pp. 261–71. University of New Mexico Press, Albuquerque.

Young, Bilone W. and Melvin L. Fowler 2000 *Cahokia: The Great Native American Metropolis*. University of Illinois Press, Urbana.

Young, Gloria A. and Michael P. Hoffman 1993 *The Expedition of Hernando de Soto West of the Mississippi, 1541–1543*. University of Arkansas Press, Fayetteville.

Index